Wordsworth's revisionary aesthetics

Wordsworth's
Revisionary Aesthetics

THERESA M. KELLEY

Associate Professor of English
The University of Texas at San Antonio

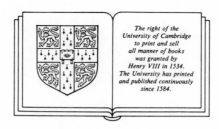

The right of the
University of Cambridge
to print and sell
all manner of books
was granted by
Henry VIII in 1534.
The University has printed
and published continuously
since 1584.

CAMBRIDGE UNIVERSITY PRESS

Cambridge
New York   New Rochelle   Melbourne   Sydney

Published by the Press Syndicate of the University of Cambridge
The Pitt Building, Trumpington Street, Cambridge CB2 1RP
32 East 57th Street, New York, NY 10022, USA
10 Stamford Road, Oakleigh, Melbourne 3166, Australia

First published 1988

Printed in Great Britain at
the University Press, Cambridge

British Library cataloguing in publication data
Kelley, Theresa M.
Wordsworth's revisionary aesthetics.
1. Wordsworth, William, 1770–1850.
Aesthetics.
I. Title.
821'.7   PR5892.A34

Library of Congress cataloguing in publication data
Kelley, Theresa M.
Wordsworth's revisionary aesthetics / Theresa M. Kelley.
p.   cm.
Bibliography.
Includes index.
ISBN 0 521 34398 4
1. Wordsworth, William, 1770–1850 – Aesthetics.
2. Wordsworth, William, 1770–1850 – Criticism and interpretation.
3. Aesthetics, British – 19th century.
I. Title.
PR5892.A34K44   1988
821'.7 – dc19   87-18771 CIP

For Thomas
and in memory of my mother
Theresa Marie Kelley

Contents

vii

Contents

Plates

Acknowledgements

I wish to thank several friends and teachers who have read part or all of this book at various stages. Dewey R. Faulkner offered encouragement and specific suggestions as I began. Stephen Parrish and Thomas A. Baylis continued to read as I wrote. Jean H. Hagstrum, who directed my dissertation on another topic, gave this book the same unwavering support throughout. During two summer seminars of the National Endowment for the Humanities in 1979 and 1982, the directors and fellow participants read earlier versions of several chapters. Ronald Paulson, who directed the first seminar, and Anne Mellor, who directed the second, have continued to support my work far beyond the limits of each seminar. Others read individual chapters or queried major issues: Elizabeth Napier, Kathleen Nicholson, Alan Liu, Stephen L. Carr, Marshall Brown, Gene W. Ruoff, Susan J. Wolfson, Cynthia Chase, Reeve Parker, Mary Jacobus, and Alan Bewell. Peter J. Manning has read most of this book more than once. On this and other occasions, I have learned much from his generous critical practice. Janann Stark and Joyce M. Hyde prepared the typescript with intelligence and great good will. I am grateful to The Society for the Humanities at Cornell University and its Director, Jonathan Culler, for a year-long fellowship during which I finished this book and worked on another. Jonathan Culler and the staff of the Society graciously encouraged both projects. Elizabeth Dipple read the entire typescript and offered timely advice as I prepared it for publication.

I would also like to thank Maurico Gonzalez and Timothy Summa, who are responsible for most of the photographic reproductions used in this book. For valuable support and research materials I am grateful to the National Endowment for the Humanities, The University of Texas at San Antonio, Cornell University Library, the Henry E. Huntington Library and Art Gallery, the Humanities Research Center

Acknowledgements

at The University of Texas at Austin, Yale University Library, Yale Center for British Art, the Boston Museum of Fine Arts, and the Library of Congress. I also thank Kevin Taylor, Caroline Drake, and Linda Matthews of Cambridge University Press for their patient and thorough preparation of this book for publication.

Abbreviations used in text and notes

B   *The Borderers.* Ed. Robert Osborn. Ithaca: Cornell
            University Press, 1982.
CEY   Reed, Mark L. *Wordsworth: The Chronology of the
            Early Years, 1770–1799.* Cambridge, Mass.: Harvard
            University Press, 1967.
CMY   Reed, Mark L. *Wordsworth: The Chronology of the
            Middle Years, 1800–1815.* Cambridge, Mass.:
            Harvard University Press, 1975.
EY   *The Letters of William and Dorothy Wordsworth:
            The Early Years, 1787–1805.* Ed. Ernest de Selin-
            court. 2d edn, rev. Chester L. Shaver. Oxford: Claren-
            don Press, 1967.
Fourteen-Book *The Fourteen-Book Prelude.* Ed. W. J. B. Owen.
   Prel.   Ithaca: Cornell University Press, 1985.
Guide   Wordsworth, William. *A Guide through the District
            of the Lakes.* In vol. 2, *Prose* (see below).
HG   *Home at Grasmere.* Ed. Beth Darlington. Ithaca:
            Cornell University Press, 1977.
MY, 1   *The Letters of William and Dorothy Wordsworth:
            The Middle Years, 1806–20.* Ed. Ernest de Selincourt,
            2 vols. 2nd edn: Part 1, 1806–11, rev. Mary
            Moorman. Oxford: Clarendon Press, 1969.
LY, 1   *The Letters of William and Dorothy Wordsworth: The
            Later Years, 1821–28.* Ed. Ernest de Selincourt. 2nd
            edn, rev. Alan G. Hill. Oxford: Clarendon Press, 1978.
P. Bord.   *Preface* to *The Borderers.* (see above.)
Poems, 1807 *Poems, in Two Volumes, and Other Poems, 1800–*
            1807. Ed. Jared Curtis. Ithaca: Cornell University
            Press, 1983.

Abbreviations used in text and notes

Prose	*The Prose Works of William Wordsworth*. Eds. W. J. B. Owen and Jane W. Smyser. 3 vols. Oxford: Clarendon Press, 1974.
Prel.	*The Prelude, 1799, 1805, 1850*. Eds. Jonathan Wordsworth, M. H. Abrams, and Stephen Gill. New York: W. W. Norton, 1979.
Prelude	*The Prelude*. Eds. Ernest de Selincourt and Helen Darbishire. 2nd edn, rev. Oxford: Clarendon Press, 1959.
Prel. 1798	*The Prelude, 1798–99*. Ed. Stephen Parrish. Ithaca: Cornell University Press, 1977.
PW	*The Poetical Works of William Wordsworth*. Eds. Ernest de Selincourt and Helen Darbishire. 5 vols. 2nd edn. Oxford: Clarendon Press, 1949.
RC	*The Ruined Cottage and the Pedlar*. Ed. James Butler. Ithaca: Cornell University Press, 1979.

Introduction

THIS BOOK is about Wordsworth's aesthetics and, in particular, the rhetorical competition between its sublime and beautiful figures. Like Thomas DeQuincey, who praised the Arab dream in *The Prelude* and as *"ne plus ultra* of sublimity," modern readers tend to assume that Wordsworth's poetic achievement is his celebration of Romantic sublimity and transcendence.[1] If this reputation has of late become something of a liability in the eyes of some readers, most still admire what DeQuincey admired: those close encounters with the sublime that recur throughout Wordsworth's poetry. Because it registers competing versions of Romantic sublimity, the Arab dream offers a point of entry into this critical debate. What DeQuincey probably meant by "sublimity" in this instance was "greatness of style and subject," a definition that would have satisfied most eighteenth-century theorists. Modern theorists have emphasized the transcendent vision of the sublime speaker or hero. The Arab dream suggests a more critical view of sublime transcendence. Although the dreamer (or the speaker himself in the 1832–50 poem) wants to help the Arab Don Quixote bury his "treasures," a stone and a shell, to save them from being destroyed by a deluge, he cannot because the Arab rides off, abandoning the dreamer to other narrative quests and solutions in the expanded *Prelude*.[2] As an isolated figure who refuses help and company, Wordsworth's Arab Don Quixote dramatizes the underside of sublime transcendence – a rebellious disregard for the rest of society. Like all sublime figures, Wordsworth's Arab wants to be alone.

Even in eighteenth-century treatises on aesthetics, these versions of the sublime collide when writers who set out to praise Milton's sublime style end up praising Milton's Satan, the hero whose sublimity so attracts and repels Romantic writers. For Keats and Hazlitt, Romantic sublimity was as much a liability as an achievement.

Introduction

According to Keats, isolation and self-aggrandizement are endemic to the "wordsworthian or egotistical sublime." Although Wordsworth is not the declared object of Hazlitt's charge that poetry or imagination is by nature "an exaggerating and exclusive faculty," the charge echoes terms he used on other occasions to praise or blame Wordsworth's poetry. For Hazlitt, what the (sublime or Wordsworthian) imagination lacks is understanding, that faculty which "seeks the greatest quantity of ultimate good, by justice and proportion."[3]

In this century critics have been more enthusiastic about the Wordsworthian sublime. In his influential survey of eighteenth-century theories of the sublime, Samuel Monk argued that its Romantic apotheosis occurs in Wordsworth's poetry. For Geoffrey Hartman, Wordsworth's stance as a "halted traveller" before the sublime is a resonant image of what Romanticism is about: a moment in which the longing for apocalypse or transcendence is laid bare. And in the last decade the sublime has become a major critical theme – or ideology – with specific methodological investments in, for example, sublime figures that compulsively reenact the indeterminacy of figures.[4] In Wordsworth's Arab dream, the speaker's ambivalence about the Arab suggests why modern readers might also question a single-minded regard for Romantic sublimity. Even as the speaker admits that the Arab's quest is attractive, he recognizes a competing set of concerns. If all trot off as the Arab chooses to do, he observes, no one will be left to tend "wives," "children," "virgin loves" – "whatsoever else the heart holds dear" (154–55, p. 158). Readers of the Arab dream who have been similarly attracted by the figure of an Arab Don Quixote do not attach much value to this reluctant but instructive expression of misgiving. Yet surely abandoning what the heart holds dear has social and, I will argue, poetic consequences. These concerns are not all that matters to Wordsworth's speaker, but they do matter.

This study argues that for most of his career Wordsworth was at least as suspicious of the sublime as Keats and Hazlitt were because, like them, he recognized that sublime transcendence might become little more than sublime egotism. Wordsworth's suspicion of the sublime prompted a "twofold" aesthetics that is critical to his emergence as a major poet. The two poles of this aesthetics, the sublime and the beautiful, derive from a well-known antithesis in earlier aesthetic theory, in part familiar to Wordsworth by way of Edmund Burke. But whereas Burke primarily describes differences between sublimity and beauty, and suggests their opposition, Wordsworth presents this opposition as an aesthetic conflict whose rhetorical complexity is a singular poetic achievement. As a quasi-Burkean aesthetic of social norms and hierarchies, the Wordsworthian beautiful opposes the wilful self-aggrandizement of the revolutionary or Satanic sublime, advocating instead communicability and a sense of known limits in art as well as society. If this account of the beautiful clearly evokes Burkean and Tory values, it also engages the poetic project Wordsworth announced in the 1800 *Lyrical Ballads* – to create a poetic speech adequate for a community of speakers and listeners.

This aesthetic conflict is absent in poems Wordsworth composed before the middle of the 1790s. Like the poets of sensibility and those of his contemporaries who supported France during the early phases of its revolution, he initially identified the sublime with original genius and human freedom. Thus in the 1793 *Descriptive Sketches*, he echoes Thomson's praise of "Britannia" in *The Seasons*:

> Oh give, great God, to Freedom's waves to ride
> Sublime o'er Conquest, Avarice, and Pride,
> To break, the vales where Death and Famine scow'rs,
> And dark Oppression builds her thick-ribb'd tow'rs.[5]

Although this freedom belongs not to English imperialism but to revolutionary France, the style and aesthetic preference of the passage are otherwise faithful to the Thomsonian model. Wordsworth would never again offer so unequivocal a celebration of the sublime. After 1793, he began to ask pressing questions about the value of sublime isolation and transcendence as opposed to the preservation of communities (living and dead) and communicability. Long after Napoleon's final defeat, this political occasion continued to structure Wordsworth's aesthetics. In poems he composed or revised after 1800, the revolutionary sublime is a resonant image of poetic figures that speak for, or of, what resists representation (political as well as linguistic), whereas the beautiful is an image of poetic figures that aspire to full or adequate representability.

Despite obvious and important similarities between this aesthetics and its predecessors, two features of Wordsworth's aesthetics are distinctive. First, Wordsworth repeatedly describes sublimity and beauty as successive, then competing, categories. Even when he does not, vestiges of this aesthetic progress haunt those poems where sublimity and beauty are in conflict. Second, more than any earlier writer on aesthetics, he dramatizes the rhetorical implications of aesthetic differences. This claim requires some explanation. As critics have long recognized, the earliest treatise on aesthetics, Longinus's *On the Sublime*, is explicitly concerned with the rhetoric of the sublime style. And in less explicit ways, so are Burke's *Enquiry concerning the Origin of Our Ideas of the Sublime and the Beautiful*, Kant's *Critique of Judgement,* and a number of other eighteenth-century treatises in which aesthetics and rhetoric are presented as parallel inquiries. Yet none of these writers explored the difference between sublimity and beauty as insistently as Wordsworth did. The logic of this insistence derives, I think, from the lingering power of Wordsworth's early recognition that the revolutionary sublime is an uncanny double of the transcendent freedom and self-consciousness which modern readers find in Kant's account of the sublime. More than the older Burke, who also rewrote his earlier preference for the sublime in the light and shadow of revolutionary France, Wordsworth chose to embody the practical and irrevocable difference between sublimity and beauty in the turns and counter-turns of poetic figures.

The first goal of this study is to describe the role of Wordsworth's revisionary aesthetics in the early as well as the mature stages of his poetic career. The second aim is to examine the relation between this aesthetics and Wordsworth's understanding of the representational task of poetic language. The sublime and the beautiful articulate extreme views of what poetry may or may not represent. In Wordsworth's poetry, on one side of the moment of "blockage" – which Neil Hertz has identified in the literature of the sublime – is the sublime, which promotes the mind's sense of being halted before unexpressed or unexpressible ideas.[6] On the other side is the beautiful, whose occasion for speech is the threat of its loss. On this side too are arrayed the interests of language, especially poetic language, as an expressive vehicle always eager (or anxious in some versions of this debate) to counter the inexpressibility which the sublime figures. Whether the beautiful is read as a figure of compensation or representation (or both), it signals the value which texts and speakers necessarily attach to the expression of meaning and thus to words or figures that bring meaning to the surfaces of texts. Unlike Hazlitt, who supposed that the imagination is by nature a sublime, self-aggrandizing power and the understanding something outside the imagination, in Wordsworth's aesthetics of sublimity and beauty both belong to the imagination; together they perform the essential representational tasks of his art, much as the autobiographical speaker of *The Prelude* undergoes an aesthetic education "by beauty and by fear" that prepares him for his work as a poet. The double project of this education is to allow sublime utterance, yet somehow contain it within the poetic forms and figures of the beautiful.

Prior to Wordsworth, the representational status of aesthetic determinations was a persistent theme among aesthetic theorists, especially Longinus, Burke, and Kant. Wordsworth's version of this theme is distinguished by its excavations of hidden, sublime figures and its efforts to compose the poetic surfaces which those figures disrupt. And, unlike Kant's, his aesthetics is continually subject to ideological pressures. As Wordsworth turned against revolutionary France, the revolutionary sublime became a major vehicle for his investigation of what is at stake in all contests for power over language – whether those contests take place in political centers of power like the French senate, or in poetic speech. For the next thirty years, he entertained or half-invented several versions of the sublime: the revolutionary sublime, a transcendent consciousness that resembles the sublimity of Kant and Hegel, and the "intense unity" of a less problematic (and less frequently presented) sublime.

Throughout this period Wordsworth remained attentive to his earlier recognition of the essential and difficult relation between language and power in all acts of representation. In this regard the sublime and the beautiful assisted his mature understanding of a reiterated contest between the need to represent meaning, and the difficulties which impede that representation. Much like Browning, who would later define poetry as "putting the infinite within the finite," Wordsworth asserts that poetry is, like religion or theology, bound to the task of providing "sensuous incarnation" for "transcendent" meaning and yet equally bound to recognize the difficulty, even the improbability, of that task.[7] So described, even in the late 1790s Wordsworth's aesthetic project anticipated the values some have assigned to a later, Biedermeier phase of Romanticism or to Victorianism. My point here is not to imply that the early Wordsworth was a Victorian in Romantic guise. Instead, I will argue that the rhetorical tension that marks both his early and late revisionary aesthetics is a thoroughly Romantic achievement. As such, it claims these Romantic analogues: Blake's contraries of circumference or bounding line vs. exploding (or imploding) form; the shifting, transgressive boundaries of character and estate in Emily Bronte's *Wuthering Heights*; Shelley's Mt. Blanc as one of many images that resist yet invite figuration and rhyme; or Keats's figures of apostrophe, whose double nature (expressive, inexpressive; present, absent) repeats the larger pattern of Wordsworth's aesthetics.[8]

My thinking about Wordsworth's poetry and aesthetics owes much to recent critics, in particular Geoffrey Hartman and Herbert Lindenberger, whose divergent accounts of Wordsworth's poetical character have instructed my own.[9] Like W. J. B. Owen, I argue that beauty and sublimity are paired aesthetic values in Wordsworth's poetry and prose. However, whereas Owen concludes that Wordsworth's aes-

Introduction

thetic principles are primarily Burkean, I argue that a number of singular differences mark Wordsworth's relation to Burke. For Albert Wlecke, the Wordsworthian sublime is the "sense sublime" of "Lines composed a few miles above Tintern Abbey," where phenomenological wholeness keeps at bay aspects of the sublime that Wordsworth develops in other poems. The range of Thomas Weiskel's *The Romantic Sublime* is more inclusive.[10] Although his argument is often unnecessarily difficult, its attention to the rhetorical and semiotic features of the Romantic sublime is exemplary. According to Weiskel, the Wordsworthian sublime presents a struggle whose contours are nominally Burkean but more insistently Kantian, Hegelian, and most of all oedipal. I question whether this struggle is also Wordsworthian and Romantic.

Like Weiskel, other critics who are equally preoccupied with the sublime tend to neglect Wordsworth's use of other figures and contexts to mediate sublime encounters. Two recent studies suggest how we might understand the poetic effects of such mediations. David Simpson argues that Wordsworth's metaphors refigure rather than dismiss reality. Such figurings and refigurings are, I suggest, the project of the Wordsworthian beautiful. Using a more explicitly thematic approach, David Pirie calls needed attention to the antithetical spirit in Wordsworth's poetry, which Pirie presents as the difference between "grandeur and tenderness,"[11] but because these terms appear in a cancelled passage of the expanded *Prelude* and are later revised for inclusion in *The Excursion*, I interpret them as an already domesticated version of a more persistent rhetorical competition between sublimity and beauty.

Because it has become very nearly a critical commonplace to assume that the Wordsworthian sublime repeats the critical gestures of the Kantian model, I want to summarize how these two models differ, and suggest why they differ. Were the issue one of philosophical rigor, the Kantian model would have the strongest claim on our attention. The world of transcendent, supersensible ideas which the Kantian sublime makes available to human consciousness is probably the best that has been thought or said on the subject.[12] Yet it is a model that defines itself outside the pressures of history and human failure. Published in 1790, a year after the Fall of the Bastille, Kant's third *Critique* avoids the potential for boundless self-aggrandizement which Wordsworth and his contemporaries identified with the revolutionary sublime.[13] It also seeks to avoid, with limited success, the troubled relation between rhetorical figures and the sublime which is in varying degrees at issue for Longinus, Burke, and Wordsworth. Unlike Kant, Wordsworth's

6

conception of the sublime is fraught with subjective measures of its political and semiotic hazards. Here one contrast will suffice to indicate the degree of difference between the two models. Whereas Kant neutralizes the sublime by making its existence depend on the operations of the reason, Wordsworth supposes that reason acts on behalf of the beautiful. Thus cordoned off from the sublime (and the French Revolution), reason serves ends unlike those Wordsworth believed revolutionary leaders often made it serve. To prevent the dream of reason from creating sublime monsters, Wordsworth assigned it to the beautiful, where it would function within the framework of social, human affections.

If Kantian disinterestedness was not possible for Wordsworth, it was in varying degrees also not possible for other Romantic writers for whom revolutionary France became a haunting image of disruptive powers which Kant had inadvertently allegorized. Romantic rebels like Victor Frankenstein, his monster offspring, and Napoleon limn the darker side of the freedom to soar beyond natural limits which Kant excludes or at best minimizes by attaching the mind's recognition of its sublimity to the realm of supersensible ideas. Post-structuralist critics who have used the Kantian model to define the Wordsworthian and Romantic sublimes have in effect tried to legitimize an absorption in and by the sublime, which Wordsworth and other Romantic writers could not afford. The irony of this strong misreading and its attachment to what Jerome Christensen has called the "romance of the other"[14] should not be missed: such absorption repeats the sublime self-aggrandizement which Kant's definition excludes. Moreover, it has influenced critics who otherwise have little tolerance for Romantic sublimity and transcendence. On several occasions Jerome McGann has taken Wordsworth's poetry to task for its sublime self-absorption.[15] Although I grant that Wordsworth felt the attraction of the "wordsworthian or egotistical sublime" as strongly as any Romantic writer, this study attempts to show that because he also understood the hazards of the sublime as well or better than any of his contemporaries, he harnessed it to a reiterated aesthetic contest with the beautiful. This contest, not an uncritical allegiance to the sublime style and its figures, is the scene of Wordsworth's aesthetic instruction.

This study approaches Wordsworth's aesthetics by way of his prose commentaries on aesthetics and landscape. Although all of them witness Wordsworth's desire to construct a coherent aesthetic model, none of them presents such a model. Yet collectively they suggest why he illustrated aesthetic principles with natural analogues and why these analogues could not suffice. In brief, they are no more and no less than mapping strategies for an aesthetics that at once resists and invites schematization. For this reason, the role of place, topography, or landscape in this aesthetics is characteristically (or maddeningly) Wordsworthian. As a poet he never, I think, needed to "raise" or remove himself from an obsession with place as such.[16] But the adhesiveness with which he insisted on the proximity between literal places and their figures tends to obscure the extent to which sublime and beautiful "places" are figures. Nature or, more precisely, landscape or topography is in Wordsworth's poems oddly numinous. That is to say, it is not strictly animist in either the primitive or the Ovidian sense. Instead, its aura of animation is more like receptivity – as if it were a container or receptacle for human history. The first part of this formulation Wordsworth implies in phrases like "forms perennial of the ancient hills." One argument of this study addresses the second part – the claim that Wordsworth historicizes places. This conception of place is not genuinely abstract, though it hinges on an attitude toward landscape which might be called "cartographic" – hence my frequent use of the term *topography* in this study. In Wordsworth's poems nature is map-like or, as he says in the first *Essay upon Epitaphs*, like "an image gathered from a map," one which assumes that spirit is the inhabitant of its places. In Wordsworth's aesthetics poetic figures manage the "crossings" between the letter of sublime and beautiful landscapes and their spirit by asserting their proximity.

In his *Guide through the District of the Lakes*, Wordsworth asserts that nature's earliest "dealings" with the surface of the earth produce sublime, undifferentiated forms. Subsequent "dealings" tend toward the production of beauty, which transforms sublime mountain forms by modifying their primitive contours. According to this model of aesthetic progress, the sublime is below, the beautiful above. However, in the manuscript fragment which W. J. B. Owen and Jane W. Smyser have titled "The Sublime and the Beautiful," he describes an aesthetics that is potentially riddled with fissures and disruptions.[17] The theme of this second account is an aesthetic progress in the mind that roughly corresponds to the one Wordsworth attributes to nature in the *Guide*. The difference between the two models is the struggle for dominance which ensues in the second as soon as the mind is able to entertain beauty as well as sublimity. To call attention to the importance Wordsworthian speakers attach to the retrieval of this aesthetic conflict, I suggest that Wordsworth's *Guide* and his unfinished manuscript on aesthetics imply two different models of archeological excavation – models that reflect contemporary hypotheses about the geological history of the earth. These Wordsworth knew from a variety of popular and scientific sources, including travel narratives, Enlightenment theories concerning the age of the earth and its formation, and early nineteenth-century discussions of the geology of the Lake District and the Alps. In the first of the models suggested by Wordsworth's *Guide*, a simple excavation of an uninterrupted aesthetic sequence images – or seeks to image – a similar sequence in the mind. In the second, aesthetic rivalries complicate the work of poetic excavation as sublime depths show themselves unwilling to remain "below," and beautiful surfaces work to suppress sublime intrusions. We can, I think, still use archeological figures to describe this second model simply because a recurrent longing for the first kind of excavation continues to structure this more complicated relation between sublimity and beauty.

To put the relation between them as a modern archeologist might, we could say that the *Guide* model is the ideal of excavation, whereas the manuscript fragment comes closer to actual practice in the field, where repeated disruptions of the original sequence in which strata were deposited make it difficult to determine which came first and how artifacts embedded in different strata are related to each other. Wordsworth's fragment on aesthetics uncomfortably acknowledges this difficulty by granting that the sublime and the beautiful compete for precedence in the mind. His major poems more frequently register this kind of archeological excavation as speakers encounter repeated disruptions of a simple aesthetic progress. Like the "archeology" of Michel Foucault's *Les Mots et les Choses* or *The Archeology of Knowledge*,[18] this second use of archeology as a figure emphasizes the gaps or baffling discontinuities that occur in Wordsworth's poetry when one aesthetic figure gives way to another. The aesthetic tension that marks these moments suggests a dialectical spiral something like Hegel's, except that what looks like synthesis in Wordsworth's aesthetics is more likely to be the beautiful, whose suppressions eventually yield to other sublime disruptions. If this tension is dialectical, its penchant for disequilibrium is probably more Blakean than Hegelian.[19]

Despite important differences, Freud's use of archeology as a figure for psychoanalysis provides an instructive parallel for Wordsworth's aesthetic project. Presenting himself as "a conscientious archeologist" in his preface to "A Case of Hysteria," Freud claims for psychoanalysis the certitudes of archeology as a science and method,[20] much as Wordsworth constructed a model for nature's successive "dealings" which he hoped to impose on poetic figures that undermine an uninterrupted aesthetic sequence. Even as psychic topographies rarely,

Introduction

if ever, yield either a fixed stratigraphic sequence or a single place for psychic artifacts, neither do Wordsworth's efforts to portray the mind's aesthetic "dealings" achieve the stability posited by his archeology of nature. For both Wordsworth and Freud, the mind's archeologies are created by an ego whose self-defense and self-definition require frequent disruptions and occlusions of psychic stratigraphies. For the older Freud and for post-Freudian readers of such defenses, the search for psychic origins, like Wordsworth's efforts to retrieve the sublime as "other," is persistently undermined as the mind contaminates what it retrieves.[21] Both writers present stratified psychic topographies that may and often do shift without warning, like pieces in a kaleidoscope, to create a new archeology and thus to require yet another excavation.

One difference between Freud and Wordsworth concerns what they retrieve and where they get it. This study deals primarily with the textual strategies which Wordsworthian speakers use to retrieve suppressed knowledge – i.e., what they know but choose not to declare. The parallel Freudian project deals with what has been repressed, which finds its way into texts and speech, if it finds its way at all, via figures that produce dislocated images of what is repressed. Yet insofar as Wordsworth's sublime and beautiful figures enact the same dislocating strategies, the parallel remains instructive. Like the older Freud, Wordsworth seems to have been as much interested in how the mind defends itself against the sublime as he was in the sublime itself. In this sense the sublime is important because it is an occasion for rhetorical and figurative strategies that enable the poetic effort to retrieve (or not to retrieve) it.

In Wordsworth's poems this aesthetic conflict between poetic surfaces and depths often makes it difficult to pull one layer back and distinguish it from another or several others beneath it. It is as if Wordsworth had inscribed aesthetic figures on a stratigraphic map whose layers have been fused together or laminated. Let me try to explain what happens to speakers or readers of such passages by considering the layers or strata in one of the most celebrated "sublime" encounters of Wordsworth's poetry, the sequence in *The Prelude*, VI, that begins when the speaker discovers that he has unwittingly crossed the Alps. My contentions are that the Ravine of Arve passage is less indebted to the sublime than it is to the beautiful for its figuration and that the aesthetic difficulty with it and the apostrophe to the Imagination that precedes it is that they tend to stick together despite their aesthetic and rhetorical differences.

The speaker's apostrophe to the Imagination is, as many readers have noted, a virtual textbook of the sublime as figure and landscape. The scene is vast; its parentage is hidden in the abyss or absent. Thus its paradoxical "home" is infinitude. The speaker is lost – lost in the Alps and lost to himself as sense experience, desire, and will evaporate before a sublime abyss. Yet in the Ravine of Arve passage that follows, the same tenor is given vehicles which press instead toward the code of representability which the beautiful advances. Here an explicitly Kantian image of the sublime like "the immeasurable height" of forests is subtly contained by the chiastic figures of "woods decaying, never to be decayed," by figures of paradox ("stationary blasts of waterfalls") and by figures whose tendency toward personification far exceeds that of the apostrophic account of the Imagination: "rocks that mattered," "black drizzling crags that spake," "raving stream." All are likened to "features" on a monumental "face," to "characters of the great apocalypse." These figures are doubly bound: they represent natural phenomena without fully humanizing them and yet they do so by giving them human attributes. The synedochic effect of this pattern of figuration is both to recognize the alien, other, or sublime aspect of the scene and to encase it in quasi-human figures which limit this otherness.

Two features of these passages are striking; they constitute a sequence, and the lines that conclude the first announce a slippage toward the figurative investments of the second. If at first the mind is submerged beneath its sublimity, those "banners militant," it is soon submerged beneath an "access of joy / Which hides it like the overflowing Nile" (6:525–48, pp. 216, 218). The double domestication of this last figure suggests what is at issue in these lines. The uncontained, destructive power of floods and deluge, which is in this and other poems a figure for revolution and the sublime, is here contained by a tamed version of itself – the annual overflow of the Nile – not a catastrophe but an anticipated and welcome irrigation. Substitutions of this kind are so close that their sublime and beautiful aspects are distinguished with difficulty, if they are distinguished at all. Yet the Nile simile and the Ravine of Arve passage usher in a different mode of figuration and a different aesthetic. Weiskel inadvertently admits as much when he dismisses the chiastic figures of the Ravine of Arve or Gondo Gorge passage by saying, "this is simply not the way Wordsworth writes or thinks, not his kind of greatness."[22] I argue to the contrary that this is indeed how Wordsworth thinks, and this too is his kind of poetic greatness. The shift in critical judgment that encouraged modern readers to recognize the workings of an apocalyptic, visionary imagination where earlier readers had recognized only nature,[23] has done much to revise early twentieth-century critiques of Wordsworth and Romanticism. But another shift in critical perspective is needed, one that more willingly scrutinizes how Wordsworth crafts poetic figures for specific ends.

The next two chapters of the study describe Wordsworth's conception of an aesthetic progress in nature and in the mind. The first compares the aesthetic claims presented in his *Guide through the District of the Lakes* and manuscript fragment "The Sublime and the Beautiful" to earlier aesthetic theory, especially that of Burke and Kant. The second examines the scene of aesthetic instruction where the progress from sublimity to beauty occurs. Chapters 4, 5, and 6 consider the stages of Wordsworth's aesthetic progress: his critique of revolution and the egotistical sublime, the revisionary aesthetics of the expanded *Prelude*, and the aesthetics of containment displayed in poems he composed or published after 1806. Chapter 7 reviews this aesthetic history by tracing its emergence in "torrent" poems Wordsworth composed over a thirty-year period. The last chapter considers the relation between Wordsworth's aesthetics and his theory of poetic language. The appendix summarizes textual evidence that suggests Wordsworth composed his fragmentary essay "The Sublime and the Beautiful" before and after 1811, the date usually assigned to this manuscript. Although this sequence of topics traces a line of development from Wordsworth's early, ambivalent attraction to the sublime to his mature conception of the beautiful, it provides a convenient anchor, not a rigid formula, for describing aesthetic engagements that frequently defy chronology.

2

Archeologies

Antiquities, or remnants of history, are, as was said, *tanquam tabula naufragii* [like the planks or tablets of a shipwreck]: when industrious persons by an exact and scrupulous diligence and observation, out of monuments, names, words, proverbs, traditions, private records and evidences, fragments of stories, passages of books that concern not story, and the like, do save and recover somewhat from the deluge of time.   Francis Bacon, *The Advancement of Learning*[1]

BACON'S SKEPTICISM about the accuracy and completeness of "antiquities" – those antiquarian records that occupied the time of so many eighteenth-century clergymen – summarizes a persistent theme in Wordsworth's aesthetics. At times insistent that it is possible to retrieve sublime origins and figures, at others he implies that this effort is flawed in conception, since excavations almost always disturb or, at best, misread partial evidence. The figures of deluge and shipwreck that Bacon uses to show why such records are incomplete also haunt Wordsworth's poetry, especially those passages in which sublime figures threaten to engulf speakers. And, like Bacon's *tabula*, literally "planks" but in this context a figure for written or inscribed tablets, the fragments of aesthetic history Wordsworth scrutinizes are at once material and figurative. Their material aspect is especially apparent in his prose on aesthetics, where he proposes models of aesthetic retrieval that affirm the value of archeological excavation as a way to recover part of the past. However much some writers might have disdained Casaubon-like collections of data, few could deny their value for the study of history after Winckelmann's accounts of excavations at Herculaneum and Pompeii.[2]

Wordsworth seems never to have used the term *archeology*, yet he was attentive to contemporary investigations of the kind we would now call archeological. To be sure, his view of them is ambivalent. He was fascinated with sites of interest to archeologists or, as he would probably have said, antiquarians. But he repeatedly warned against what the Solitary in *The Excursion* calls the "antiquarian humour," the tendency to "skim along the surfaces of things," collecting rocks and artifacts with little if any interest in what they represent – a history without written records.[3] In his *Reply to 'Mathetes'*, Wordsworth's most cutting portrait of antiquarian foolishness, he mocks the naivety common to primitive societies and modern interpreters of artifacts those societies leave behind. He could also be impatient with antiquarian friends who amassed more data than he needed or wanted. Hence his reply ("a pox on your antiquarianism") to Sir Walter Scott's offer of authentic chronicles of the Rising of the North after Wordsworth had drafted a fictive reconstruction of the event in *The White Doe of Rylstone*.[4] Wordsworth's fascination with archeological inquiries is less strident, yet it exerts much greater pressure on his poetry and, I will argue, his aesthetics.

A Guide through the District of the Lakes

From his first visit to Salisbury Plain in 1793, his interest in stone circles like Stonehenge reflects his absorption in the idea of an unrecorded past. In his *Guide through the District of the Lakes*, he imagines what the region might have looked like before primitive peoples settled there. He then peoples (or re-peoples) this imagined vacancy with successive inhabitants.[5] In the 1822 edition of his work, he expanded a brief allusion to Roman and Druid sites in earlier editions with a note and sonnet on "Long Meg and Her Daughters," a stone circle near Penrith which he first saw in 1820 or early 1821. Echoing William Stukeley's hypothesis concerning Stonehenge, he assumes that the Penrith circle is "a complete place of Druidical worship."[6] Like Stukeley and many others, Wordsworth was wrong about the provenance and age of this and similar sites. Yet the archeological cast of his interest is instructive. The speaker of the sonnet asks "Long Meg" to speak about her origins because these, not simply the existence of a stone circle near Penrith, draw him to the place.

Wordsworth sketches the archeological impulse of his aesthetics in successive revisions of his *Guide*, which he revised more extensively than any other piece of prose, and his unfinished manuscript on aesthetics, "The Sublime and the Beautiful," which is troubled by aesthetic tensions that the *Guide* minimizes.[7] I begin with the aesthetic models presented in this published work because they offer a more schematic account of aesthetic differences. First published anonymously in 1810 as the text for Rev. Joseph Wilkinson's *Select Views in*

Cumberland, Westmoreland, and Lancashire, the work was later revised and reissued under Wordsworth's name. Expanded versions present two different views of his aesthetics of landscape. The first, which appears in the anonymous text of 1810 and all subsequent editions, compares the topography of the Lake District to a wheel. The second, a description of sublimity and beauty as nature's successive "dealings" in the region, first appears in the 1820 edition. Whereas the first account is wholly concerned with surveying the present appearance of the region, the second imagines an aesthetic progress in the region that mirrors its geological history.

To introduce readers to his subject, he asks them to visualize the Lake District as if it were "an image borrowed from a map," something like a three-dimensional model of the Alps which he had seen at Lucerne (2:176–77). This substitution of a map-like view for an actual map like those typically issued with guidebooks of the period emphasizes the act of representation inherent in map-making. It also assigns readers the task of imagining a bird's eye view of the region. Wordsworth explains that to look at its Lucerne prototype, which apparently resembled the three-dimensional maps that are sometimes found in the visitor centers of national parks, the spectator climbed a platform and looked down at an accurate, detailed representation of "mountains, lakes, glaciers, rivers, woods, waterfalls, and vallies, with their cottages, and every other object contained in them." Wordsworth's apparent pleasure as this spectator is a model for the pleasure he hopes readers will have: "this exhibition affords an exquisite delight to the imagination, tempting it to wander at will from valley to valley, from mountain to mountain, through the deepest recesses of the Alps" (2:170).

Were Wordsworth primarily a guidebook writer or a poet who celebrated nature for its (or her) own sake, delights of this kind would surely suffice. But he adds that the model affords a "more substantial pleasure" because it allows spectators to see how "the sublime and beautiful region, with all its hidden treasures, and their bearings and relations to each other, is thereby comprehended and understood at once" (2:170). As much aesthetic as it is topographical, this pleasure promotes an even more schematic and less picturesque model of the Lake District than its prototype at Lucerne:

I know not how to give the reader a distinct image of these [the main outlines of the country] more readily, than by requesting him to place himself with me, in imagination, upon some given point; let it be the top of either of the mountains, Great Gavel, or Scawfell; or rather, let us suppose our station to be a cloud hanging midway between those two mountains, at not more than half a mile's distance from the summit of each, and not many yards above their highest elevation; we shall then see stretched at our feet a number of vallies, not fewer than eight, diverging from the point, on which we are supposed to stand, like spokes from the nave of a wheel. *(Prose, 2:171)*

As an approximate representation of Lakes topography, Wordsworth's wheel image registers his conception of *topography* as the "mapping of places." What he wants to show the reader is not the Lake District as such but an imagined model of its contours. Because no map can record every feature of a terrain, map-making requires a pre-selection of relevant data and presupposes an ideology.[8] Thus a Marxian economic map of an industrialized nation is different from one that reflects a Keynesian or "supply-side" perspective. The control which economic maps exert over the realities they are said to "represent" is relatively self-evident. Although topographical maps seem to offer more "natural" or "real" images, these also require a selection of data and a conventional system of representation. Such maps typically emphasize land contours and give less attention to roads and trails, as the amateur who tries to read them as if they were road maps soon learns.

Wordsworth's imagined overview of the Lake District falls mid-way between economic and topographical maps. The wheel image identifies topographical contours, but it also selects data more obviously than a topographical map might seem to do: the hub of the "wheel," a point situated above and between Scawfell and Great Gavel, is not the true center of the region. It is, however, the center of Wordsworth's image of the region, much as certain economic factors would be the focus of maps drawn from different economic perspectives. As an image that organizes the sublime and beautiful features of the Lakes, it declares a subtle preference for the aesthetic containment appropriate to the beautiful.

From this perspective, the debate about whether Wordsworth invented this image or stole it from a local dalesman is amusing but misleading. If Wordsworth stole it from someone, so did DeQuincey and Coleridge, and probably the dalesman as well. Coleridge's use of the image of an "old coach-wheel" to suggest the relation between seeing "abstractly" and the beautiful tells us more about the role of the beautiful in Wordsworth's adaptation of the same figure. When we look at such a wheel "abstractly," Coleridge argues, we see it as beautiful because we note "how its rays proceed from the centre to the circumferences, and how many different images are distinctly comprehended at one glance, as forming one whole, and each part in some harmonious relation to each and all."[9] Although the role of the beautiful in establishing this aesthetic control is as suppressed in

Wordsworth's text as it is declared in Coleridge's, the wheel-image summarizes the advantages the beautiful offers Wordsworth as the poet and essayist who would like to be able to map his aesthetic progress as surely as he surveys the region represented by the model at Lucerne. Later editions make this point even more explicit by locating "sublime or beautiful features" on this "wheel" (*Prose*, 2:174). The difference between this image and the circle as a Platonic image of perfection is suggested by Wordsworth's placement of the image in his text. First he describes the region, then he introduces the wheel as an analogous form, not an ideal one. As such, it is a conventional model or representation, used with this clearly in mind. But it is not an ideal to which the world of appearances bears an imperfect resemblance. Platonic distinctions between sublunary and ideal realms are simply not appropriate to the Wordsworthian beautiful, concerned as it is with recognizing relations and proportions in the phenomenal world and in language.

In a passage Wordsworth may have written in 1819 or 1820, he introduces another, more antithetical view of the Lakes. The new passage, which appears in the 1820 edition, the first to bear Wordsworth's name and his choice of title,[10] describes how the "*boundary-line*" of the larger lakes of the region was formed:

> That unformity which prevails in the primitive frame of the lower grounds among all chains or clusters of mountains where large bodies of still water are bedded, is broken by the *secondary* agents of nature, ever at work to supply the deficiences of the mould in which things were originally cast. Using the word *deficiences*, I do not speak with reference to those stronger emotions which a region of mountains is peculiarly fitted to excite. The bases of those huge barriers may run for a long space in straight lines, and these parallel to each other; the opposite sides of a profound vale may ascend as exact counterparts, or in mutual reflection, like the billows of a troubled sea; and the impression be, from its very simplicity, more awful and sublime. Sublimity is the result of Nature's first great dealings with the superficies of the earth; but the general tendency of her subsequent operations is towards the production of beauty, by a multiplicity of symmetrical parts uniting in a consistent whole. (*Prose*, 2:181)

This conception is indebted to earlier aesthetic theory, to theories of the earth's formation, including Thomas Burnet's *Sacred Theory of the Earth*, and to early nineteenth-century discussions of the stratigraphy and geology of the Lakes. In Wordsworth's *Guide* each of these pre-texts is assimilated to an aesthetic progress from the sublime to the beautiful.

As Marjorie Nicolson has observed, the mountains and abysses which were for Burnet the "ruines" of a once-paradisal earth became the landscapes of the eighteenth-century sublime. Specifically, the

Archeologies

eighteenth-century admiration for the boundless, infinite character of
the sublime echoes Burnet's mournful descriptions of the post-diluvial
world as an infinite, boundless Chaos come again.[11] Revising this
source as he invokes it, Wordsworth insists that his use of the term
deficiences applies to the forms themselves, not to the "stronger
emotions" which those forms excite in the mind. Because this sublimity is the result of nature's *first* dealings, it implies a distinctly
un-Burnetian premise – there was no original paradise, no perfectly
smooth globe. Wordsworth instead assumes that the earth was
originally deficient and so in need of nature's "subsequent
operations." In brief, because the sublime is primitive and incomplete,
it needs the beautiful as its successor.

By suggesting that sublime mountain forms are deficient not because
they are indistinct, but because they lack completion, Wordsworth
questions Burke's famous declaration that sublime objects and expressions tend to be indistinct.[12] As straight, parallel lines that reflect each
other, the simplicity of these mountain forms echoes the argument of a
number of eighteenth-century treatises on rhetoric and aesthetics that
simple rather than ornate figuration is essential to the "sublime style."
(For the moment I ignore the debate over Milton's sublime style which,
Addison and others agreed, was not simple.)[13]

Wordsworth's discussion of the sublimity of simple mountain forms
also queries William Gilpin's disapproval of rugged, parallel mountain
"lines." Gilpin argued that such forms lacked "picturesque beauty,"
the aesthetic hybrid he used to describe, among other "lines," the
boundary-line of lakes in the North of England.[14] Despite Uvedale
Prince's more cautious (and more manageable) definition of the
picturesque as "a sudden roughness or variation," nineteenth-century
tourists and guidebook writers often threw Price's caution to the
winds, describing scenes as "picturesquely sublime" or "picturesquely
beautiful" with abandon. Neither Wordsworth nor Coleridge found
this blurring of aesthetic distinctions edifying.[15] Wordsworth's charge
in *The Prelude* that the picturesque was a "strong infection of the age"
(*Prel.*, II:155–61, p. 424) did not prevent him from appropriating
Gilpin's attention to outline and form in the Lake District. However,
he did so to advance a different aesthetic argument. As "a multiplicity
of parts within a consistent whole," the architectonic features of
Wordsworthian beauty reiterate Coleridge's argument that the beautiful is "Multeity in Unity" and demonstrates how "the many, still seen
as many, becomes one." This assessment echoes Francis Hutcheson's
influential definition of beauty as "Uniformity amidst Variety." In
notes he probably composed in 1808, Coleridge offers a distinction

between ancient and modern art, derived from Schlegel and possibly Schiller. Whereas sublimity characterizes modern art, "grace, proportion, and elegance" – traditional attributes of the beautiful – characterize ancient art.[16]

If much of what Wordsworth argues in the *Guide* echoes eighteenth-century aesthetic theory, his identification of sublimity and beauty as successive phases in "nature's dealings" has no precedent in earlier aesthetic theory. Despite the eighteenth-century enthusiasm for primitive, "Ossianic" poetry, no previous discussion of sublime landscapes and bards offered so specific a transfer of the idea of primitive poetry and poets to a similar archaism in nature. This conception also modifies contemporary antiquarian and geological hypotheses that were central to nineteenth-century archeology.

As John R. Nabholtz has argued, Wordsworth makes some use of Thomas Whitaker's *The History and Antiquities of the Deanery of Craven*, which he read in 1807, which begins by observing that Yorkshire was gradually "soften[ed] down from Deformity to Grandeur, and from Grandeur to Beauty" and thus gradually "reduce[d] ... to tractable and productive shape." Whitaker adds that the processes by which "a Substance so hard and stubborn as limestone-rock should have been smoothed into shapely knolls, or moulded into soft and regular alterations of hill and valley" are less well understood, although the evident result is the transformation "of angles and right lines" into "graceful curves." The figure he uses to represent this process is especially apposite to the Wordsworthian beautiful: it is "as if some plastic hand had formed the original surface over again for use and beauty at once."[17] Whitaker's description may owe something to Joseph Addison's suggestion that beauty delights because it "gives a Finishing to anything that is Great or Uncommon." But it probably owes more to late eighteenth-century geological thought.[18] Wordsworth fuses Whitaker's two earliest stages (deformity and grandeur) into one epoch of primitive sublimity to insure a strong antithesis between sublimity and beauty. He then secures this antithesis by refusing Whitaker's explicit equation of beauty with use and his implicit one between sublimity (Whitaker's deformity or grandeur) and uselessness.

Wordsworth's account of an aesthetic progress in nature's successive "dealings" makes tactful use of contemporary speculations about stratigraphy and, in particular, discussions of the stratigraphy of the Lake District which began to appear around 1800.[19] Erasmus Darwin summarized more than a century of discussion of the stratigraphy of the earth in *The Botanic Garden* when he describes the "hidden strata" that record the earth's evolution.[20] Like Buffon (whose analysis of the earth's continual and successive variations implies a recognition of geological strata) and Hutton, as well as Playfair and Cuvier a few years later, Darwin grants the role of strata as demarcations in geological time. Cuvier's fossil research further implies the relation between fossils and strata which John Frere declared in a letter published in 1800 in *Archaeologia*, the London periodical of the Society of Antiquaries. Using his analysis of strata in a gravel pit near Hoxne in Suffolk as a case in point, Frere urged readers to consider the historical evidence suggested by finding artifacts embedded in different strata.[21] Later in the nineteenth century archeologists began to use stratigraphic maps to chart the location and relation of artifacts found during excavations.

In 1841 Wordsworth reminded the eminent geologist Rev. Adam Sedgwick of his promise twenty years earlier to contribute some remarks on the geology of the Lakes to Wordsworth's *Guide*. Sedgwick obliged with a series of letters which appear in subsequent editions of "Hudson's" *Guide*, essentially Wordsworth's *Guide* in a more accessible format. The two men had met in 1822, while Sedgwick gathered data in the North of England for a stratigraphic map of the region modelled on William "Strata" Smith's 1815 stratigraphic map of England.[22] Wordsworth's renewal of a request he had made twenty years earlier signals the importance he consistently attached to geological principles.

By the early 1820s, if not before, he had met several geologists whose stratigraphic investigations then focused on the Lake District. Local speculations about the stratigraphy of the region were frequently featured in *The Lonsdale Magazine*, a short-lived Kendal publication which Wordsworth read. Jonathan Otley contributed three essays to the journal in 1820, its first year of publication. Of these, one gave an explanation of the floating island of Derwentwater, a subject that fascinated Wordsworth, while a second offered the first extended account of the stratigraphy of the Lakes.[23] In this essay and in subsequent works, Otley explained that the central peaks of the region, including Scawfell, Great Gavel, and Helvellyn, among others, are older than the surrounding limestone. For reasons which are still being debated, these peaks were gradually lifted up and tilted so that they rise above the more recent limestone which encircles them with a fringe of smoother rock.[24] Wordsworth had already encountered a similar geological configuration in the Alps. According to Ramond de Carbonnières, whose popular French translation of William Coxe's guidebook Wordsworth used extensively during his 1790 tour of the

Continent and for the composition of *Descriptive Sketches*, the central mountainous zone of the Alps is older than the surrounding "secondary" peaks. Ramond and contemporary geologists like de Saussure believed these younger peaks had been deposited by a deluge.[25]

By 1822, then, when Wordsworth added the phrase "and sublimity" to the end of his description of the peaks at the "hub" of his wheel-image, he had a fairly specific knowledge of the stratigraphy of the Lake District:

> From the circumference to the centre, that is, from the sea or plain country to the mountain stations specified [Great Gavel and Scawfell], there is – in the several ridges that enclose these vales, and divide them from each other, I mean in the forms and surfaces, first of the swelling grounds, next of the hills and rocks, and lastly of the mountains – an ascent of almost regular gradation, from elegance and richness, to their highest point of grandeur and sublimity.   (*Prose*, 2:173)

As visible artifacts of an earlier epoch, Scawfell and Great Gavel reveal the existence of an aesthetic as well as a geology which would otherwise be buried by nature's beautifying operations, manifested in the Lakes by the gentler contours of the surrounding limestone. The pre-history for this notice of sublime features in the midst of a beautified terrain probably began several years earlier. Wordsworth's identification of the sublimity of the peaks at the center of this wheel image owes something to William Green's 1819 *The Tourist's New Guide*, which declares that Scawfell is "the most sublime and commanding elevation in England."[26] Green's remark is doubly indebted to Otley, who was his companion during the 1816 Scawfell ascent described in Green's *Guide*, and the author of an 1818 "Pocket Map" of the region which challenged earlier claims that Helvellyn was the highest peak of the Lake District. According to Otley's more accurate elevation chart, the Scawfell Pikes are higher.[27] Thus if Wordsworth made use of Otley's geological hypotheses in 1822, his acquaintance with them may have developed from interests he had in common with Otley and Green. Finally, Otley's geological hypotheses may have prompted one other *Guide* revision. In the 1823 edition Wordsworth expanded an 1810 reference to deposits of schist and limestone on the fringe of the mountains of the Lake to include "free-stone," a variety of limestone or sandstone which Otley described in his 1820 letter to *The Lonsdale Magazine*.[28]

The differences between the versions of Lakes stratigraphy described in the 1820 and the 1822 *Guides* can be illustrated by imagining a modern stratigraphic map for each of them. Unlike nineteenth-century stratigraphic maps, which used cross-sections and labels to indicate different strata, modern ones use transparent overlays to represent each of the strata excavated at a given site. The contours of each are depicted by lines on a single overlay, and the placement of the artifacts discovered at the site is marked on the appropriate overlays by a conventional system of notation. Finally, these transparent "strata" are superimposed in the sequence determined for their original deposition. Looking down through the transparent overlays of such a map, we would see its reconstruction of the entire stratigraphic sequence. Or, by pulling individual overlays away from the rest, we would be able to see which artifacts belonged to which "strata." Either method allows us to see more of earlier, hidden strata than could those nineteenth-century travellers who stood on a platform to look look down at a relief map of the Alps, or readers of Wordsworth's *Guide* who imagined looking down on the Lake District from a point suspended midway between two of its major peaks.

A modern stratigraphic map of the relation between sublimity and beauty as it is presented in the 1820 *Guide* would show how nature's earliest "dealings" had been gradually softened and made to form a coherent whole. Beauty would dominate the transparency that corresponds to the surface. Without this imagined map it would be impossible, or at least impractical, to find out what lies beneath the surface. Lacking modern coring equipment, we would have to locate an area where the order in which strata were first deposited had been disturbed, much as nineteenth-century geologists had to do. Or we might look down through the transparent layers of a stratigraphic map of the aesthetic relations described in the 1822 *Guide*. This map would show how the original deposition of strata had been disturbed as earlier strata intruded into later ones. In Otley's geological analysis these intrusive strata are occasionally visible as outcroppings. In Wordsworth's aesthetics they reveal the continued presence of sublimity in a topography whose surface is dominated by the production of beauty.

For Wordsworth the sublime is down, hidden, and primitive, yet occasionally it re-emerges. As a guide, a poet, and the mental traveller who resembles them both, he is the archeologist of this aesthetics. He excavates, finds artifacts, and, with the aid of an aesthetic progress made visible in the strata of the Lakes, he seeks to locate those artifacts on stratigraphic maps of his imagining. This aesthetics displays the archeologist's fascination with depths rather than with relics found scattered on the surface. Like Winckelmann, who hoped to rescue "much older cultures from the abyss of time" by establishing "a provisional order for what had been outright Chaos,"[29] Wordsworth hoped to identify an order for the depths as well as the visible surfaces of the mind's aesthetics. And, much like Winckelmann, he did so in part to manage the mind's sublimity, whose powers and forms he associated with primeval Chaos. Like Frere and other nineteenth-century writers who recognized that where artifacts were embedded mattered as much as what they were, Wordsworth pays nearly as much attention to where the mind experiences sublimity and beauty – whether in topographies or in texts – as he does to what the mind experiences.

Early nineteenth-century investigations of the stratigraphy of the Lake District offered Wordsworth a model for his own investigations, begun years before, of the sublime and the beautiful as successive strata in the mind's aesthetic progress, while Otley's account of the intrusion of the earlier strata that comprise the central peaks of the region suggested (or confirmed) the potential for sublime intrusions into a surface modified and composed by the beautiful. As the eighteenth-century antiquarian Rev. Henry Rowlands suggested "archeology" typically does, Wordsworth's aesthetics of retrieval relies on "inference" and "conjecture" to supplement available records.[30] Lacking a written record of the mind's aesthetic progress, he must instead look for artifacts of "possible sublimity" (*Prel.*, 2:334–37, p. 82) and recognize the presence of the beautiful in texts as well as landscapes.

Because Wordsworth's aesthetic model is based on inference and conjecture rather than a transparent archeological record, it provides only a partial representation of the mind's aesthetic engagements. Like maps in general, it abstracts and summarizes details and complexities of the world it depicts. As such, it is a figure for the problems of representation that trouble his unfinished manuscript on aesthetics. There an uneasy equilibrium between the depths and surfaces of the mind's aesthetic "progress" indicates a suppressed aesthetic conflict.

"The Sublime and the Beautiful"

Commentaries on Romantic aesthetics have given little attention to "The Sublime and the Beautiful," the only philosophical account of the mind's aesthetics Wordsworth attempted.[31] One reason for this neglect is the fact that it ends without fully explaining the role of the beautiful in the mind's aesthetic determinations. Because its opening paragraphs summarize that role, this omission is less critical than it appears to be. The structure of its argument presents more serious difficulties. One critic complains that it shifts methodological grounds at least twice, proceeding in some sections as if sublimity and beauty designate what goes on in the mind and in others as if they summarize external criteria. Yet in most of this essay and in his much later letter denouncing the construction of the Kendal and Windermere Railway, Wordsworth makes his position clear enough. Aesthetic distinctions are learned not found in landscape.[32] If the ambivalence of some sections of his manuscript on aesthetics betray genuine difficulties in his contentions about mind, landscape, and aesthetic response, they also record his response to Kant and Burke and his invention of a model that differs from theirs.

As the manuscript begins or, more precisely, as it takes up its argument in mid-sentence, Wordsworth announces the traits of this model:

Though it is impossible that a mind can be in a healthy state that is not frequently and strongly moved both by sublimity and beauty, it is more dependent for its daily well-being upon the love & gentleness which accompany the one, than upon the exaltation or awe which are created by the other. – Hence, as we advance in life, we can escape upon the invitation of our more placid and gentle nature from those obtrusive qualities in an object sublime in its general character; which qualities, at an earlier age, precluded imperiously the perception of beauty which that object if contemplated under another relation would have been capable of imparting.   (*Prose*, 2:349)

Like Ann Radcliffe and other advocates of the doctrine of sensibility, Wordsworth assumes that aesthetic response is an index of moral feeling: a "healthy" mind is in this context one that is ethically sound.[33] He also makes use of Burke's opposition between an authoritarian sublimity that inspires exaltation and awe and a placid, domesticated beauty, and its suggestion of a progress from sublimity to beauty.[34] In other ways Wordsworth's account of the mind's progress from sublimity to beauty differs from Burke, from Kant, and even from the aesthetic model he ascribes to nature in the *Guide*. In his manuscript on aesthetics, he argues that if an object potentially evokes sensations of sublimity *or* beauty, the mind is more likely to think it sublime. Under other conditions the same object might instead appear beautiful. This modification of the fixed aesthetic progress outlined for nature initiates a strong rivalry between sublimity and beauty. Whereas the first is more imperious in early stages of the mind's aesthetic education, in later stages beauty will gain precedence. Placid though it is, it aids the mind in its escape from the sublime by showing how the same object can be perceived "under another relation." As someone who lived mostly in a mountainous region, created views in at least one landscape garden, and read picturesque guidebooks that incessantly describe points of view, Wordsworth understood that seeing objects from different locations alters visual (as well as aesthetic) relations between the perceiver and objects in the field of vision.[35]

For Wordsworth, the aesthetic conflict is not, as it was for Kant, between the mind and nature's magnitude or might but between the mind's sublimity and the mind's beauty. Instead of reacting against the power and patriarchal authority of nature or the precursor-poet by sublimating them – as the mind is said to do in Weiskel's neo-Kantian reading of the Wordsworthian sublime[36] – the mind grows capable of experiencing as beautiful scenes it once regarded as sublime. And if the mind is at first largely unable to avoid sensations of sublimity, it gradually learns to do so. Beauty's "invitation" masks its powerful interventionism, fully equal (in later years or in the later stages of the mind's aesthetic development) to the imperious sublime.

To this account Wordsworth adds an intriguing qualification: this aesthetic progress does not necessarily occur early in life. Its onset depends on when one visits mountainous regions for the first time. Thus an adult stranger to scenes of this kind will be like a child insofar as aesthetic response is concerned. But whether the perceiving subject is a child or an adult, Wordsworth reiterates, "the sublime always precedes the beautiful in making us conscious of its presence" (*Prose*, 2:50).

From this review of how and when the mind perceives sublimity and beauty, Wordsworth turns to the three parts of the sublime as they exist in objects: "a sense of individual form or forms; a sense of duration; and a sense of power" (*Prose*, 2:351). This discussion is not, however, concerned with these as primary qualities of objects (strictly speaking, only the first might be so construed), but as qualities which the mind can be expected to associate with objects that excite sensations of sublimity. The principle he seeks to demolish by tracing the relations among power, form, and duration is Burke's assertion that obscure or indistinct forms or expressions are sublime.[37] Wordsworth says of the mind's response to the Pikes of Langdale:

But if they be looked at from a point which has brought us so near that the mountain is almost the sole object before our eyes, yet not so near but that the whole of it is visible, we shall be impressed with a sensation of sublimity.

(*Prose*, 2:351)

As W. J. B. Owen has observed, this argument echoes Burke's claim concerning the mind's absorption in the sublime and consequent inability to reason about what it experiences.[38] Yet Wordsworth also disallows Burke's famous corollary principle that this occurs because sublime forms are indistinct. Wordsworth's assessment of the role that individual forms have in impressions of sublimity assumes that the mind recognizes the idea of infinity under the aspect of duration:

Duration is evidently an element of the sublime; but think of it without reference to individual form, and we shall perceive that it has no power to affect the mind. Cast your eye, for example, upon any commonplace ridge or eminence that cannot be separated, without some effort of the mind, from the general mass of the planet; you may be persuaded, nay, convinced, that it has borne that shape as long as or longer than Cader Idris, or Snowdon, or the Pikes of Langdale that are before us; and the mind is wholly unmoved by the thought; and the only way in which such an object can affect us, contemplated under the notion of duration, is when the faint sense which we have of its individuality is lost in the general sense of duration belonging to the Earth itself.   (*Prose*, 2:351)[39]

In cancelled versions of a related passage, Wordsworth attempts to clarify how individual form communicates ideas of duration and power to the mind. He suggests that the outline of such forms conveys power "by dim analogies to active [power *del*.] force as expressed by the [? to] parts of the human body such as shoulder or head or neck" (*Prose*, 2:351–52). In successive formulations of this passage, the quality which Wordsworth seeks to express is a kinetic force whose potential motion is implied by its outline. The final version acknowledges the paradox of arguing that a stationary object might express the idea of motion:

A mountain being a stationary object is enabled to effect this in connection with duration and individual form, by the sense of motion which in the mind accompanies the lines by which the Mountain itself is shaped out. These lines may either be abrupt or precipitous, by which danger & sudden change is expressed; or they may flow into each other like the waves of a sea, and, by involving in such an image a feeling of self-propagation infinitely continuous and without cognizable beginning, these lines may thus convey to the Mind sensations not less sublime than those which were excited by their opposites, the abrupt and precipitous.
                    (*Prose*, 2:352)

The infinitude that characterizes the Wordsworthian sublime is, then, primarily temporal, whereas Burkean obscurity is primarily spatial. Moreover, unlike the power of the Burkean sublime, that of the Wordsworthian sublime is communicated when the mind perceives the motion that is immanent in mountain forms, which seem to stride through time from an archaic past much as they stride through space toward the boy of *The Prelude*, 1. Movement in space is thus made an analogue for duration, perceived diachronically as movement through endless time.

The direction of the argument shifts when Wordsworth attempts to deal with an inconsistency in his discussion of duration. Because a child's sensation of sublimity is likely to be too caught up in "awe or personal apprehension" (*Prose*, 2:353), few children are likely to recognize an idea of duration in their experience of the sublime. This inconsistency is never really resolved in Wordsworth's long consideration of the role of fear in sublime experience. At times, more frequently in poems written after 1806, he skirts the problem by assigning eternality – and thus duration – to the beautiful. Given this impasse, it is little wonder that he chose not to finish the manuscript.

To return to the line of argument that Wordsworth takes up at this point (or gap) in the text: "personal apprehension" designates the kind of fear which had provoked considerable debate among eighteenth-century theorists. It is, moreover, the kind of fear Burke said was essential to sublime experience.[40] The fact that the opening section of the essay omits fear from its otherwise traditional and Burkean catalogue of the emotions which attend the sublime suggests Wordsworth's recognition of the difficulties which arise whenever fear, even a carefully circumscribed fear, is granted a role in the sublime. For some eighteenth-century poets and theorists, fear insured the mind's subservience to God as the highest illustration of the sublime; for others, fear had no essential role in sublime experience, however it was defined. This debate is singular not because its speakers always responded to opposing arguments convincingly, which for the most part they did not, but because its irresolution for more than a century signals a persistent uneasiness about the presence or absence of fear in aesthetic response.

In "The Pleasures of the Imagination," Addison argued that the final cause of our delight in "greatness" is that it leads us to the contemplation of God.[41] Elsewhere in *The Spectator* he noted with approval Longinus's claim that the sublime need not be accompanied by the *pathetick*, a term eighteenth-century writers identified with fear and the sublime.[42] Prior to the publication of Burke's *Enquiry* in 1758, other writers were no less cautious than Addison had been. John Baillie defined the sublime as that which elevates the mind by giving it "the Consciousness of its own Vastness." He explained that while both sublimity and fear "are felt upon viewing what is great and awful," fear is merely accidental and sublimity essential. The sublime elevates, whereas fear sinks and contracts. Baillie concluded that if the mind experiences too much "dread," the sensation of sublimity may be entirely destroyed.[43]

Baillie's analysis of fear signals the emerging impasse in British aesthetics. As long as the elevation of the Longinian sublime could be attributed to God or divine creation, there could be no contest between

27

God and the human mind. But once that elevation was attributed to the mind as well, a potential conflict developed between God or nature's sublimity as a manifestation of God's power, and the mind's sublimity. To some extent this conflict has been implicit in the admiration for Longinus, who described elevation as the basis of the sublime style and made only passing mention of the sublime in nature.[44] Still, for those who identified the sublime with God, elevation belonged to Him, not to the essayist or orator.

Burke emphasized rather than minimized the conflict between the mind's elevation and pride on the one hand and its fear of God on the other, by arguing first that fear and pain rather than elevation are the sources of the sublime, and second, that awe or terror accompany our idea of God's sublime power:

> Whilst we contemplate so vast an object, under the arms, as it were, of almightly power, and invested upon every side with omnipresence, we shrink into the minuteness of our own nature, and are, in a manner, annihilated before him. And though a consideration of his other attributes may relieve in some measure our apprehensions; yet no conviction of the justice with which it is exercised, nor the mercy with which it is tempered, can wholly remove the terror that naturally arises from a force which nothing can withstand.[45]

The problematic character of this argument emerges when Burke identifies sublime fear with rebels (reformed or not) against God. He asserts, for example, that we feel awe and fear in reading Milton's description of Satan in *Paradise Lost*, or the Old Testament account of Job's initially rebellious, then fearful encounters with his God. The claim which Burke seeks to prove by citing these texts concerns how obscure images induce fear as clear ones cannot, but his choice of texts speaks to, or incites, a rather different theme, that of the rebellion or subservience of men and fallen angels to God.[46] Although the allusion to Milton is probably guided by a retrospective attention to John Dennis and to Addison, who both commented at some length on the sublimity of the epic conception and style of *Paradise Lost*, Burke captured the attention of subsequent writers on aesthetics as his predecessors had not.[47]

Of those writers who responded to Burke, a few rejected fear altogether. But many more argued that some kind of fear is present in the sublime, although they could not agree about whether fear was an agent or merely an accident of that experience.[48] A third group granted Burke's thesis that fear is the source of the sublime, then used it to emphasize the antithetical natures of the sublime and the beautiful. These writers argued that whereas the sublime suggests greatness and power, and evokes feelings of terror, awe, or humility, the beautiful exhibits proportion and order, and evokes feelings of love and gentility.[49]

Unlike Richard Payne Knight, who argued rather evasively that fear is present in the sublime but contributes nothing essential to it, Kant responded directly to Burke's analysis of fear and self-preservation by challenging Burke's assertion that "no passion so effectually robs the mind of all its powers of acting and reasoning as fear."[50] Quite simply, Kant disallowed fear's theft by redefining the sublime as that which comes into being when the imagination attempts to encompass nature's magnitude (the "mathematically sublime") or to resist its might (the "dynamically sublime"), but fails to do either. At this critical moment reason intervenes, and recognizes in this failure a power or "faculty of judgement" which surpasses nature and sense experience. This faculty – not nature's might or magnitude – is the sublime.[51] Kant categorically denied the presence of fear in the mind's contemplation of God.

For Wordsworth and for Coleridge, Kant and Knight were both wrong, but for different reasons. Coleridge concluded that fear did not exist, either as accident or agent, in sublime experience.[52] Wordsworth argues to the contrary that a limited fear is part of the sublime. Otherwise his disagreements with Kant mirror Coleridge's. In his essay on aesthetics, Wordsworth recapitulates the section of Kant's third *Critique* with which Coleridge also took issue.[53]

Because "The Sublime and the Beautiful" exhibits both Wordsworth's fascination with the Kantian model and his recognition of its incompatibility with his own, it offers a singular account of how one Romantic poet, perhaps the poet of the Romantic sublime, struggled with the implications of a philosophical system which he could neither master nor fully grant. Like Coleridge, he claims that the sublime can only exist when the mind experiences a sense of "intense unity" and the "comparing power" is suspended. By this he means the role which Kantian reason performs to aid the imagination at the moment of its defeat before the spectacle of nature's magnitude or might:

To what degree consistent with sublimity power may be dreaded has been ascertained; but as power, contemplated as something to be opposed or resisted, implies a twofold agency of which the mind is conscious, this state seems to be irreconciliable to what has been said concerning the consummation of sublimity, which, as has been determined, exists in the extinction of the comparing power of the mind, & in intense unity.   (*Prose*, 2:356)

This discussion of opposition and resistance echoes Kant, who argues that "the sublime is that in comparison with which everything else is small." Lest his reader think that the sublime refers to nature,

however, he modifies this definition to indicate that the sublime owes
its existence to the mind and in particular to reason: "the sublime is
that, the mere ability to think which shows a faculty of mind
surpassing every standard of sense."[54] The mind discovers its own
sublimity as the imagination attempts to encompass nature's magnitude or to resist its might. Wordsworth echoes both Kantian poles, but
emphasizes the mind's resistance to nature's might, Kant's "dynamically sublime" (Prose, 2:354–56).

Kant argues further that nature's might "has no dominion over us,"
because while we resist it and find it fearful, it is fearful only in the
limited sense that it can claim physical mastery over us, but not – and
the distinction is crucial for Kant – intellectual mastery. Thus the
"dynamically sublime" is produced by a conflict within the mind,
whose "rational faculty" (Vernunft-vermögen) secures its intellectual
"self-preservation" (Selbsterhaltung) in order to countermand the
physical superiority of nature's "might."[55] He earlier explains that the
intellectual hazard which the mind experiences before nature's might
or magnitude requires the assistance of reason (Vernunft), which
bridges the "abyss" of the transcendent discovered by the imagination
(Einbildungskraft) when it attempts to encompass or resist nature.
From the "harmonious" conflict or "subjective play" between imagination and reason emerges a new, nonsensuous standard which allows
the mind its superiority without denying nature its physical dominion.[56] Reason's encounter with nature in the "dynamically sublime" is
so replete with allusions to resistance, power, danger, and alternative
modes of self-preservation that Kant's disclaimers about personal fear
are not altogether convincing. Frances Ferguson has argued that
Kant's effort to legislate the solitary, isolated character of the sublime
by placing it under the aegis of reason is fraught with danger from
within.[57] Here Kant attempts to neutralize that danger by projecting it
outward, onto the mind's encounter with nature.

Wordsworth's attempts to define the sublime are marked by a
similar ambivalence. Although he occasionally presents it as though it
were Coleridge's "endless allness," notably in "Tintern Abbey,"
where the speaker argues that nature guides the mind to "a sense
sublime / Of something far more deeply interfused,"[58] he more often
grants the presence of fear in the midst of a sense of unity. The sublime
encounters of The Prelude also display Kantian recognitions of the
sublime as that which allows the mind to transcend limits imposed by
sense and the phenomenal world. However, one essential difference
between Kant and Wordsworth is the role and place each assigns to
reason in those recognitions and their aftermath. For Wordsworth, the

progress toward the sublime is intuitive and imaginative, not rational, whereas Kant's progress toward the sublime requires that imagination step aside so that intuitive reason may recognize what the imagination cannot.[59]

In "The Sublime and the Beautiful" Wordsworth acknowledges the contradiction between his claim that "intense unity" and the "extinction of the comparing power" are necessary to sublime response and his (Kantian) counter-assertion that the mind resists nature's might, then offers to introduce a principle "which will remove the main difficulties of this investigation" (2:354). No principle is forthcoming. Instead he introduces a famous landscape, the Fall of the Rhine near Schaffhausen in Switzerland, to demonstrate how the mind can resist nature's might and still experience intense unity. This use of a scene which was a familiar visual and verbal text for nineteenth-century readers and travellers is, I suggest, a covert response to Kant's third *Critique*, which lists "the lofty waterfall of a mighty river" as the last in a series of scenes in nature which "exhibit our faculty of resistance as insignificantly small in comparison with their might."[60] Allusions to nature are infrequent in the third *Critique*. Moreover, Wordsworth had already repeated the key points of the argument concerning the "dynamically sublime" in which this list appears.

In the center of the Rhinefall is a massive boulder divided into two crags, around and through which the waters of the Rhine descend with considerable force. Wordsworth explains that because this rock has opposed the mass of waters that surge around it "for countless ages," together the rock and the waterfall demonstrate a continuous "state of opposition and yet reconcilement." By means, then, of an unending paradoxical relation, the mind's resistance can, like that of the rock to its surrounding waters, be included in the sublime if, and only if,

The mind, either by glances or continuously, conceives that power may be overcome or rendered evanescent, and as far as it feels itself tending toward the unity that exists in security or absolute triumph.   (*Prose*, 2:356)

Wordsworth considers a similar relation between sublimity, resistance, and duration in "An Unpublished Tour" (*Prose*, 2:317). In both texts, resistance implies self-confidence about one's capacity to survive the hazards of opposing a mighty force, a self-confidence that is absent from Burke's discussion of fear and the sublime, and only made available in the Kantian model when reason steps in to secure a triumph in the realm of supersensible ideas. But for Wordsworth, the sublime fear of Burkean and Kantian aesthetics is circumscribed by the mind's capacity to resist or to engage in an all-encompassing unity, much as the rock near Schaffhausen perpetually opposes the waters that surround it and yet remains part of the sublimity of the scene.

If Burkean fear provided a useful focus for debate by later theorists, Kant's addition of reason and a reactive phase to the sublime undermined the basis for regarding the sublime as a category separate from the beautiful. For once it is assimilated to the sublime, reason ceases to function as a means of distinguishing between the two. Whatever their other disagreements with Kant's third *Critique*, several nineteenth-century German theorists appear to have drawn the conclusion which is implicit in the Kantian model. Thus Schiller, Herder, Schelling, and Schleiermacher suggested that the sublime and the beautiful might belong to a single aesthetic, which Schiller called beauty.[61] Yet given the revolutionary epoch which coincided with Kant's publication of the third *Critique*, as well as the larger role of reason in his philosophy, it is hard to imagine Kant having done otherwise, any more than it is possible to imagine the older Burke of *Reflections on the Revolution in France* wishing to celebrate the revolutionary fear and terror which he had so effectively represented as sublime forty years earlier.

Although the risk of sublime, revolutionary chaos also haunts Wordsworth's mature aesthetics, he chooses not to endorse Kant's inclusion of reason in the sublime. Instead he identifies reason or "the comparing power" as the agent of the beautiful. Traditionally the aesthetic of symmetry, order, and proportion, the beautiful owes its existence to reason and an Apollonian preference for appropriate limits in life and art. Calling this agent a counter-sublime, as one recent critic has,[62] re-engages the Kantian model using different terms: a "counter-sublime" is still a phase of the sublime. As that which can be known or defined, the Wordsworthian beautiful requires a balance of parts and wholes, of center and periphery which is alien to the Wordsworthian sublime, whose "intense unity" and fear momentarily obstruct the mind's capacity to reason about parts and wholes. As beauty's agent, reason suppresses the sublime by subjecting it to scale and effacing its incomparability and immeasurability. The beautiful also compels the mind's return to definable limits and to the human present from an archaic, pre-human past. By restoring a pre-Kantian opposition between reason and the sublime, and rejecting specific features of Burkean aesthetics, Wordsworth restrains sublime fear even as he grants its continuing and necessary presence in the mind. The aesthetic model which he generates to accomplish these tasks features a constant movement between the sublime as the chaotic but powerful origin of the mind's aesthetic progress in the child and in the adult, and the beautiful as the aesthetic which suppresses or domesticates the mind's earlier sublimity. With this model Wordsworth re-engages the sublime energies which Kant had wished to displace, and yet makes certain that those energies would be checked by the beautiful.

Other cross-currents between Wordsworth's aesthetics and that of Kant, Schiller, and Hegel are by turns ironic and confirmative. In all the critical works, including the third *Critique*, Kant advocates a reason that serves transcendent self-consciousness because he believes it essential to ethical action and thought. In the case of the sublime, Kantian reason makes strong claims for individual freedom and the rights of humankind, as opposed to rights insured by Burkean custom and inherited property.[63] But because Wordsworth's understanding of the sublime tends to be satanic insofar as he believes that sublime, transcendent self-consciousness may be perverted, he rejects the Kantian model for the same reason that Kant invented it. Briefly stated, the transcendent self-sufficiency of Kantian reason is what Wordsworth feared most, whereas Kant feared action and thought which do not emerge from transcendent reason.

In *On the Aesthetic Education of Man*, Schiller justifies the moral force of the Kantian aesthetic by presenting it as the play between the "freedom" made possible by reason, and the demands of the sensuous world. As Schiller elaborates this model, he introduces a series of binary, opposing pairs that resemble Wordsworth's opposition between sublimity and beauty. The last of Schiller's pairs subdivides beauty into two types – one "melting" (*schmelzende*) the other "energizing" (*energische*).[64] Although the persistent tension between these types of beauty recalls a similar tension in Wordsworth's aesthetics, neither this pair nor the sensuous and rational drives to which this subdivision of beauty responds are exactly equivalent to Wordsworth's categories. At its most complex, the tension between Wordsworthian sublimity and beauty owes much to the fact that neither is wholly sensuous or transcendent, that neither possesses all the moral or ethical advantages. Unlike Kant, and to a lesser extent Schiller, Wordsworth is more attentive to sublunar or sensuous manifestations of the sublime.

The Wordsworthian sublime most closely approximates the Kantian model (albeit without reference to a transcendent reason) when it registers what Hegel later called the negativity of the sublime – its existence outside appearance, beyond or (as Wordsworth characteristically presents it) below the phenomenal world.[65] The negativity of the Kantian and Hegelian sublime can be, and sometimes is, a compelling presence in Wordsworth's aesthetics. Yet what complicates his attraction to this version of the sublime is his sense that it is (*pace* Kant and Hegel) only one version. The other, the sublimity of revolutionary heroes, villains, and chaos come again, is never far behind Wordsworth's celebrations of sublime negativity. In *On the Sublime*, where a reluctant notice of sublime phenomena in nature and history is at odds with his main argument concerning the mind's sublime freedom,[66] Schiller signals the dilemma that articulates Wordsworth's aesthetic engagements – the pressure of history on the sublime as well as the beautiful.

Although Wordsworth might have written more on quarto sheets which have since been lost (two are clearly missing from the middle of the last section), no other evidence suggests that he ever completed the manuscript on aesthetics. In its last pages he continues to insist that readers should not use landscapes as objective criteria for aesthetic judgments, yet he repeatedly calls attention to "forms of nature" which are particularly suited to excite sensations of sublimity or beauty (*Prose*, 2:358). This shift in emphasis – from a discussion of the relation between the mind's aesthetic response and the objects which are likely to excite that response to a discussion of the objects themselves – displays the epistemological difficulty which Kant had dexterously avoided, but which Wordsworth and post-Kantian German theorists could not avoid because they supposed that aesthetic judgments do in some sense report a complex relation between a perceiving subject and an aesthetic object. In turning his attention toward landscape in "The Sublime and the Beautiful," Wordsworth takes refuge in the relative security of nature's visible analogues for hidden aesthetic processes.

In a series of letters to Jacob Fletcher in 1825, Wordsworth hints at his own dissatisfaction with his earlier efforts to define sublimity and beauty. In the last of these letters he concludes, "I am far from thinking that I am able to write satisfactorily upon matters so subtle – yet I hope to make a trial and must request your patience until then."[67] This disclaimer is curious since he had almost certainly made one or several "trials" before this time. In the same letter, he argues that the title of Longinus's treatise *Peri Hypsous* should not be translated as *On the Sublime*. In part this objection calls attention to a semantic swerve in Boileau's historic French translation which English translators repeated. But the objection also finesses a tension in Wordsworth's aesthetics. He argues that, properly translated, ὑψος (the Greek *hypsos*) refers to "animated, impassioned, energetic or if you will, elevated writing."[68] So far, Wordsworth is right. But his next observation that those who translate *hypsos* as "sublime" "deceive[ ]

34

the english Reader, by substituting an etymology for a translation" is partly wrong about the etymology of the two terms. More importantly, it evades the historical affinities that existed by the end of the eighteenth century between Longinus's "elevated writing" and the sublime.

Wordsworth's mistaken suggestion that *sublime* is etymologically related to *hypsos* probably derives from earlier efforts to establish an etymological link between the two terms. In 1611 John Florio defined the sublime as "high and aloft, extolled, above us, lofty. Also the upper post of a doore."[69] The first part of this definition, which echoes the literal translation for the Greek *hypsos*, is in fact not an etymology but an interpretation of the second part, which is more or less an accurate translation of the etymological compound for *sublime*, *sub* + *limen*, meaning "up to" + "lintel."[70] Florio and later lexicographers broadly construed this etymology, defining the sublime as "elevated, aloft" and thus legitimating its association with *hypsos*. Because Samuel Johnson grounds his definitions of *sublime* and *sublimity* in their Latin forms (*sublimis* and *sublimitas*), his *Dictionary* is one possible authority for the etymological link which Wordsworth describes.[71]

Wordsworth's remark to Fletcher that "much of what I observe you call sublime, *I* should denominate grand or dignified" suggests a scale of aesthetic judgment akin to the one Coleridge proposed;[72] but it does not demonstrate a necessary distinction between Wordsworth's idea of the sublime and the topic of Longinus's treatise, which is concerned, as Wordsworth acknowledges, with not only grand or dignified writing but with writing that is impassioned, energetic, and elevated. All these terms characterize Wordsworth's discourse about sublime experience. His reluctance ("or if you will, elevated") to include the last of these attributes is prompted, I suggest, by his recognition that this term had long been central to the claim that the title of Longinus's treatise ought to be translated *On the Sublime*, since elevation can be said to refer both to the sense of upward movement implied by the Latin etymology of *sublime* and to the literal translation of *hypsos*. What is critical about Wordsworth's objection is less its etymological confusion than its refusal to admit the common rhetorical ground which Longinian elevation shares with the Wordsworthian sublime. In similar ways and probably for the same reasons, the last pages of "The Sublime and the Beautiful" put aside questions about resistance and the sublime which occupy Wordsworth's interest earlier in the manuscript.

Although Wordsworth never completed his essay on aesthetics, other essays and poems display its characteristic strategies and turning-points. Two "excursions" that he appended to the 1822 and 1823 editions of his *Guide* dramatize the mind's progress from the sublime to the beautiful, together with beauty's suppression of the sublime. To the 1822 *Guide* he added a revised version of Dorothy Wordsworth's journal account of an 1802 excursion to Scawfell Pikes. To the next edition he added her description of a tour to Ullswater; and to the fifth and definitive edition of 1835, he added two poems, one after each excursion, which emphasize the aesthetic experience appropriate to each narrative.[73] As if to suggest that ordinary travellers may experience a progress from the sublime of Scawfell to the beauty of Ullswater, the first of the excursions abandons the public voice of a well-informed guide in favor of a less authoritarian, more anecdotal voice. This new persona is an appreciative, but initially inexperienced traveller, the paradigmatic "stranger" of "The Sublime and the Beautiful," whose aesthetic progress is a model for the reader's.

Wordsworth's decision to add the Scawfell excursion to the *Guide* owes something to the fact that Dorothy Wordsworth had already composed her recollections of one such excursion. But this journal, which existed long before he revised the *Guide* for publication in 1820, was not the only reason for his inclusion of a revised version of it in the 1822 edition. His interest in Scawfell was also prompted by the higher elevation Otley had given it in his "Pocket Map" and by Green's admiration for its sublimity. Their attention to the Pikes may in turn have reminded Wordsworth of Coleridge's 1802 ascent (or scramble) and the various chasms which threatened him throughout the climb.[74] By beginning with an excursion to Scawfell, Wordsworth announces that the sublime is the origin of the traveller's aesthetic progress in a mountainous topography. Although he preserves much of Dorothy Wordsworth's text, he deletes references to other companions so that the excursion includes only two travellers and a shepherd-guide; and he reorganizes the narrative so that the barren sublimity of the summit becomes the culmination of the speaker's experience. These slight adjustments minimize the anecdotal character of the original and emphasize the aesthetic education which the travellers undergo.

The situation in which the travellers to Scawfell find themselves before reaching the summit recalls the determinants of the Wordsworthian sublime. Like the speaker of *The Prelude*, who is frequently a stranger or someone lost in a strange landscape just prior to a sublime encounter, both travellers are strangers to the place. As Wordsworth argues in "The Sublime and the Beautiful," strangers are in such scenes like young children and hence more likely to experience sensations of sublimity when they confront a mountainous landscape for the first time. Their guide is a native who can read signs in the landscape which they misread. First they mistake a cloud on the horizon for a ship. Next they fail to recognize signs of a storm, although their "prophetic" guide warns them of its approach (*Prose*, 2:241). As strangers unable to order or identify what they see, they are susceptible to sensations of sublimity at the summit. There the speaker reports:

I ought to have mentioned that round the top of Scawfell-Pike not a blade of grass is to be seen. Cushions or tufts of moss, parched and brown, appear between the huge blocks and stones that lie in heaps on all sides to a great distance, like skeletons or bones of the earth not needed at the creation, and there left to be covered with never-dying lichens, which the clouds and dews nourish.

(*Prose*, 2:242)

The principal features of the Wordsworthian sublime are well represented on the summit of Scawfell. Because its rocks and boulders are massive and barren of vegetation, the summit looks primitive. Moreover, the speaker reads the scene as if it were a ruin of creation, much as Burnet reads such landscapes in his *Sacred Theory*. In doing so, this traveller-stranger emulates a fashionable occupation among contemporary tourists, who eagerly "read" gothic ruins as emblems of the transitoriness of human life.[75] But the history of the ruin on Scawfell is so archaic that without these few physical remnants it would be lost to human memory; for the rocks which are scattered there seem to have been cast off after creation and without design. As such, they signify a past whose beginning cannot be determined.

By imposing a literary topography of sublimity and beauty on a natural one, the poem "To —: On Her First Ascent to the Summit of Helvellyn," which Wordsworth appended to the Scawfell Excursion in the 1835 *Guide*, insists that travellers create aesthetic experience much as poets and prophets do. The poet advises the traveller to

> halt,
> To Niphates' top invited,
> Whither spiteful Satan steered;
> Or descend where the ark alighted,
> When the green earth re-appeared.   (*Prose*, 2:243–44)

Both scenes recall events in Genesis and *Paradise Lost*; each exhibits a different aesthetic. The first, the top of Mount Niphates, is the spot on earth where Milton's Satan "alights" on his way to Eden.[76] The second is the site of Noah's recognition of the first sign that God has begun to fulfill his promise of renewing the earth after flooding it.

Because of its topographical elevation and identification with Milton's Satan, the allusion to Mount Niphates invokes the landscape and literary iconography of the sublime. The "green earth" of the second view, which echoes the phrase which Wordsworth uses in the 1800 "Prospectus" to describe where beauty "walks,"[77] subtly emphasizes the values of the beautiful in a scene which still exhibits signs of sublime devastation. When the ark "alights" on a mountaintop – in marked contrast to Satan alighting on Mount Niphates – the narrative of Genesis once again becomes prospective and, more significantly for Wordsworth's aesthetics, hopeful about the renewal of civilization in a world cleansed of earlier corruption. In one sense, then, the sequence of views illustrated by these allusions maps a Wordsworthian progress from sublimity to beauty onto the chronology of fall, Deluge, and prospective redemption.

Yet this sequence also subverts a crucial literary chronology: a later, Miltonic allusion precedes an earlier, Biblical one. Moreover, in the lexicon of Wordsworth's aesthetics, this sequence offers little aesthetic equilibrium as it moves from a Miltonic, sublime intrusion to a scene in which beauty once again walks or prepares to walk. One reason for the disequilibrium is what lies suppressed between the two allusions – the sublime *topos* of the Deluge itself. As vehicles for the speaker's congratulatory account of the addressee's first ascent and descent of Helvellyn, these allusions assist a tone that manages, rather than succumbs to, the aesthetic competition it describes. Yet they also create a stratified, literary topography whose original sequence of "deposition" is disturbed by a satanic, Miltonic intrusion.

The Ullswater Excursion retains the colloquial tone and format of Dorothy Wordsworth's journal account. Like hers, the *Guide* narrative is divided into dated entries which chat about sights and incidents encountered during the speaker's "short excursion through more accessible parts of the country" (*Prose*, 2:244). The accessibility of this route readily distinguishes it from the climb up Scawfell. Moreover, the speaker is here an experienced traveller in the Lakes whose observations reveal a consciousness never at a loss to describe what it sees. In one of Wordsworth's few alterations of the original, the speaker adds that on this excursion he saw "a place where sublimity and beauty seemed to contend with each other" (*Prose*, 2:245), an aesthetic judgment which echoes Gilpin's commentary on the Ullswater region.[78] The assessment is pre-eminently a trained, perhaps too well trained, aesthetic response. For, as Wordsworth insists in "The Sublime and the Beautiful," the mind is not at first and for some time thereafter able to perceive "images of Beauty co-existing in the same object with those sublimity" (*Prose*, 2:360).

The speaker of the Ullswater narrative displays the full range of aesthetic responses, but only from the perspective of the beautiful as the personal history of his aesthetic progress vanishes. What is left is a speaker whose ready categories recall the assured tour guide of Gilpin's essays. From the vale of Grasmere where the travellers begin, up to the pass of Kirkstone, and finally down to Brotherswater and Ullswater, the scenes are in succession "intricate," "variegated," "picturesque," "sublime," "visionary," "Ossianic," and "beautiful." Brilliant in its details, this rapid survey transforms successive aesthetic experiences into a dizzying, Gilpinesque collage.

The "Ode: The Pass of Kirkstone," which Wordsworth placed after the Ullswater Excursion in the definitive edition of the *Guide*, was composed in 1817, "chiefly in a walk from the top of Kirkstone to Patterdale," and included among "Poems of the Imagination" in the 1827 *Poems*.[79] It begins with a summary of the scenes which the speaker surveys from the pass and ends by emphasizing the value of human habitation in the valley below (*Prose*, 2:251–53). The sublime and the beautiful are the implicit aesthetic perspectives of the pass and the valley. The speaker's topographical location throughout the ode is the pass itself, where travellers can look down into several valleys, but because its aesthetic perspective shifts from the sublime to the beautiful in the third stanza, the ode provides a review of the progress from sublimity to beauty which is a theme in both excursions.

In the opening lines the speaker suggests that the boulders that are strewn in the pass look like remnants of some ancient cataclysm, either an earthquake or the Flood:

> save the rugged road, we find
> No appanage of human kind;
> Nor hint of man, if stone or rock
> Seem not his handy-work to mock
> By something cognizably shaped;
> Mockery – or model roughly hewn,
> And left as if by earthquake strewn,
> Or from the Flood escaped.   (*Prose*, 2:251)

As if to people the landscape in spite of itself, the speaker offers several human analogues for the rock formations at the pass: Druid altars, an Egyptian monument, a tower, a tent. But none of these, he asserts, ever would have been, or even could be, inhabited by "human kind." The scene appears to be too archaic, perhaps too savage, to have been created even by the earliest inhabitants of the regions. Like the topography of Scawfell, that of the pass recalls Burnet's description of the post-diluvial world. The sublime is implicit in the *Guide* account of a place so chaotic, archaic, and primitive that it never has accommodated human life.

In the second stanza the speaker looks down on the valley below and mocks the "uneasy game" of ownership (enclosed fields and buildings) and responsibility that culture requires of its members (*Prose*, 2:251). The speaker's declaration that the "genius" of the pass can erase all "memory" of the life below suggests a probable cause for the mind's uneasiness in the presence of nature's sublimity and its own. In the last two stanzas the beautiful calls the mind back to its humanity and rationality.

The shift toward beauty's human perspective begins in the third stanza when the speaker calls the pass "savage." Much of the stanza is devoted to a discussion of the "aspiring Road," which serves as a guide analogous to what human beings require

> When life is at a weary pause,
> And we have panted up the hill
> Of duty with reluctant will.   (*Prose*, 2:252)

Once travellers reach the pass of this Bunyanesque "hill of duty," they should be grateful, the speaker suggests, for "the rich bounties of Constraint." In the strained quasi-allegorical diction of the stanza, the moral which the speaker laboriously attaches to the road and its summit at Kirkstone Pass ignores the sublimity of the place as well as its genius.

In the final stanza the sublime is trivialized as "delight / That wore a threatening brow," and rejected because it is outside the bounds of human existence as it is found in the valley of the Ullswater:

> Though habitation none appear,
> The greenness tells, man must be there;
> The shelter – that the perspective
> Is of the clime in which we live.   (*Prose*, 2:252)

Wordsworth argues in "The Sublime and the Beautiful" that the refuge which the beautiful offers in its focus on human life makes it the aesthetic response whose "love and gentleness" we seek to escape the sterner sublime emotions of "exaltation and awe." The same aesthetic preference is visible in the much earlier "An Unpublished Tour," where Wordsworth lists the "influx of thoughts" suggested by the sight of the ocean "spread without limits": "hardship and enterprize, a homeless life, endless wanderings, and infinite dangers" (*Prose*, 2:302). Yet aesthetic escape from these dangers is itself fraught with danger for the sublime[80] as the foundation of the mind's aesthetics, even as it is the foundation for nature's successive "dealings" with the earth's surface. As the "Ode: The Pass of Kirkstone" indicates, when the progress from sublimity to beauty is viewed from beauty's perspective, the distinct aesthetic character of the sublime may be obscured. Thus in the last stanza of the ode, the speaker proposes that the scene in the pass teaches us how to appreciate the beautiful:

> —Who comes not hither ne'er shall know
> How beautiful the world below.   (*Prose*, 2:253)

In a manuscript variant of the second of these lines, Wordsworth makes the same association between cultivated valleys and the beautiful which he had introduced earlier in the *Guide*: "How beautiful the world [*corrected to* Vale] below" (*PW*, 2:280n.). Here the mind's experience of the sublime becomes little more than a temporary halt for the wayfaring stranger who might otherwise mock the exacting responsibilities of human life, much as the speaker had done in the second stanza.

If no other section of Wordsworth's *Guide* offers as complete an exposition of how the aesthetics of a mountainous topography produces analogues for the mind's aesthetics, neither does any other section of the *Guide* or "The Sublime and the Beautiful" leave the beautiful (finally presented in the guise of "Faith" in things human) quite literally with the last words:

> Hope, pointing to the cultured Plain,
> Carols like a shepherd boy;
> And who is she? Can that be Joy!
> Who, with a sun-beam for her guide,
> Smoothly skims the meadows wide;
> While Faith, from yonder opening cloud,
> To hill and vale proclaims aloud,
> "Whate'er the weak may dread, the wicked dare,
> Thy lot, O man, is good, thy portion fair!"   (*Prose*, 2:253)

In announcing his farewell to the "desolate Domain" of the Pass of Kirkstone so that he might celebrate the neat, fixed personifications of Hope, Joy, Faith, and human life, the speaker of the ode reduces the sublime to a dispensable antechamber. Indeed, the Horatian structure of the ode suggests that the beautiful exerts control throughout the poem, even though the sublime appears to dominate the perspective of the first two stanzas. As a stanzaic form in which the rhyme and number of lines are regular once they have been established, the Horatian ode is peculiarly unfitted to the expression of sublime themes. Wordsworth's predecessors tended to regard the "wild" Pindaric as the ode form best suited to the sublime style.[81] The ode with which the *Guide* concludes would seem, then, to have been dedicated to the offices of the beautiful from the beginning. From this perspective, the sublime primarily affords a fitting occasion for contrast. In reiterating this aesthetic and topographical preference elsewhere in the 1820 *Guide*, Wordsworth reverses his own aesthetic progress in order to argue:

Now, everyone knows, that from amenity and beauty the transition is easy and favourable; but the reverse is not so; for, after the faculties have been elevated, they are indisposed to humbler excitement.   (*Prose*, 2:229–30)

Despite its seeming disregard for the "humbler excitement" of the beautiful, the goal of this assertion is to sustain the capacity to appreciate the beautiful as well as the sublime.

Beauty's capacity to supplant the sublime is the critical point in Wordsworth's aesthetics. The beautiful may offer rhetorical and visible shape to the mind's effort to recuperate the sublime. But it may also allow the mind to forget its sublimity. Although first and necessary to the mind, the sublime is succeeded by the beautiful, which promotes the categories and limits of conscious life and poetic expression. As a guide and a poet, Wordsworth seeks to recuperate the sublime much as the two travellers of the Scawfell Excursion travel back and up to a scene of "chaos and old time." As a topography in which outcroppings expose an earlier sublimity, the Lake District provides a natural emblem for Wordsworth's aesthetic progress from the sublime to the beautiful and back again.

3

The scene of aesthetic instruction

It is easy to find hidden things if their places are pointed out and marked, and, in
like fashion, if we wish to track down an argument we should know places.

Richard McKeon[1]

RICHARD MCKEON'S ADVICE about the importance of places in
argument reiterates a thoroughly classical conception of rhetorical
places as the topics of argument and invention. As Cicero, Quintilian,
and other classical writers emphasized, orators discover what they can
say by consulting commonplaces or *topoi*. And, as Frances Yates
observes, the classical art of memory may also have depended on
topoi. Orators who wished to remember speeches could "deposit" key
images in designated *loci*. In early rhetorical practice, such *loci* may
have been indistinguishable from *topoi* in that the images or key ideas
mentally deposited were likely to be *topoi*, the traditional turning-
points of arguments.[2] As aids to argument and recollection, classical
loci and *topoi* show the advantage of knowing places. Cicero illustrates this point by telling the story of how the poet Simonides
discovered the art of memory. While attending a banquet given by
Scopas, a nobleman of Thessaly, Simonides was called out of the
banquet hall by divine visitors. During his absence the ceiling of the hall
collapsed, killing the host and the other guests and disfiguring the
bodies so badly that relatives could not identify the dead. But
Simonides, who remembered where everyone had been sitting, could.[3]
The death of Scopas and his other guests dramatizes the potential loss
of images or ideas that help speakers remember.

The role of places in Wordsworth's aesthetics is rhetorical as well as
literal. Like Quintilian, whose account of *loci* and *topoi* Yates cites,
Wordsworth's conception of the scene of aesthetic instruction relies on
a persistent confusion of actual places with rhetorical ones. In several
poems he composed between 1798 and 1805, aesthetic conflicts are
identified with commonplaces of earlier aesthetic theory. These are not

43

The scene of aesthetic instruction

the first of Wordsworth's poems to be concerned with the rhetorical properties of place, but they are among the first to read places as scenes of aesthetic conflict between sublimity and beauty, figured either as the difference between sublime and beautiful landscapes or, more resonantly, as the difference between competing aesthetic figures.

"Prospectus" for *The Recluse*

In the "Prospectus" to *The Recluse*, probably composed in January 1800 for inclusion in *Home at Grasmere* and first published with *The Excursion* in 1814, Wordsworth uses the diction of the Miltonic sublime to announce his epic subject.[4] The text is well known, perhaps even better known than the lines about man's fittedness with nature which so exasperated William Blake. I quote more of the epic invocation than critics usually do to emphasize its twofold aesthetic program:

> All strength, all terror, single or in bands,
> That ever was put forth in personal forms –
> Jehovah, with his thunder, and the quire
> Of shouting angels and the empyreal throne –
> I pass them unalarmed. The darkest Pit
> Of the profoundest Hell, chaos, night
> Nor aught of [blinder ms. D] vacancy scooped out
> By help of dreams can breed such fear and awe
> As fall upon us often when we look
> Into our minds, into the mind of Man,
> My haunt and the main region of my song.
> Beauty, whose living home is the green earth,
> Surpassing the most fair ideal Forms
> The craft of delicate Spirits hath composed
> From earth's materials, waits upon my steps,
> Pitches her tents before me when I move,
> An hourly Neighbour.[5]

"Fear and awe" announce the role of the sublime in Wordsworth's subject, the "mind of man." The speaker's boast, that this "region" inspires him with sublime emotions as the regions of heaven, hell, chaos and night do not (he passes *them* "unalarm'd"), indicates his intention to "out-sublime" the epic poets who are his predecessors, especially Milton, who was after Homer the sublime poet of all ages for eighteenth-century writers.[6] Because the Miltonic trio of hell, chaos, and night belongs to pre-Biblical history, brought into time and speech with the creation of time in Genesis and reclaimed for modern (fallen) civilization and Wordsworth's time by *Paradise Lost*, it obliquely introduces the temporal priority of the Wordsworthian sublime. Eighteenth-century writers agreed that the sublime was boundless, vast, infinite, and thus much like chaos. Wordsworth emphasizes the atemporality of sublimity and chaos.

If the boast of the "Prospectus" ended here, its commitment to the eighteenth-century cult of the sublime, original genius would be axiomic, as Geoffrey Hartman in fact implies by considering only the first part of the passage quoted here.[7] But the speaker goes on to summarize beauty's guardianship of his imaginative progress. Like the Biblical word of the gospel of John,[8] beauty's "tents" shelter the poet as he traverses the sublime "haunt and main region" of his song. In the 1800 *Home at Grasmere* this image serves an ethos of shelter and wholeness and declares Wordsworth's invention of a place from which to take the measure of his poetic powers (*HG*, Ms. D, 146–51, p. 49). As an agent of the speaker's "real estate," the beautiful legislates Wordsworth's effort to represent visionary experience. Because its domain is spectral and unavailable to human expression, the sublime is a force or a quality, not a visible agent or presence. It thus "haunts" the mind in the double sense that it inhabits it and makes it spectral. Read in this fashion, the mind's sublime "haunt" finds its naturalized, humanized antagonist in the "living home" of the beautiful. To the hazard of crossing a place where the sublime is present, the beautiful responds by setting up its own tents for the benefit of the speaker.

Two earlier poems sketch aspects of this aesthetic conflict. In the sonnet "Written in Very Early Youth," probably composed by 1791,[9] the speaker describes a Miltonic "blank of things" that brings a "calm" and "harmony" that are "home-felt" and "home-created." The aesthetic coordinates of these images are mixed: blankness recalls the sublime landscapes of Burnet and other writers on the sublime, yet it precedes (and perhaps announces) a domestication of place which is beauty's gift to the speaker in the 1800 "Prospectus." In "A Night-Piece," begun in 1798 and probably completed two years later,[10] the speaker's vision of a "dark abyss" or, in an early manuscript, a "gloomy vault" includes most of the features of sublime experience in Wordsworth's poetry. He is alone, the vision is unexpected. The substitution of "dark abyss" abandons a more topographically exact phrase for one that secures the sublimity of the scene on Wordsworth's (and Thomas Burnet's) terms. As such visions do, this one soon closes, leaving the speaker's mind "not undisturbed by the delight it feels." This response follows Burke's formula: whereas our response to the beautiful is unalloyed pleasure, we respond to the sublime with a mixture of pleasure and pain. A manuscript variant which substitutes "deep joy" for delight suggests both sublime depths and the fourth of

Dr. Johnson's definitions for the adjective *sublime* – "elevated by joy." (*PW*, 2:209n.).[11] This mixed aesthetic response yields in the last lines to "peaceful calm," a shift that indicates some movement toward the tranquil aesthetic pleasure offered by the beautiful.

Although "Fidelity" is unquestionably a minor poem, it clearly illustrates how a sublime scene of instruction can be made beautiful, or at least made to reflect its values of community and communicability. Probably composed in 1805 and first published in the *Poems* of 1807,[12] it dramatizes what Burke had said men fear most about the sublime – possible loss of life or, to use Kant's phrase, its threat to "self-preservation."[13] A shepherd finds a faithful, presumably hungry, dog that has stayed with its master's body in an isolated mountain recess on Helvellyn for three months. Hedged by "A lofty precipice in front, / A silent tarn below," and "remote from public road or dwelling, / Pathway, or cultivated land; / From trace of human foot or hand," the scene is topographically sublime. In an early manuscript Wordsworth calls it a "forlorn Abyss" and an "unfriendly spot." Like the amended text of "A Night-Piece," this inversion of height for depth declares their symbolic reversibility. Sublime, fearful places signify abysses even when the literal vehicles are mountains or plains. By calling it a "place of fear," the speaker makes it clear that he responds to its sublimity.

If "Fidelity" is, as Wordsworth's 1815 classification indicates, concerned with the faculties "of Sentiment and Reflection," its notice of values that do not belong to this "place of fear" or "savage place" suggests how beauty can be made unobtrusively present in a sublime place. In one manuscript variant the discovery of the body receives more attention. A "company" arrives, as one does in the 1805 and 1850 versions of the Drowned Man episode in *The Prelude*, and the narrator describes the skeleton in detail. But in the published poem the fearful sublimity of the scene and discovery is given less weight; domestic values dominate instead.[14] Until he realizes that the "barking sound" he hears belongs to a dog that is "not of mountain breed," the shepherd approaches the animal not knowing whether it is feral or domesticated. Later, the suggestion of feralness still lingers – the dog's motions are "wild and shy" and its cry is "unusual" to the shepherd's well-trained ear. Once the speaker realizes what has happened to its owner and why the dog has remained, the matter of its feralness is explained: it is alien and wild in *this* environment. In other words it embodies, as the title of the poem declares, the hold of domestic affection in so extreme a case; for such an animal could have become feral during its long tenure as "a dweller in that savage place." While it is true that the body of its owner is now a skeleton, the dog has not feasted on it. This is, after all, not Byron's *Don Juan*, but one of Wordsworth's "Poems of Sentiment and Reflection."

The domestic code of the narrative is retrospectively confirmed by the contrasts with which the poem begins. The "place of fear" is defined by its difference from the civilized world of domestic affections and codes of behavior (in this case presumably "a dog is a man's best friend"), and by the network of roads, paths, and houses which represent human "settlement." Because the dog, the speaker, the shepherd, and the dead man belong to the world in the valley below, they are all aliens in a mountain recess. More subtly, the dog's "love sublime" deflects the reader's attention from the fearful, savage sublimity of the scene, which is never actually *named* as such although its attributes and the shepherd's response to it make its aesthetic character evident. Here the named version of the sublime is Johnsonian "elevation," less hazardous than the fearful sublime. "Fidelity" sketches two concerns that recur in Wordsworth's aesthetic engagements: a reluctance to acknowledge sublime fear and the opposition between this sublimity and domestic or social norms.

In "Stepping Westward," composed in 1805, the speaker specifies the aesthetic progress he undertakes as he walks westward in "one of the loneliest parts of that solitary region" (*PW*, 3:76).[15] The poem begins as a woman queries his direction. He agrees that it would be a "*wildish* destiny" to travel so by "chance," yet he wonders who would not continue "with such a sky to lead him on." Unlike Donne, Wordsworth's speaker insists it is a "kind of *heavenly* destiny" to travel westward into a "region bright." The woman's initial greeting ("What, you are stepping westward?") indicates the boundlessness of the sublime more than the scene itself: "'twas a sound / Of something without place or bound." Yet moving westward also leaves behind the human sweetness of the woman's query, which has "the very sound of courtesy." Once again, the images that represent the speaker's progress project the aesthetic terrain of later poems, especially the 1805 *Prelude*. By proclaiming the sublimity which is the speaker's goal even as it reminds him through "courtesy" of the world of human connectedness he leaves behind, the sound of the woman's voice suggests a parallel office for the beautiful. It too may give Wordsworthian speakers a "spiritual right" to travel in sublime "region[s]" even as it reminds them of the limits which will be imposed on speakers so doubly bound.

A more implicit dramatization of aesthetic differences operates obliquely in "Michael," a poem in which the values of pastoral and paternal care oppose values implied by the figure of Michael as someone whose first love is nature. By virtue of its place in the sub-genre of early nineteenth-century pastoral or georgic, this poem ought to celebrate pastoral values being encroached upon by industrial society.[16] This is the reading given by David Simpson, who argues that Michael's world is disrupted by external forces – the notice of a legal hold on the land which arrives from the city where surplus and the division of labor reign. Otherwise, Michael's pastoral life illustrates economic self-sufficiency, a fullness of life and work without division of labor or the production of surplus.[17] Margorie Levinson argues that by keeping the land and letting Luke go rather than making the land "capital intensive" (by selling wool at market, for example), Michael suffers the economic and spiritual consequences of objectifying the son. In Marxian terms, Wordsworth would seem to replace use value for Luke's exchange value on the open (city) market.[18] Although I agree that Michael's decision to send Luke off to make money and thereby keep the land clearly establishes his sense of what comes first, the poem is built on this irony not betrayed into it. From this perspective, the metonymic substitutions that issue from Michael's exchange of Luke for the land are the poetic terrain the Wordsworthian speaker of the poem explores as he invites another generation of poets or a "few gentle hearts" to make their own poetic tale of the losses that riddle the poem.

As Dorothy Wordsworth says of the ruined sheepfold, Michael's decision reveals a "heart unevenly divided" between love of his son and a strong need to keep the land which is his life and work. As a poem which displays this choice without supervising it, "Michael" echoes the double perspective of Virgil's *Eclogues*, which query the role of pastoral in a changing world.[19] Wordsworth's poet-speaker is divided between his affection for this story as

> the first
> Of those domestic tales that spake to me
> Of Shepherds, dwellers in the valley, men
> Whom I already loved; – not verily
> For their own sakes, but for the fields and hills
> Where was their occupation and abode,   (*PW*, 2:81, ll. 21–26)

and his sympathetic portrait of Michael's absorption in the land, with its echoes of a similar absorption and consequent lack of moral links to society in the character of Rivers, the villain of Wordsworth's early *Borderers*. In one sense, the poem would have us read its pastoralness as the aura projected by a small community whose "domestic tales" and valley abodes elicit the speaker's love and suggest the values of the

Wordsworthian beautiful. Yet Michael's dilemma and choice suggest that the shepherd's solitary absorption in his land may one day find itself in unresolvable conflict with social needs and principles, among them keeping a family together and handing a pastoral way of life on to a son. Wordsworth's 1815 classification of "Michael" among "Poems of Affection" calls attention to the conflict in "affection" which Michael must confront. In aesthetic terms the fault line of that conflict is the difference between sublime isolation in nature and the domestic, social relations which the beautiful celebrates.

In each of these poems, the scene of aesthetic instruction is a specific place whose significance is ultimately less topographical than rhetorical. The value of these places is, then, their representation of aesthetic differences and turning-points. In the early JJ *Prelude* manuscript of 1798, Wordsworth proposes that when these differences are "impressed" on landscape, they initiate the mind's aesthetic education:

> ye through many a year
> Thus by agency of boyish sports
> Impressed the stream[s] the woods the hill[s]
> Impressed upon all form[s] the characters
> Of danger & desire & thus did make
> The surface of the universal earth
> With meanings of delight, of hope & fear,
> Work like a sea —   (*Prel. 1798, 125*)[20]

In this passage nature's "ministry" is primarily Burkean: "danger" and "fear" recall the Burkean sublime, while "delight" and "hope" suggest the gentler climate of the beautiful. Where "desire" belongs is less clear. Were this Burke, desire might indicate the beautiful, especially feminine beauty. But Wordsworth suggests that desire is a corollary to danger, without making clear how the two are related. Despite this ambiguity, these lines sketch the task that nature's "forms" perform for the mind's aesthetics. Much as metals are impressed with images that indicate their value as insignia or legal tender, so do aesthetic "characters" make "the surface of the earth ... work like a sea."

The Prelude, 1

In Book 1 of the expanded *Prelude*, Wordsworth elaborates the education "by beauty and by fear" which he had sketched in the JJ manuscript six years before. Like the account of nature's successive dealings in his *Guide*, the "spots of time" in *The Prelude,* 1[21] represent stages in an aesthetic progress from sublimity to beauty. This much is obvious if we compare the boy's partly fearful and solitary activity in the first three "spots" to his joyful skating in the fourth, a transitional episode in which he acts separately but in sight of companions. In subsequent episodes of this book, the speaker more frequently than not recalls his participation in other group activities. What makes this gradual progress from the *affections* of sublimity to those of beauty merit more attention than the brief account I have just offered is the modulation in the boy's early sublime encounters. Readers who insist that in the first three "spots of time" the boy remains passive before Nature's "sterner interventions"[22] neglect intriguing differences in the way the boy organizes his perception of each scene of instruction. Not only is he not passive, he responds differently in each case. To illustrate these differences and their aesthetic consequences, I suggest that they exhibit a developing conception of space similar to the one Jean Piaget describes in his analysis of how children learn to recognize spatial relations. My point is neither that Wordsworth anticipated Piaget, nor that the "spots of time" are merely illustrations of Piagetian principles. Rather I suppose that Piaget's preference for describing cognitive strategies as mapping strategies illuminates Wordsworth's use of topography to illustrate aesthetic differences.

Piaget identifies three stages in the child's conception of space: topological, projective, and euclidean. My argument concerns only the first two. According to Piaget, at about the age of eight or nine (roughly the age given for the boy Wordsworth in Book I), children begin to investigate their surroundings, relying on topological distinctions – separation, spatial succession, contiguity, and the notion of "betweenness." Children who organize space topology can recognize a mountain cluster as a series of more or less contiguous masses, but they have no sense of how individual mountains are related one to another, nor can they predict how those relations might be changed if they were to look at the same topography from a different point of view. In the next stage, children gradually discover that where they stand in relation to objects determines the shape and limit of what they see. In short, they learn to apply projective principles to their environment. Once children know how parts are related to a whole and what belongs inside or outside a given perceptual field, they can exert some control over what they see.[23]

As a primitive means for identifying and describing places, topology designates a hidden, sublime "science of place," whereas topography articulates the projective relations among places and surfaces. As a cognitive apparatus for manipulating point of view and position, projective geometry and the rules of perspective objectify the capacity for order, proportion, and knowable limit which belong to the Wordsworthian beautiful. In the Book I "spots of time," these methods of perceiving space suggest how the boy's mind begins to "escape upon the invitation of our more placid & gentle nature from those obtrusive qualities in an object sublime in its general character" ("Sublime and Beautiful," *Prose*, 2:349).

Initially the boy Wordsworth is passive before Nature's "severer interventions" (2:370, p. 48). But with each of the thefts which constitute a sub-plot in this book, he tests physical limits as well as implicit injunctions about the risks he incurs by violating those limits (don't hang over the cliff, don't steal). In the autumn woodcock "spot of time," his "joy" while wandering alone on the heights is chastened by his recognition that he is an intruder who disturbs the peace dispensed by the moon and stars "shining o'er my head" (1:321–24, p. 46). No other topographical boundaries are specified, although the suggestion that the "solitary hills" rise up from a valley or plain is implicit, as is the idea that the boy's home – he only visits the hill – is below (1:320, 329, p. 46). Like the "place of fear" on Helvellyn that is the scene of the fatal fall described in "Fidelity," these hills are hazardous, although the boy of *The Prelude* escapes as the dead man of "Fidelity" does not. This sublime encounter demonstrates the common denominator between Burkean fear and Wordsworth's conception of a child's characteristic response to the sublime. Noting in "The Sublime and the Beautiful" that "personal apprehension" may dominate the child's sublime encounters so as to exclude the recognition of duration that is requisite to the sublime, Wordsworth argues that fear belongs primarily to the aesthetic progress which children and "unpracticed" adults must undergo. He adds that even in these cases the experience of the sublime is possible only "if personal fear & surprize or wonder have not been carried beyond certain bounds" (*Prose*, 2:353).

This condition calls attention to an instructive difference among the first three episodes of Book I, all of which describe tests conducted in a climate of fear and excitement. In the first episode the boy's movements suggest that he is worried about self-preservation: he "scud[s] away" from snare to snare. Yet the fact that he stays is itself a challenge to sublime fear. This defiance is double-edged, since it challenges both the absent owner of the trap and the boy's own "anxious visitation." In retribution for his "deed," the boy hears

> Low breathings coming after me, and sounds
> Of undistinguishable motion, steps
> Almost as silent as the turf they trod.   (1:330–32, p. 46)

The avenging spirit whose steps pursue the boy is as gothic as the ghosts who wander about dripping blood in *The Vale of Esthwaite*. In that early poem he rejects "fancy in a Demon's form" and "sweet Melancholy," which may act to "blind" the poet to the thousand words that lie / In the small orb of [ ] eye" (*PW*, 1:282, ll. 548–53). In Book I of *The Prelude* a similar exorcism of gothic forms begins with the nest-robbing episode and inaugurates the boy's spiritual inhabitation of place in the poem.

In the second "spot of time," the boy steals a bird from its natural home rather than from a man-made trap. The physical risk of this theft is greater than that of the first, but so is the speaker's retrospective exultation:

> Though mean
> My object and inglorious, yet the end
> Was not ignoble. Oh, when I have hung
> Above the raven's nest, by knots of grass
> And half-inch fissures in the slippery rock
> But ill sustained, and almost, as it seemed,
> Suspended by the blast which blew amain,
> Shouldering the naked crag, oh, at that time
> While on the perilous ridge I hung alone,
> With what strange utterance did the loud dry wind
> Blow through my ears; the sky seemed not a sky
> Of earth, and with what motion moved the clouds!
>
> (1:339–50, p. 46)

Here the speaker notes the topographical limits of the boy's landscape with care and fixes his location by relying on adverbial prepositions of place. Suspended "above the raven's nest" and "on the perilous ridge," the boy puts himself at the edge of a wilderness where children enact rites of passage toward adult consciousness. In *The Prelude*, these self-imposed rites illustrate an aesthetic progress toward adulthood that occupies years rather than months of childhood and adolescence. Because the object of theft on this occasion is a bird in a nest, not a snare, the boy robs nature, but this is given less attention in the text than the risk and triumph of getting to the nest. These lines convey, as Christopher Ricks observes, "exultation, an extraordinary nonchalance of security." The passage is also remarkable for what D. G. Gillham calls its "hidden figures," figures that deliberately blur the distinction between the boy and features of the landscape.[24] As Gillham explains, the agent of the phrase "shouldering the naked crag" is syntactically ambiguous – it ought to be "blast" but the sense of the passage requires that it be the speaker's "I" five lines earlier. This ambiguous figurative relation between the boy and the place is made more emphatic by the demi-personification of *"naked* crag" (my emphasis) and, most of all, by the way that the boy's body becomes a near appendage to the crag – "shouldering" it both in the sense of giving it a human contour and of superimposing his body on the curve of the crag.

By matching his body to the crag in this way, the boy insists (so much for passivity) that whatever limits nature imposes, he will challenge them. These challenges are, like Kant's analysis of the mind's response to nature's magnitude and might, predicated on some future capacity to override those limits by declaring them signs of a "physical" rather than "intellectual mastery" over the mind. Here the logic of the boy's aesthetic progress is closely affiliated to Burkean and Kantian principles. Yet the instructive Wordsworthian feature of this sublime encounter is the hiddenness of its figures, whose ambiguity of reference reminds us that as the boy hangs over some unspecified gap or depth, he dramatizes its (and his) primitive, sublime topology.

In the same episode the sense of impending retribution is localized in the "strange utterance" of the wind, rather than in the "breathings" of a walking spirit. The boy thus senses for the first time that behind the ordinary appearances of this world is quite another, to which the speaker alludes much later when he declares that the "forms / Of Nature have a passion in themselves" (12:89–90, p. 452). With each theft the boy recognizes something more of the visionary character of these forms and the limits they impose. Two curious revisions in the fourteen-book poem of 1832–50 place this otherwise solitary experience within a social framework. This version begins, "Nor less when spring had warmed the cultured Vale, / Roved we as plunderers" (1850, 326–27, p. 47) and substitutes "our" for "my" to describe the intended theft. The rest of the episode is essentially the same, except for the omission of two phrases in the 1805 text which, together with "high places," specify the scene of plunder as "lonesome peaks," "among the mountains and the winds." But in the coda that follows, the speaker declares: "Dust as we are, the immortal spirit grows / Like harmony in music" instead of "The mind of man is framed even like the breath / And harmony of music" (1850, 1:340–41, p. 47; 1805, 1:351–52, p. 46).[25] I note these changes to suggest that in the later version the speaker surrounds his account of a sublime experience with slight notices of values that imply the beautiful but do not insist that it become part of the sublimity of the scene. The more obvious of these values is the new sociability of this boyhood plundering. The second is the phrase "cultured Vale," which supplies a domesticated, social landscape in contrast to the "high places" of this sublime scene, much as the same phrase does in the 1817 "Ode: The Pass of Kirk-stone." Collectively, these revisions register the proximity of the beautiful even here.

In Book I, snare, nest-robbing, and skating are habitual activities; as such they describe repeated experiments with movement, theft, and limits over what may be a year's time. The first two are described as "these night wanderings" (1:325, p. 46), and the skating takes place "not seldom" and "often times" (1:474, 478, p. 52). Woodcock theft occurs in autumn, nest-robbing in spring, and skating obviously in winter. The boat-stealing episode, which advances him far beyond these habitual activities, occurs just once: it is not repeated because it need not be. In the opening lines the boy uses topological distinctions to locate objects. He finds the boat tied "*to* a willow tree ... *within* a rocky cave, its usual home" (1:374–75, p. 48, my emphasis). After untying the boat, he pushes it "*from* the shore" (1:384, p. 48, my emphasis). Each of these phrases defines the location of the boat by noting its relation to contiguous objects. Since it is almost entirely enclosed by the space created by the cave and the willow, this space can be described topologically. To put the point as a topologist might: contiguity and its absence are designated by the set of boat, willow, cave, and shore.

However, once the boy frees the boat he can no longer rely on topological principles, which cannot economically account for the successive sets of boundaries and internal relations which are created as he rows away from the willow and the cave. Since the boat is in constant motion, it must fragment whatever new topological arenas he devises. His response to his "act of stealth" (1:388, p. 48) suggests that what really troubles him is not the theft but the loss of known principles of order and place. Instead of abandoning the boat and sneaking away from the scene of the crime, he relocates the boat within another space and order. He begins by making it the starting-point of a projective field. Rowing so that the boat leaves circles on either side "until they melted all into one track / Of sparkling light" (1:392–94, p. 48), he maintains a straight course so that he will have some basis for judging whether objects in his field of vision are "in front," "behind," or "to one side" of his position. Then, by fixing his view "upon the top of that same craggy ridge, / The bound of the horizon" (1:398–99, p. 48) in imitation of eighteenth-century techniques for surveying a mountainous topography,[26] he establishes the upper limit of the landscape, noting that "behind" this ridge there is nothing "but the stars and the grey sky" (1:399–400, p. 48). Now he can locate any point or object in this new perceptual field by relating it to direction or boundary.

With the economy of a topographer's eye, he has selected the criteria necessary for constructing a bounded, three-dimensional space. However, like the children of Piaget's experiments after they construct their first projective fields, he at first believes this new field is absolute, displaying the bias toward fixed points and spaces which was part of his earlier topology of places. Although he has constructed a projective field by relating the position of objects to his own, he does not as yet pursue the logic implicit in this discovery. That is to say, he has not yet recognized that these new boundaries will change again when he abandons this fixed point of view.

As he rows farther away from the cave and boundary ridge above it, a second peak looms up "from behind that craggy steep, till then / The bound of the horizon" (1:405–6, p. 50). As he had been in earlier episodes, he is again terrified, but this time he seems to fear being disoriented. Twice he notes the former limits of his perceptual field, adding that the second peak "rose up between [him] and the stars" (1:410, p. 50). No form in nature which he has thus far characterized as having motion exhibits the wilful pursuit he ascribes to this new, black peak. The fourteen-book poem is emphatic on this point: "for so it seemed, with a purpose of its own / And measured motion like a living thing, / [it] Strode after me" (1850, 1:383–85, p. 51). So terrifying is the thought that landscape forms change that the boy refuses to examine the new world of which this peak is part. It is a world governed by time, not stasis. In each of these "spots of time," motion – whether real or imagined – is the one dimension missing from a static frame of the world which reveals the life possessed by Nature's forms. For Wordsworth, this discovery is a necessary preparation for a human imagination similarly committed to the adoption of successive aesthetic judgments.

When the second peak rises up, then, the boy cannot say what has happened, but his actions indicate what he has learned. He rows "back to the cavern / Of the willow tree" (1:414–15, p. 50). The phrase syntactically reasserts the topological sense of place which was absent while the boat was untied and in motion. Given the "fear and trembling" which marks his return, the boy would probably not have reversed his direction unless he had already recognized the projective relation between the crag and his movements away from it. Although he retreats from the shock of experiencing a world that changes with shifts in point of view, his sense of what is in the world is no longer confined to the static, bounded field he had thought was immutable. The speaker notes that in the days which followed, his brain

Worked with a dim and undetermined sense
Of unknown modes of being. In my thoughts
There was a darkness – call it solitude
Or blank desertion – no familiar shapes
Of hourly objects, images of trees,
Of sea or sky, no colours of green fields;
But huge and mighty forms that do not live
Like living men moved slowly through my mind
By day, and were a trouble to my dreams.　　(1:419–27, p. 50)

In each of the preceding episodes and in the boy's initial movements in the boat-stealing scene, the agency of fear dominates sublime encounters, not the sensation of "intense unity" which Wordsworth describes in "The Sublime and the Beautiful" (*Prose*, 2:356). In *The Prelude* the boy's "dim" sense of unknown modes of being projects another level of sublime experience, one in which a familiar place becomes "inhabited by a power"[27] that is unfamiliar or *unheimlich*. This recognition of the sublime as that which haunts ordinary human existence by making it inhabit a "spectral" world refocuses the external gothic terrors of these episodes. For the immanence of sublime forms in the known world makes gothic terror serve an interior function. That is to say, the sublime induces the boy's troubled consideration of "huge and mighty forms that do not live / Like living men" and yet move "through" his mind. This identification of "darkness" or "blank desertion" in the world of known forms introduces the mode of attention which distinguishes Wordsworth's sublime from that of Burke and Kant. For Wordsworth the child's aesthetic progress requires at first an absorption in sublime fear, and then some effort to test the limits of that fear in the dual register of trespass and hazards to self-preservation. These activities direct the mind toward some acknowledgment of forces that trouble the mind. Thus far, the sublime experiences of Book 1 confirm Kant's claim that the sublime has to do with the mind's intellectual mastery over nature's magnitude and might. But in the skating episode, the difference between the Wordsworthian and Kantian sublimes is made clear as the boy's earlier practical reasoning about projective fields asserts its relation to the beautiful.

The skating episode is the first "spot of time" which does not include a theft. But the issue is not boyish reform. He no longer steals because for the moment he has taken what he needs from nature. He knows that forms, not gothic spirits, possess a motion which implies the existence of a visionary world in the visible one. He also senses that this motion and its modes of being can be his. The multiplicity of voice and action, which sets the skating "spot" apart from earlier ones, demonstrates the proliferation of voices which will belong to the adult poet. The speaker remarks that among the boys who impersonate hounds, hare, and horn, "not a voice was idle" (1:466, p. 52). He then lists the answering sounds of precipice, trees, and hills (1:463–65, p. 52). With others and then by himself, the boy moves with an assertiveness that is new in the poem as he cuts a path on the ice across the reflection of a star, skates with the wind, then stops on his heels. A joyous manipulation of projective fields concludes the episode. For the first time he and nature seem to collaborate toward mutual ends. He prolongs the "rapid line of motion" (1:482, p. 52) produced while he skates in the direction of the wind, stopping to watch the cliffs "wheel" past, "even as if the earth had rolled / With visible motion her diurnal round" (1:485–86, p. 52). So unafraid is he now of motion among nature's forms that he deliberately elicits it.

Book I chronicles the emergence of a poetic voice that owes much to the *genius loci* tradition, but more to the boy's efforts to become the spirit of his places. To review briefly, he rejects a gothicized spirit as the source of motion and voice, locating both first in Nature and then in his mind. Thus while it is true, as Hartman points out, that Wordsworth had described the presences of Nature as "spirits" in the JJ manuscript, and that *The Vale of Esthwaite* is riddled with gothic spirits,[28] such spirits are gradually exorcised in *The Prelude*, I. As the boy transforms a primitive topology of sublime places into a projective system, he begins to create an aesthetic topography that is controlled by the beautiful. Still, the perilous hold which this aesthetic has on the speaker's recapitulation of childhood activities is made explicit much later in the poem. As a darkened image of how play beside a lake can end, the Boy of Winander passage in Book v specifies the risk of death and the desire for self-preservation that are antagonists in Wordsworth's aesthetics.

"Lines composed a few miles above Tintern Abbey"

Although "Lines composed a few miles above Tintern Abbey" in part summarizes childhood experiences more fully represented in *The Prelude*, I, in the earlier poem the scene of aesthetic instruction is complicated by a three-way conflict between the revolutionary sublime, a "sense sublime" whose "intense unity" Wordsworth describes in his fragment on aesthetics, and those "beauteous forms" the speaker hopes to remember or have Dorothy Wordsworth remember. "Tintern Abbey" is certainly not the only poem in which Wordsworth uses the figure of memory as a place or container – much the same case

could be made for various tour poems or for *The Prelude*. Yet
"Tintern Abbey" presents this figure more economically. From its
opening verse-paragraph, where strong enjambments declare the
text's enclosure of its speaker's recollections, to the final verse-
paragraph where Dorothy Wordsworth's mind is made a future
repository for what the speaker may not always be able to recall, the
figure of memory as a place and container recurs even though it is
hedged by potential reversals of its power.[29]

To cite only one example, since these moments in the poem are well
known to its readers, the speaker claims that the "beauteous forms" of
the scene have not been "as is a landscape to a blind man's eye" (*PW*,
2:260, ll.22–24). We unravel the "turnings intricate" of this syntax to
mean: the speaker has kept this scene in his mind's eye, even as a blind
man (who could neither see nor recollect what he had seen unless not
blind from birth) cannot. What retards this reading is Wordsworth's
double negation: this landscape has not been for the speaker what it
would have been had he been blind. As a rhetorical strategy directed as
much against the speaker's wish to affirm as it is directed toward our
wish to believe his affirmations, this litotes and those that follow in the
poem unleash a Wordsworthian irony which manages doubt and fear
at least as much as it manages belief. As a poem that makes the Wye
scene a mansion for Wordsworthian recollections, "Tintern Abbey"
elaborates the role of memory as an interior shelter created and
preserved by the beautiful.

The opening stanza exemplifies the acts of invention and enclosure
by which the beautiful makes sublime places safe for human habitation. First the speaker binds past to present by declaring, then twice
repeating, the number of years that separate him from his earlier visit
("five years," "five summers," "five long winters"), in order to bend
past and present time around the moment of this speech. As successive
acts of bounding and placement, these lines assert the speaker's
rhetorical possession of the topography he describes and his license to
invent it. Next strong enjambments, principally from verbs to their
objects, secure the monumental and textual perimeters of the scene.
One goal of this gradual enclosure is to include the speaker there,
"under this dark sycamore." References to the "thisness" of the place
("these" plots, hedgerows, farms, and so on) further declare his
proximity to the scene (*PW*, 2:259, ll. 1–18). I review these much
discussed lines to emphasize how the speaker gradually achieves, in the
sense suggested by the French cognate *achever*, the "place-ness" of the
Wye scene. Unlike the poet Gray and the tour guide Gilpin, well
known to Wordsworth and his contemporaries as promoters of the

picturesque tour and poem in general and the Wye scene in particular,[30] Wordsworth's speaker does not comment at all about the ruined abbey, its grounds, or its picturesque inhabitants. Instead, by emptying this well-known place of its usual inhabitants, then barely re-peopling it with an unseen "Hermit" (*PW* 2:259, ll. 18–21), Wordsworth re-invents the Wye as a complex scene of aesthetic instruction.

As several readers have observed, the title of the poem may both retrieve and suppress the fear that dominated Wordsworth's response to the revolutionary sublime by 1798. J. R. Watson notes that the complete title, "Lines composed a few miles above Tintern Abbey, July 13, 1798," does not match the chronology indicated by the Wordsworths' itinerary, which specifies that they were *above* Tintern Abbey on July 11 and on their way to Bristol on July 13. Geoffrey Little adds that some elements of the scene described as being above the abbey were in fact located at John Thelwell's farm at Llyswen, seventy-five or eighty miles upstream.[31] Yet quasi-fictional topography is hardly unusual in Wordsworth's tour poetry. And, as Mark Reed has suggested, "July 13" may simply indicate the day on which Wordsworth completed the poem he had begun two days earlier while walking downstream toward the abbey.[32]

However, because this date also doubles as the anniversary of two events in revolutionary France which Wordsworth recalls in other poems, and because his suppression of the revolutionary sublime is among the most reiterated aesthetic patterns of the expanded *Prelude*, readers are probably right to suspect that he altered the topography and chronology of his return visit to the Wye for a reason. Watson reminds us that Wordsworth and Jones arrived at Calais on July 13, 1790, a date Wordsworth recalled in 1804 as he composed Book VI of *The Prelude*. If this July 13 was a time of great hope and joy, it later marked a darker anniversary. On July 13, 1793, Charlotte Corday killed Marat in his bath, an event memorialized as pro-Jacobin propaganda in David's *The Death of Marat*. This, as much as the Wye, Watson suggests, may be the occasion whose anniversary Wordsworth creates in the "five years" of the opening verse and paragraph of the poem. Against the pressures, then, of a highly stratified recollection, the speaker of the poem seeks to balance the darker image of revolutionary terror by superimposing the image of his return to the Wye. Seen from the mental and topographical vantage-point of the Jacobin sympathizer Thelwell's farm far above Tintern Abbey, then, the "picture of the mind" which Wordsworth offers in "Tintern Abbey" gathers a number of negative images around a more positive one.

An intriguing cooperation between the beautiful and the "intense unity" of the Wordsworthian sublime shelters the poem against the hazard of its stratified sense of place and the revolutionary sublime. The agency of "beauteous forms" prompts both the gift of "aspect more sublime" and the domesticating virtues of the Wordsworthian beautiful, those "little, nameless, unremembered, acts / Of kindness and of love" (ll. 22–35). This recognition of visionary and domestic realities as the two gifts of "beauteous forms" registers the dual aesthetic nature of the scene. Calling this second gift "more sublime" subjects it to comparison. Yet in "The Sublime and the Beautiful" Wordsworth insists that to experience the sublime the mind's "comparing power" must be suspended. Phrases like "more sublime" and "sublimer" do appear in earlier aesthetic theory. Moreover, Shelley uses the second in *Adonais* and in "Hymn to Intellectual Beauty," where it marks the sublunary speaker's recognition of the inaccessibility of a "sublimer world."[33] Shelley's phrase suggests a similar perspective in Wordsworth's earlier poem, where "beauteous forms" (an 1820 revision for "these forms of beauty") legislate the speaker's presentation of a higher, hence "more sublime" gift. The implication is of course that "beauteous forms" are also in some sense "sublime." If they are, the sublimity at issue is likely to be the sense of elevation which Dr. Johnson preferred, not the fearful response to the revolutionary sublime which the speaker keeps at bay in this poem.

The speaker implies an equally intriguing aesthetic cooperation when he describes his "recompense" for the disappearance of boyhood joys:

> And I have felt
> A presence that disturbs me with the joy
> Of elevated thoughts; a sense sublime
> Of something far more deeply interfused,
> Whose dwelling is the light of setting suns,
> And the round ocean and the living air,
> And the blue sky, and in the mind of man:
> A motion and a spirit, that impels
> All thinking things, all objects of all thought,
> And rolls through all things.   (ll. 93–102)

The power of this sublimity to project a transcendent reality that "rolls through all things" turns the speaker back to the surfaces, those "beauteous forms," for the anchor and guide that they provide. Jerome McGann has charged that in "Tintern Abbey" Wordsworth displaces revolutionary and thus ideological inquiry to introduce a de-politicized "sense sublime." For McGann, this displacement exemplifies the transcendent lurch of Wordsworth's poetic achievement and its major liability.[34] Yet this claim assumes that to write and read ideologically, we must do so explicitly. As Frederic Jameson observes, the way of ideology – in poems, in criticism, and in culture – is more often oblique,[35] much as it is in Wordsworth's 1798 poem celebrating a return to the Wye that surreptitiously uncelebrates the revolutionary sublime.

The return to visible surfaces from unseen presences re-engages the aesthetics of containment with which the poem began. In the famous (or infamous) concluding address to Dorothy Wordsworth, he hopes that his preceding "exhortation" might be deposited in her mind so that her memory will be "as a dwelling-place / For all sweet sounds and harmonies" (ll. 140–41). These will, he hopes, shelter her from whatever "solitude, or fear, or pain, or grief" might be her "portion" in later life (ll. 143–44). Both what is to be remembered ("lovely forms," "sweet sounds and harmonies") and the consolatory promise of this remembrance indicate the presence of the beautiful. Like beauty's "tents" in the "Prospectus," its shelters in memory provide a place of safe-keeping for the speaker's discourse about the Wye, his past, and the sublime. While this praise of Dorothy Wordsworth's memory as a "dwelling-place" does not supersede the sublime recognition of a reality whose "dwelling" is everywhere, it does offer the speaker hope for a habitation as fixed and enclosed as the previous one is not.

This difference between a sublime "dwelling" and a beautiful one is embedded in several, allied pre-texts for Wordsworth's text. Like the sublime "haunt" of the "Prospectus," that of "Tintern Abbey" is sensed, not seen, whereas the "dwelling-place" of memory is described as though it were substantial and visible. Yet, unlike beauty's tents in the "Prospectus," it is a fixed habitation, not one that moves before the speaker. In the 1798 poem, these resonances are fixed by Words-worth's allusion to Milton's and Sidney's translations of the eighty-fourth Psalm. Milton's translation from the Hebrew – which found its way into the Anglican hymnal – begins, "How lovely are thy dwellings fair"; Sidney's translation begins, "How lovely is thy dwelling." Much as Wordsworth seeks a shelter within the text of "Tintern Abbey," the psalmist seeks God as a refuge (variously described in the Psalms as a "shelter," a "tent," or a "tabernacle")[36] from his enemies or from his own spiritual or physical isolation. Wordsworth secularizes the psalm-ist's need, but not his spiritual longing.

This longing for the beautiful as a refuge from the sublime structures Wordsworth's most sustained representations of this aesthetic con-flict, beginning in the 1790s, when he composed early versions of *The*

Borderers and the poem he later published as *Guilt and Sorrow*. In these poems critical displacements bring the threat of revolution and social disorder obliquely home to England. In the thirteen-book *Prelude* of 1805, a revisionary aesthetics recuperates what the earlier "Lines composed a few miles above Tintern Abbey, July 13, 1798" barely acknowledges.

4

Revolution and the egotistical sublime

In early as well as late versions of *Guilt and Sorrow* and *The Borderers*, rhetorical placements and displacements shape the aesthetic conflict and revolutionary history with which these poems are concerned. In "Adventures on Salisbury Plain," a female vagrant and a sailor suffer the aftermath of the English war against revolutionary America in which one was a reluctant actor and the other a bystander.[1] *The Borderers* dramatizes Wordsworth's ambivalence toward the French Revolution as an image of sublime power. Divided between participating in the villain Rivers's sublime style and resisting it – the two poles of the Wordsworthian sublime – he distances this struggle by placing it in the north of England during the reign of Henry the Third. Paradoxically, this strategy brings revolutionary France "home," where it is made safe by two prior displacements: revolutionary struggle is removed from France and moved back to the thirteenth century. The second displacement permits the invention of a figurative topography whose "depth of field" is, like that of The Salisbury Plain poems, temporal and spatial.

By projecting versions of *Guilt and Sorrow* and *The Borderers* onto topographies that belong to the past or allude to it, Wordsworth indicates the aesthetic task he assigns to landscape in these poems. As a relic of an ancient, primitive people and its ritual sacrifice, Stonehenge is the scene of Wordsworth's first critique of the sublime. Like a classical orator, he chooses structures (Stonehenge is "that *fabric* scarce of earthly form," my emphasis) and a topography that will allow him to locate the *topoi* he needs to speak of public and personal histories that intersect. Because the past conveys sublime terrors and visions, it asserts that the sublime may resist permanent burial and rise up to the surface of the text, much as the body of a drowned man may rise to the surface of a lake. These figures of burial and exhumation, which are explicit in the 1799 and 1805 *Preludes*, are implied in earlier poems when characters see ghosts of their past or stumble on structures that are relics of the past. The archeological pattern of *The Borderers* is more complex. As "antiquities" from the reign of Henry the Third and before, the landscapes and characters of the play dramatize a struggle with revolutionary action and principles that looks backward, as Wordsworth says, looking back on the tragedy in the 1840s, "into the depths of our nature."[2] In the tragedy the Wordsworthian sublime is prior, hidden deep in a history that is partially visible in the ruins or "antiquities" which dot its landscape.

Unlike Schiller, whose admiration for the sublime tends to skirt the possibility that sublime self-consciousness may, under the pressure of history and circumstance, become wilful tyranny, in *The Borderers* Wordsworth dramatizes the pressure of French history on his understanding of what an historical or tragic sublime might entail.[3] In this poem and in versions of *Guilt and Sorrow*, Wordsworth presents a satanic image of the negativity Hegel emphasizes in his account of the sublime. For Hegel, negativity marks the other worldly, transcendent nature of the sublime, whose approximate material representations emphasize its negative relation to the phenomenal world. For Wordsworth, sublime negativity may, and often does, invite a more satanic reading as sublime heroes and villains scorn limits on their powers and ambitions, or challenge the society whose norms such limits reflect. This is not, indeed, the sublime of Hegel or Kant. Yet Wordsworth's satanic reading foregrounds possibilities as implicit in the Kantian aesthetic as they are explicit in the older Burke's Tory rejection of the revolutionary sublime.

In *The Borderers* and versions of the poem Wordsworth finally titled *Guilt and Sorrow*, the act of telling tales (false or true) assists and complicates aesthetic conflict. Both poems restrain the sublime by encasing it in tales or by using tales as narrative barriers against its intrusions. In the three versions of *Guilt and Sorrow*, tales of sublime isolation help to create bonds between teller and auditor. In *The Borderers* characters tell or recall tales that are more often false than true. Those that are "true" (or at least not disproved within the play) assert the values of the human community, its laws and its benevolence. Although it is by no means neatly diagrammed in these poems – nor is it ever in Wordsworth's poetry – the aesthetic principle at issue in so emphatic an attention to tales and tellers is the role which the beautiful might or might not play in life and in art. At its most hopeful, tale-telling knits a community of tellers and auditors, much as traditional ballads are said to do. But just as ballads may disturb the community of teller, auditor, and tale,[4] so may tale-telling, par-

ticularly in *The Borderers*, defy the bonds it appears to assert. Because
the tales Rivers tells or has told in *The Borderers* disrupt the social
order by undermining its values (belief in the goodness of parents, in
the innocence of a beloved, etc.), this poem presents special problems
for Wordsworth's aesthetics. For behind the appeal of tale-telling as a
counterforce to an alienating sublime is the beautiful as the aesthetic
that contains or seeks to contain words and actions within a manageable human framework. So regarded, tales are parables about the
enclosure and coherence of beautiful landscapes. For this reason, those
tales that question or deny the principle of composed surfaces and
texts necessarily challenge the presumption that all tales are self-
contained fictions.

The Salisbury Plain Poems

In all versions of the poem Wordsworth published in 1842 as *Guilt
and Sorrow*, landscapes image the sublimity of the traveller's (or guilty
sailor's) experiences. He is lost or rather, with "all track quite lost" he
must "wilder [ ] on" through the storm ("Adventures on Salisbury
Plain," 165–66, p. 128).[5] *Wilder* suggests interior as well as exterior
confusion: he is lost in a wilderness and confused, hence *be*wildered.
His "glimpse" of "a naked guide-post's double head"[6] dramatizes the
semiotic nature of sublime figures. They point in two directions –
toward external, visible analogues and toward interior experience –
and they are only intermittently displayed. For this and later Wordsworthian travellers, "glimpses" are the temporal and spatial norm of
sublime vision. As a verb or noun that means "fugitive" or "evanescent" glances, or to seeing something between barriers,[7] *glimpse*
suggests the fleeting, transient character of the sublime. To capture it,
it must be "sited" in texts and in landscapes, placed much as artifacts
are placed on stratigraphic maps. Like the guidepost the sailor or
traveller glimpses, sublime guideposts are not stable signs: they appear
and disappear in ways that declare the visible limits of nature and
language to be mere appearance. Instead, what the traveller encounters on Salisbury Plain is presented as the absence of signs. The second
version, "Adventures on Salisbury Plain," is more explicit about
relationships between the void or emptied landscape and that absence:

> No swinging sign creak'd from its cottage elm
> To bid his weary limbs new force assume;
> 'Twas dark and void as ocean's watry realm
> Roaring with storms beneath night's starless gloom;
> No gypsey cower'd o'er fire or furze or broom;
> No labourer watch'd his red kiln glaring bright,

Nor taper glimmer'd dim from sick man's room;
Along the heath no line of mournful light
From lamp of lonely toll-gate stream'd athwart the night.

(172–80, p. 128)

The lack of human signs, which negatively defines the sublimity of the scene, implies another aesthetic standard. Were this scene inhabited, these signs (no gypsy, no labourer, etc.) would be reversed: the traveller would see, at the very least, a labourer, a gypsy, and some light, however mournful. So reversed, the scene would hardly be beautiful, but it would dimly register a social presence. In brief, here the semiotic measure of sublime negation is the language of the beautiful, not an Hegelian recognition that the sublime negatively registers a world beyond or behind the landscape of Salisbury Plain.

In the 1792 "Salisbury Plain," the first version of what later became *Guilt and Sorrow*, human sublimity and beauty are plotted without commentary along natural lines. Whereas the hungry savage roams "naked and unhouzed" in landscapes that offer no comfort, and yet is "strong to suffer" because he has no recollection of a better existence, vagrants who now roam hungry and "unhouzed" by the economic consequences of expensive wars are broken by similar hardships (1–11, p. 21) because they have become accustomed to the domestic comforts which a civilized society offers. This opposition between primitive and civilized man previews the *Guide* opposition between nature's sublimity and beauty. But in subsequent revisions Wordsworth presents the aesthetics of nature as something distinct so that its figurative status as a vehicle for the mind's aesthetic experience is made clear. In "Salisbury Plain," a "voice" from within Stonehenge warns the narrator–traveller to turn away from this scene of torture ("Salisbury Plain" 82–90, p. 23). But in "Adventures on Salisbury Plain," the first version to distinguish the narrator from the traveller, now a discharged sailor who has committed murder, the narrator addresses Stonehenge as an image of the sailor's guilt:

Thou hoary Pile! thou child of darkness deep
And unknown days, that lovest to stand and hear
The desart sounding to the whirlwind's sweep,
Inmate of lonesome Nature's endless year;
Ever since thou sawest the giant Wicker rear
Its dismal chambers hung with living men,
Before thy face did ever wretch appear,
Who in his heart had groan'd with deadlier pain
Than he who travels now along thy bleak domain?

(154–62, p. 127)

66

By assuming and transforming the message that a gothic voice delivers in the earlier version, the speaker asserts that the sublime scene is an exteriorized image of an interior guilt.

This revision summarizes Wordsworth's sense of the difference between the gothic and the sublime. Gothic fiction projects a sublime surface but little, if any, sublime depth. Until Ann Radcliffe created the gothic villain Schedoni, whose deeds lead him into a Dantesque journey of the soul through its own darkness,[8] the typical gothic villain is a hollow or flat character. His evil, power, and sublimity are surface phenomena that only rarely indicate the existence of interior states. The genre of gothic fiction exhibits a parallel fascination with surfaces. Even after 1789, when gothic novels began to offer suppressed portraits of revolutionary struggle as sublime villains seek to over-power predictably beautiful maidens (and laws and societies),[9] these images of revolution and the sublime are at best faint versions of a displaced reality, largely because they are preoccupied with external struggles and the surfaces of characters. Like Radcliffe's Schedoni, Wordsworth's guilty sailor in "Adventures on Salisbury Plain" sug-gests that the sublime must be recognized as an interior or hidden force. By transforming a gothic voice from without into the narrator's recognition of the sailor's guilt, Wordsworth asks readers to under-stand that bloodshed and murder are irrelevant if they are presented as thrills like those the Marquis de Sade recommended to tempt a jaded reading public,[10] but much to be feared as signs of interior states of mind.

Gone too from this second version is the hope Wordsworth expresses in his 1793 *Letter to the Bishop of Llandaff*, where he acknowledged the disasters of war, including regicide and violence, but claimed that they are temporary waystations along the revolution-ary path. Wordsworth argued that when the new French nation emerged phoenix-like out of revolutionary destruction, it would be possible to look back on earlier, more violent stages as necessary, evil, but transient. So violent a path is necessary, he explained, to eliminate the poverty which the Bishop of Llandaff chose not to see from his royalist perspective on the regicide of the French king.[11] But in "Adventures on Salisbury Plain" he argues instead that sublime forces are not simply manifestations of a power outside humankind, but forces within the mind that urge destruction and will remain after a war or revolution is concluded.

The sailor's history also illustrates the muddied moral terrain of revolutionary turmoil. The narrator explains that as the sailor returned from two years abroad, he was conscripted by "the ruffian press gang" to serve in the American Revolutionary War. Returning to England a second time, he is denied preferment in exchange for his wartime services. As he travels home without the means to support his family, his "mood" becomes desperate. Near his home he murders and robs a traveller, then flees the scene of the crime. This scenario is more troubling than the female vagrant's history, which includes no comparable crime, because it shows how individual human responsibility can become enmeshed in forces that extend far beyond individual will.

In other ways, the female vagrant is a compelling figure of aesthetic differences and management. Awakened by the sailor in the "lonely spital,"

> at once her spirits fail
> From fear by instant recollection bred;
> For of that ruin she had heard a tale
> Which now with freezing thoughts did all her powers assail.
>
> Had heard of one who, forced from storms to shroud,
> Felt the loose walls of this decayed retreat
> Rock to his horse's neighings shrill and loud,
> While his horse paw'd the floor with furious heat;
> Till on a stone that sparkled to his feet
> Struck, and still struck again, the troubled horse.
> The man half-raised the stone with pain and sweat,
> Half-raised, for well his arm might lose its force
> Disclosing the grim head of a new-murder'd corse.
>
> Such tales of this lone mansion she had learn'd,
> And when that shape, with eyes in sleep half drown'd
> By the moon's sullen lamp she first discern'd,
> Cold stony horror all her senses bound. (204–20, p. 129)

The female vagrant's unwitting transfer of a dream image of the murdered corpse onto the sailor produces a fleeting revelation of his guilt. He *is* the murdered corpse because guilt figures him as his crime. Without knowing it, she had brought the hidden crime to light. As a figure for sublime knowledge buried beneath the surface of texts, she indicates how figurative interventions can bring what is hidden momentarily out of hiding. But while the reader, the speaker of the poem, and the traveller "know" what lies hidden, she is unconscious of the interior horror for which the scene and her first sight of the sailor are figures.

The female vagrant's own history displays the linguistic and ethical concerns of the beautiful. Although she is one of Wordsworth's "disasters of war," unlike Margaret in *The Ruined Cottage* and *The Pedlar*, she survives and still acts as a social being. The fact that she, like the sailor, is destitute and mourns the loss of all whom she has loved gives her at least as much provocation to commit crime. Yet she is untouched by the darker, moral ravages of the sublime landscape and her history. She can tell her tale of lost happiness and be comforted as the sailor cannot. Moreover, as she talks, she invents a species of human community. Listening to her tale, the sailor grieves and, the narrator explains, "the more he griev'd, she loved him still the more" (594, p. 147).

The irony of reception in the poem is that whereas she gains "new delight and solace new" once she tells her life story, the sailor is terrified by her disclosures. As he explains after the first instalment of the tale, which prompts him to have grim night thoughts of ghostly wanderers over Salisbury Plain, "your tale has moved me much and I have been / I know not where" (419–20, p. 139). One other difference between the two early versions of *Guilt and Sorrow* suggests Wordsworth's recognition of this quality in the female vagrant. In the earlier version the traveller, who has committed no murder, comforts the female vagrant while she tells her tale by calling her attention to the dawn (334–36, p. 32). In the second and third versions she ends her tale, then comforts the sailor by calling *his* attention to the dawn (568–70, p. 146). Considered along with other aspects of the sailor's crime and Wordsworth's handling of it, this revision probably registers alienation, not punishment. The point is not that the sailor deserves no comfort, but that he can find none. Like other sublime figures, he is isolated. And from the perspective of the Wordsworthian beautiful, to be isolated is to be comfortless.

By making her history into a figure for the sailor's internal pain ("By grief enfeebled I was turned adrift, / Helpless as sailor cast on desart rock," 469–70, p. 141), the female vagrant transforms the despair that had prompted the sailor to murder into a descriptive simile. She thus invents an image that is "true" for them both, but because it is for her not literally but figuratively "true," it demonstrates her symbolic control over the tale she tells and the one he doesn't tell. Similarly, the three years she has wandered before meeting him echo and extend the three hours he "wilder'd on" (166, p. 128) after fleeing Stonehenge.

These appropriations of sublime figures suggest how the beautiful can make sublime figures its own. Here the kind of figure used depends on its aesthetic function. Figures that are tropes in the strict sense of the term (i.e. "turnings" from literal meanings) designate the otherness of the sublime. Those that express similitudes that broaden the meaning of an image in ways Coleridge called "organic" or "symbolic"[12] typically serve the beautiful as the aesthetic of mimetic faith – the conviction that words can be adequate to meaning.

The most singular revision of the poem is the place chosen for the sailor's gibbeting in "Adventures on Salisbury Plain." Although the scene of his crime is his native region, he confesses and is executed in the "City." There, contrary to the contemporary practice of gibbeting a body at the scene of the crime, his body is gibbeted. This practice, like dissection, was reserved for those who had committed particularly heinous murders. After execution, the body of the murderer was hanged either in chains or gibbet irons, a metal frame which held the limbs together, usually at the scene of the crime. Unless dissected, gibbeted bodies could not be buried and might thus remain on display for years.[13] Unlike dissection for the purposes of anatomical study (which Victor Frankenstein does better than he ought), gibbeting in chains or, as Wordsworth's speaker says, "in iron case," is intended to hold the body parts together. These alternative punishments are bizarrely reciprocal: dissection insures that the body will be split apart, gibbeting that it will be held together; and whereas the dissected body can be buried, the gibbeted one cannot. It must instead be exposed to "idle thousands" (820–28, p. 154). The differences between gibbeting and dissection call attention to the brutality and compensation specific to each form of punishment. Burial compensates the body for dismemberment, and the chains or "iron case" of the gibbet, which kept the body parts together in some semblance of their human configuration, compensate the body for public humiliation.

In "Adventures on Salisbury Plain" and *Guilt and Sorrow*, Wordsworth tries to minimize the horror of this punishment, first by locating it outside the topography with which the poem is mainly concerned and then by omitting the gibbet scene altogether in the final version. Yet he retains the narrator's description of the curious public which such a punishment *would* have attracted had it occurred:

> His fate was pitied. Him in iron case
> (Reader, forgive the intolerable thought)
> They hung not: – no one on *his* form or face
> Could gaze, as on a show by idlers sought;
> No kindred sufferer, to his death-place brought
> By lawless curiousity or chance,
> When into storm the evening sky is wrought,
> Upon his swinging corse an eye can glance,
> And drop, as he once dropped, in miserable trance.
>
> (658–66, pp. 281, 283)

In "Adventures on Salisbury Plain," the *anaclasis* of drop/dropped links the glance of the kindred sufferer to the sailor's earlier trance before another gibbet, the place where his guilt first found external sign in the poem. In *Guilt and Sorrow*, the potential identification between kindred sufferer and murderer is denied because there is no gibbeting.

The gain of these revisions for Wordsworth's aesthetics of community and representability is apparent: no gibbet, no crowd of idlers peering at "*his* form or face." The omission of this audience makes a "clearing"[14] in the text for the benevolent, social perspective initiated by the narrator's direct address to the reader. Both are, the speaker implies, more likely to pity than gawk. For them, gibbeting elicits the primitive cruelty which society may exhibit at the sound of gunfire, at the spectacle of a hanging, or at the scene of a gibbet. By excluding the gibbet scene in the 1842 text, Wordsworth insists that the narrative is in the end controlled by the values of the beautiful: benevolence and a community of feeling that includes the reader, the narrator, and the pathetic subject. This pathos displaces the sublime pathos of the unnamed "kindred sufferer," who exists only as a negative possibility in *Guilt and Sorrow*. This sufferer would presumably display a kindred past, one whose sublimity is its alienation from society.

More than any single revision, this new conclusion questions the attractions of the sublime. For if in "Salisbury Plain" and "Adventures on Salisbury Plain" only the female vagrant represents the values of the beautiful, in *Guilt and Sorrow* the burden of conscience that is the theme of the new title is finally lifted for the narrator and reader, whose conspiracy of pity insures their distance from the sailor, his guilt, and his fate. In part this revision echoes Wordsworth's earlier protest against gibbeting in "An Unpublished Tour," probably written in 1812. There he objects to the implied moral logic of the practice, calling it a "relic of barbarism." The later version also reflects a legal fact: in 1834 gibbeting was abolished, as dissection had been two years earlier.[15] Wordsworth's parallel removal of the gibbet scene asserts the emergence of a society and narrative frame whose values are a surety against the crimes and energies of the sublime. Yet this revision also emphasizes an aesthetic perspective that is implied by his initial choice of the Spenserian stanza for the first version of the poem.[16] As a form invented to present a long, allegorical narrative in well-defined stanzaic units, the stanza imposes limits, even as Wordsworth's revisions of "Salisbury Plain" progressively limit its sublimity.

Much as the gibbeting of the sailor takes place far from the place of his crime, so does Wordsworth's first investigation of the hazards of sublimity take place on Salisbury Plain, far from the arenas of his personal and public histories. Yet this region also became a *topos* of his aesthetics because of what he brought to it in 1793 – several years of uncertainty about revolutionary France and his responsibility as an English citizen, as an early supporter of the republican cause, and as the father of an illegitimate French child. By projecting some of this uncertainty onto Salisbury Plain, he fictionalized turmoils that were not resolved then or for some years afterward. In *The Borderers* place is differently displaced. Instead of taking the turmoil of revolution to France, as he would in the 1805 *Prelude*, he brings it home, a gesture that invites a sharpened perspective on the common ground which aesthetics and ethics share in the tragedy.

The Borderers

In the early 1790s Edmund Burke implicitly revoked his youthful fascination with the sublime by linking it to revolutionary France and by proclaiming the value of custom and hereditary rule. He denounced the Revolution as "terrifying," "astonishing," and "sudden," calling it the work of an "infernal faction," a "night and hell," a "spectre" and a "questionable shape." In November, 1793 he wrote: "I should certainly wish to see France circumscribed within moderate bounds."[17] Here redundancy betrays an underlying aesthetic opposition. Not only is France to be circumscribed, it must also be placed within bounds. Both terms reiterate his youthful definition of the beautiful. And in 1789 he rejected the "unbounded power" of revolutionary France by opposing it to those customs and laws that insure "the perpetuation of society itself."[18] For Burke, the preservation of society requires the beautiful, whose composition and balance echo the social symmetry and stability of the pre-revolutionary era.

Wordsworth also links unbounded power and energy to the sublime, and a sense of limit or containment with the beautiful. But whereas the older Burke was eager to suggest that the beautiful ought to win, in the early *Borderers* Wordsworth indicates that neither aesthetic can win because both describe basic impulses in the human mind. Yet he too fears the chaotic energy of the sublime, which threatens to disrupt the well-ordered surfaces of society and language. In *The Borderers* the hazards of the sublime prompt inquiries about the efficacy or inefficacy of tales as agents of social order, language, and the beautiful; the power and character of the sublime style; and the representational capacity of sublime landscapes.

As a quasi-gothic drama about a struggle among a daughter, her father, a lover of hers whom he has rejected, and a gothic villain who manipulates other characters to gain his own Iago-like ends, *The*

Borderers exhibits the antagonisms typical of such struggles, which usually include a third element, the community whose authority the villain either falsely assumes or otherwise subverts.[19] Burke's reading of the French Revolution offers a similar pattern. The revolutionary cause is the villain, the disrupted community pre-revolutionary France, and the queen represents both the House of Bourbon and the sexually threatened heroine.[20] What distinguishes Wordsworth's tragedy from its gothic and Burkean precedents is its more complicated reading of the revolutionary conflict between sublimity and beauty. Whereas Rivers acts out sublime villainy and a heritage that includes Milton's Satan and the gothic villain, Herbert and Matilda affirm the social order and benevolence of the beautiful. Mortimer is caught in the middle: he wants to be a sublime rebel yet he cannot wholly abandon the values Herbert and Matilda represent.

Setting and genre serve competing rhetorical strategies in *The Borderers*. What the setting conceals, the action of the tragedy discloses. Thus if the ostensible setting is the Border region between England and Scotland, an area that includes Liddisdale, the Tweed and Esk, and Cheviot Beacon,[21] the concealed center of the play is a smaller area near, or visible from, Penrith Beacon. With the exception of a brief reference late in the play which indicates that Mortimer is near Rosslyn Glen and Edinburgh, all the action of the play, including places off-stage that characters mention, can be located on a map of the Penrith–Stainmore region.[22] Written through and against other texts and figures, Wordsworth's dramatic representation of Penrith Beacon displaces the gibbet so critical to the scene in *The Prelude*, replacing it with a figurative topography created from literary artifacts. Two scenes in the tragedy establish Penrith Beacon as its concealed center. In the first of these scenes, as Rivers and Mortimer take Herbert toward the dungeon where Mortimer is supposed to murder the old man, Rivers explains where they are in relation to their camp:

> Did I not mention to you
> That as we mounted up the open steep
> I saw a distant fire in the north-east?
> I took it for the blaze of Cheviot Beacon;
> With proper speed our quarters may be gained
> Early tomorrow evening.　　　　(2.3.17–22, p. 142)

In the diagram of Lake District landmarks that appears in James Clarke's *Survey of the Lakes*, Penrith Beacon is the elevated point of view from which Cheviot Beacon is visible to the northeast;[23] see Plate 1. A second scene, in which members of Mortimer's band discuss

Rivers's treachery and history, returns to this "open steep," identified as "an eminence – a Beacon on it" (3.4, p. 202). William Gilpin's description of Penrith Beacon suggests that it is the beacon in question:

In the offskip, beyond the castle, arose a hill, in shadow likewise; on the top of which there stood a lonely beacon ... This beacon is a monument of those tumultuous times, which preceded the union; and the only monument of the kind now remaining in these parts.[24]

Called the "Border Beacon" in the 1805 *Prelude* (6:242–45, p. 198), Penrith Beacon is the only remaining marker of the disputed thirteenth-century Border which is the locale of Wordsworth's tragedy. As an artifact that points to others that are buried in the landscape and in the past, this monument is another sublime guidepost. Its "double head" points back to what is hidden, buried, and yet to be excavated but also forward to a struggle for power on the border between sublime vision and tyranny and the beautiful.

To locate this aesthetic struggle in the vicinity of Penrith Beacon, Wordsworth echoes and revises several guidebook descriptions of the region as well as contemporary discussions of the French Revolution as a drama or spectacle. With the characteristic tyranny of his picturesque eye, Gilpin trivializes the dramatic potential of the scene: "with regard to the adorning of such a landscape with figures, nothing could suit it better than a group of banditti."[25] In *The Borderers* Mortimer and his band are not simply picturesque adornments. Instead, Wordsworth's choice of genre invests character and setting with the dramatic power suggested by William Hutchinson's description of the view from Penrith Beacon as "a vast theatre, upwards of one hundred miles in circumference, circled with stupendous mountains." The aesthetic determinants of this "vast theatre" are sublime: "a dreary prospect extended to the eye, and all around a scene of barrenness and deformity ... all was wilderness and horrid waste, over which the wearied eye travelled with anxiety."[26]

As the sublime landscape that induces anxiety not Alpine exhilaration, Penrith Beacon is an apt setting for a drama about the different moral terrain of revolution and its difference from the pageant of unbounded, joyous "Freedom" depicted in the 1793 *Descriptive Sketches*. By choosing the genre of tragedy to present his reassessment of the revolutionary sublime, Wordsworth simultaneously elaborates a theatrical figure that appears in other contemporary reactions against revolutionary France and queries the contemporary identification of the sublime with tragedy.[27] In August 1789, Burke described the Revolution as "this monstrous tragi-comic scene." Camille Desmoulins, who aided revolutionary forces during the Fall of the Bastille but was himself guillotined by the Jacobins in 1794, called the Revolution a *torrent révolutionnaire* which drowns its actors in its undertow. Looking back on events Desmoulins had known first hand, Thomas Carlyle depicted the French Revolution as the great theatrical spectacle of the age.[28]

Because the Wordsworthian sublime denotes forces beyond and beneath the surfaces of language, consciousness, and society, a sublime topography like Penrith Beacon necessarily refers to concealed places and origins. For this reason it is not named in *The Borderers*. Similarly, the 1842 revision of the last scene presents Matilda's refusal to name Rivers as an attempt to ward off sublime terror. In the 1797–99 text she exclaims: "Rivers! oh! / The name has terror in it" (5.3.145–46, p. 278); in the 1842 text she merely says, "Name him not" (2205, p. 279). In the tragedy Penrith Beacon functions then, as an unnamed, but visible analogue for the way characters entertain or defend against competing aesthetic impulses, often as they tell tales that advance one set of aesthetic values even as they call another into question.

In *The Borderers* the powers of the beautiful are rarely matched to those of the sublime. In marked contrast to the female vagrant's tale in "Adventures on Salisbury Plain," the tales told in *The Borderers* are almost always intended to sever human, social ties. Only two tales in the tragedy effect or sustain such ties. The first is the one which an old pilgrim tells Matilda. The effect of the second, a tale of her father's exploits which Matilda once told Mortimer, is weakened by its position in the narrative. Mortimer tells it after Rivers has questioned the truth of Herbert's tale of his past.

When Matilda meets the old pilgrims who tell her of the decree restoring her father to his baronial rights, one of them tells her that years before all of them had shared the shelter of a cave during a storm. His tale recalls a world in which the values of the beautiful prevail for all those who participate in the closed set of speaker, hearer, and tale:

> No doubt you've heard the tale a thousand times.
> It was a dreary afternoon – and we
> Were worn with travel, when a storm o'ertook us
> In a deep wood remote from any town.
> A cave that opened to the road presented
> A friendly shelter, and we entered in ...
> We sate us down. The sky grew dark and darker.
> I struck my flint, and built up a small fire
> With rotten boughs and leaves such as the winds
> Of many winters in the cave had piled.

75

Meanwhile the storm fell heavy on the woods.
Our little fire sent forth a cheering warmth
And we were comforted, and talked of comfort.

(2.2.25–30, 33–39, p. 138)

The tale summarizes the values of the beautiful, whose shelter is talk as well as place. It also predicts the return of this aesthetic to power. This, at least, is the hope of those who tell it and it is the standard against which other shelters and talk of shelter later in the play will be measured. In the 1842 text, the pilgrim specifies the aesthetic register of Herbert's love for his daughter. "He said to me, that he had seen his child, / A face (no cherub's face more beautiful) / Revealed by lustre brought with it from Heaven" (716–19, p. 139). In the context of the pilgrim's tale, this aesthetic also describes the figurative shelter of their mutual affection.

Yet until the last scene, the action of the tragedy is dominated by the version of the sublime with which this poem is concerned. Herbert is abandoned and dies unrescued. The difference between Herbert's fate and that of obvious Shakespearean antecedents, Lear and Gloucester, is instructive. They are at least rescued (although rescue comes too late for Lear). In the subplot of Wordsworth's tragedy, the impoverished Robert leaves Herbert to die because, as a poor man with a family to feed, he fears reprisal should he end up with a dead man on his hands. His wife Margaret's exhortations that Herbert be helped are clouded by the profit motive. She reasons that the old man may be rich or well placed and that he or his heirs may reward them. In the *Ur-Borderers*, the ironies and make-shift ethics of the couple's poverty are not so vehemently declared.[29] Unlike "Salisbury Plain" and especially "Adventures on Salisbury Plain," where the sailor's guilt is counter-balanced by the female vagrant's insistent care for him and for the domestic tragedies they encounter, in *The Borderers* the mutual care which ought to sustain those ravaged by war and economic distress is too often absent. The domestic, civic virtues that belong to the beautiful lack authority until late in the play. Only then does it prevail against a sublime code of action and rhetoric.

Because he "has deeply imbibed a spirit of enterprize in a tumul-tuous age," as Wordsworth says in his early preface "On the Character of Rivers" (3–4, p. 62), Rivers belongs to that class of men who rise to prominence during periods of extreme political turmoil. The irony implicit in the phrase "spirit of enterprize" is appropriate to any of the identities that readers have suggested as sources for Rivers – young men of revolutionary France, the English Jacobin John Oswald, or Wordsworth himself.[30] For all these, revolutionary France was a land of opportunity. For the Jacobin Oswald, the enterprise was bloodshed, for the speaker of *The Prelude*, the enterprise seems to have been as much rhetorical as political. Seeing the "babel" of the French senate and its decrees, he suggested he might be eager to become a speaker for revolutionary hopes.[31] Because he so clearly belongs to the class of men who might be called sublime rebels against authority, Rivers is a satanic figure for the transcendent political and imaginative freedom which Kant, Schiller, Hegel and some post-structuralist critics have identified with the sublime.[32] Rivers dramatizes the other side of sublime isolation and transcendence – self-aggrandizement in the name of transcendent freedom.

As a "shadow" who recalls Wordsworth's "former self," Rivers is dangerous because he uncannily (or cannily) assumes the "sublime" voice of the autobiographical speaker of *The Prelude*. Like him, Rivers urges Mortimer to seek God "in darkness and in tempest." In the two-part *Prelude* of 1798–99, the relevant phrases are "in storm and tempest" and "in grandeur and in tumult" (*Prel. 1798, 352, 372,* p. 63). The most damaging Wordsworthian echoes occur as Rivers remembers the growth of his criminal mind, which began after he was betrayed by shipmates into abandoning his ship's captain on a deserted island. Of the period between this act and his decision to banish his remorse for it, he says, "three sleepless nights I passed in sounding on / Through words and things, a dim and perilous way" (4.2.102–3, p. 236). According to Burke, the "way" of sublime speech is "dim and perilous" because it is obscure. For Wordsworth, what is perilous is the self-justification which the sublime facilitates. Like the boy Wordsworth who leaves companions and is instructed by a sublime Nature, Rivers says of himself:

> Oft [I] left the camp
> When all that multitude of hearts was still
> And followed on through woods of gloomy cedar
> Into deep chasms troubled by roaring streams,
> Or from the top of Lebanon surveyed
> The moonlight desart and the moonlight sea;
> In these my lonely wanderings I perceived
> What mighty objects do impress their forms
> To build up this our intellectual being,
> And felt if aught on earth deserved a curse,
> 'Twas that worst principle of ill that dooms
> A thing so great to perish self-consumed.
> – So much for my remorse. (4.2.127–39, p. 238)

The "thing so great" that should not "perish self-consumed" is Rivers or, in a thorough perversion of Kantian aesthetics, Rivers's "intellectual being." These echoes of lines and cadences which reappear in Wordsworth's later poems and, more importantly, in the voice of an authorial persona, emphasize the troubling proximity between Wordsworth and his villain. Here the sublime isolation common to Rivers and to the boy of *The Prelude* enhances their sense of election at the expense of their social being. In *The Prelude* this sublime effect returns to haunt its speaker.

It is hardly surprising that the 1842 *Borderers* minimizes verbal parallels between Rivers and the speaker of *The Prelude*. Urging Mortimer to see their plot against Herbert in heroic terms, in the early version Rivers argues that external forms and surfaces are merely outward shows, and that what matters is the hidden source for which things are the mere "spectacles of forms" (2.1.98–102, p. 130). In the 1842 revision he merely observes, "Yes, they / Men who are little given to sift and weigh / Would wreak on us the passion of the moment" (644–46, p. 131). The declaration still shows Rivers's canny assessment of human behaviour, but it expunges his sublime speech. In another 1842 revision, Wordsworth "unsays" Rivers's sublime words by omitting the speech in which he tells Mortimer that he will be "more awful and sublime" if he kills Herbert (2.1.77–78, p. 128).

As an "energetic character [who] uses his power for evil purposes,"[33] Rivers is a troubling test case for the claim that the mind can sympathize with or participate in the sublime. Specifically at issue is Wordsworth's argument that the mind ought to be able to experience "intense unity" whether it resists or participates in the sublime power or energy it confronts (*Prose*, 2:254–56). As Milton's Satan in Wordsworthian dress, he is the same nemesis that troubled earlier writers on aesthetics, who attempted to explain (or explain away) Satan's attractiveness to readers by declaring its source to be Milton's style, not Satan's character.[34] In doing so they hoped to minimize the cosmic, if negative, grandeur of Satan's effect on human history. If Rivers does not achieve Satan's cosmic range of influence, he does threaten the precarious political equilibrium of the Border until the last scene of the play. What makes Rivers dangerous is his sublime speech. Like readers of *Paradise Lost*, who may be persuaded against all moral claims to the contrary that Satan is the character who justifies his ways to man, readers of *The Borderers* must keep Rivers's perfidy in mind so as not to be seduced by his eloquence.

This is the aesthetic difficulty of the tragedy, one in which its maker is implicated. When Wordsworth declares in his preface that Rivers "is betrayed into a great crime" (4–5, p. 62), we do well to query the syntactic passivity of this phrase. Who betrayed whom when Rivers left the captain of his ship on an island? Although Rivers was himself initially betrayed by crew members who needed both to rid themselves of a despised authority and to find a scapegoat, he (and perhaps Wordsworth) diminishes his culpability by arguing, much as Satan does, that someone else initiated the chain of events that led to his crime. For both Rivers and Satan, their crimes are merely repetitions of the crime by which each was "betrayed."

In his early preface, Wordsworth is careful to give his protagonist the attributes of a sublime villain: inordinate pride and will (1–31, pp. 62–63). Like other literary villains, Rivers "lays waste the groves that should shelter him" (43–44, p. 63). This image reiterates the theme which the Pilgrim's tale announces early in the play. Shelters that offer the safety and enclosure of the beautiful are prey to the sublime.[35] Rivers shows that laying waste to social and natural shelters is what sublime villains do best. Curiously, Wordsworth does not mention that in addition to the antecedents he names (Orlando, Cardenias, and Iago), Rivers is a near double for Milton's Satan, Caleb Williams, and the protagonists of Schiller's *Die Rauber*.[36] Yet in explaining Rivers's motives, he belabors his faults:

They are founded chiefly in the very constitution of his character; in his pride which borders even upon madness, in his restless disposition, in his disturbed mind, in his superstition, in irresistable propensities to embody in practical experiments his worst thoughts and most extravagant speculations, in his thoughts and his feelings, in his general habits and his particular impulses, in his perverted reason justifying his perverted instincts. (146–53, p. 67)

Because Rivers's "thoughts" and "feelings" are specified in some detail, they need not be given as a separate category, nor is the repetition of "perverted" necessary.[37] By omitting some of Rivers's antecedents and yet listing his faults more than once, Wordsworth warns readers (and himself) against being attracted to a character whose powers of speech, like those of Milton's Satan, tend to attract rather than repulse readers.

To explain how Rivers's early history can be deduced from his present conduct, Wordsworth represents that hidden history as an absent, sublime origin which we mistakenly assign more influence over present behavior than it in fact possesses:

When our malignant passions operate, the original causes which called them forth are soon supplanted, yet when we account for the effect we forget the immediate impulse and the whole is attributed to the force from which the first motion was received. The vessel keeps sailing on, and we attribute her progress in the voyage to the ropes which first towed her out of harbour. (175–81, p. 68)

To apply this figure to Rivers, we could say that "the ropes which first towed" his character out of "harbour" signify the first cause of his evil.

But we are given no information about the event for which these ropes are a figure. This elided tenor will not be made explicit until late in the play when Rivers reveals his history to Mortimer. Like the original motive for a family feud that is "lost" to later generations, Rivers's motives belong to the atemporal or pretemporal arena of sublime agency.

Earlier in the preface Wordsworth makes the origin of sublime power part of his critique. Noting Rousseau's observation that "a child ... will tear in pieces fifty toys before he will think of making one" (38–39, p. 63), he argues that Rivers exhibits a similarly "destructive use of power." Because the Rousseauist analogy implies that a destructive will-to-power is infantile, it argues against the traditional claim that the sublime belongs to elevated natures, but especially to God. He also calls attention to Rivers's perverted use of reason to aid a misguided imagination:

He is perpetually imposing upon himself; he has a sophism for every crime. The *mild* effusions of thought, the milk of human reason, are unknown to him. His imagination is powerful, being strengthened by the habit of picturing possible forms of society where his crimes would no longer be crimes, and he would enjoy that estimation to which from his intellectual attainments he deems himself entitled. (63–69, pp. 64–65)

In the tragedy Rivers calls this process "enlarg[ing] the intellectual empire of mankind" (4.2.188–89, p. 242). Wordsworth insists that a reason that is abstracted from human and natural practices lacks ethical foundations. Unlike Kant, who supposed that reason frees the imagination from sense experience and permits the mind's recognition of its sublimity, he suggests that it tempts the mind to self-aggrandizement and deception. As "an empiric – and a daring and unfeeling empiric" (*P. Bord.*, 81–82, p. 65), Rivers uses reason to construct an imagined world in which his powers, not society's, are normative. Responding to those who were suspicious of the persuasive powers of classical oratory, Hume praised classical orators who united the sublime and the pathetic. He added that such eloquence is not deceptive if it is accompanied by sound reasoning.[38] The ancient and modern difficulty Hume hoped to resolve concerns whether lawyers and public speakers rely too much on passion (or pathos in Hume's sense) and too little on reason to persuade audiences. Wordsworth returns to this issue in *The Borderers* by portraying Rivers as a speaker whose eloquence assists "a perverted reason." Because Hume hoped to persuade readers that rhetorical eloquence could assist right reason, he excluded the possibility which a more skeptical Wordsworth dramatizes: the use of sublime eloquence to assist a wrong reason.

Rivers repeatedly uses the sublime eloquence against which Wordsworth warns readers. Hearing that news of Herbert's restored barony
is about to reach Mortimer and his band, Rivers decides to shift
tactics. Instead of offering "proof" of Herbert's villainy, he will offer
passionate avowals of it. Invoking a sublime image also used by the
speaker of *The Prelude*, whose mind "turn[s] round as with the might
of waters" after he sees a blind beggar in London (7:616–17, p. 260),
Rivers says of Mortimer: "the mind of man upturned / Is a strange
spectacle" (3.2.11–28, pp. 182, 184). And when he argues, "we
dissect / The senseless body, why not the mind?" Rivers exemplifies the
spirit behind gibbeting and, to paraphrase the speaker of "The Tables
Turned," murder by a coldly analytic reason (*PW*, 4:57, ll. 26–28). To
convince Mortimer and his followers that the blind Herbert ought to
be killed, he gives a "set speech" in praise of sacrificial justice. Echoing
Portia's mercy speech in *The Merchant of Venice*,[39] he argues against
mercy, claiming that Wisdom "spares not the worm" – i.e, *Herbert*
(2.3.381–401, pp. 176–78). His personification of Justice, as she who
serves Wisdom, uses a traditional iconographic image – a woman who
weighs alternatives in a scale.[40] Like Rivers's "infant lamb," a popular
and Biblical emblem of helplessness, this Justice is a stock figure he
invokes to give an aura of integrity to an argument that subverts the
very abstract principles it personifies. If the twisted core of his
character is momentarily visible in his disdain for weakness as a
product of the "wiles of Women" and "craft of age" – a disdain that
betrays his conviction that absolute power is its own right – his
elevated figures and quasi-Biblical images achieve the desired end.

More than any other figure of the Wordsworthian sublime, Rivers
shows how sublime rhetoric undermines the critical alliance between
language and meaning. Thus when he reports Herbert's charge against
Mortimer and his followers in the later version ("he calls us
'Outlaws'," 1842, 63, p. 77), he uses quotation marks to argue that the
charge is false. Now Herbert's words mean not what he intended but
what Rivers wants Mortimer to believe: that his band simply
"guard[s] the innocent" (63, p. 77). And thanks to Rivers, who
questions the tale of Herbert's "quondam Barony" (1.1.52, p. 78)
before Mortimer recalls hearing it from Matilda, the reader takes note
of the oedipal jealousy submerged in Mortimer's story of learning to
love Matilda by hearing her tell of her father's exploits.[41] Undoubtedly
Mortimer was charmed by the teller, but he was not necessarily – and
is not during the action of the play – similarly charmed by the father.
Yet for Mortimer the image of the father was once inextricable from
that of the daughter: "when we conversed together / The old man's

image still was present: chiefly / When I had been most happy"
(1.1.69–71, p. 80). The doubt that hovers over "chiefly" is precisely
the kind of submerged doubt – in texts and in the human heart – which
Rivers's sublime discourse brings to the surface. Among the definitions
Freud quotes to his own definition of *unheimlich* is Schelling's more
critical definition, which Rivers's narrative interventions dramatize:
the *unheimlich* is what is brought to light but ought to remain
hidden.[42] From the perspective of the beautiful, which stands guard
over society and language, the sublime is responsible for unlawful
exhumations that threaten social, familial ties. Like the exposed,
gibbeted body of the sailor in "Adventures on Salisbury Plain," what
Rivers exhumes is an affront to the social code of Mortimer's
conscious meaning.

More telling still is Rivers's command of the language of the
Wordsworthian beautiful. He tells Mortimer:

> Your single virtue has transformed a band
> Of fierce barbarians into ministers
> Of beauty and order. – The old man
> Blesses their step, the fatherless retires
> For shelter to their banners.   (2.1.65–69, p. 128)

His other appropriations of beauty's figures are more violent. In the
same speech he uses *benevolence* as near-synonym for "the wholesome
ministry of pain and evil" (2.1.72–74, p. 128). Finally, he undermines
the beautiful when he argues that murdering Herbert (which he
mistakenly believes Mortimer has done) is not murder, but a justified
act of nature:

> Murder! what's in the word?
> I have no cases by me ready made
> To fit all crimes. Carry him to the camp!
> You have seen deeper – taught us that the institutes
> Of nature, by a cunning usurpation
> Banished from human intercourse, exist
> Only in our relations to the beasts
> That make the field their dwelling. If a viper
> Crawl from beneath our feet, we do not ask
> A licence to destroy him: our good governors,
> Wise thinkers! have by forms and ceremonies
> Hedged in the life of every pest and plague
> That bears the shape of man, and for what purpose
> But to protect themselves from extirpation?   (3.1.92–105, p. 216)

The logic of this argument depends on a remarkable wrenching of the
image "beasts." Rivers tells Mortimer that he has, unlike those who
make laws prohibiting the extermination of pests and the bringers of

plague, recognized Herbert for what he is – a beast of the field. This catachresis is justified, Rivers implies, because Herbert's "treachery" lowers him to the class of beasts that make the field their dwelling. By using the term *dwelling* to assist his claim that Herbert should be exterminated, he converts a sign of Herbert's and Matilda's human-heartedness into the sign of Herbert's guilt, and subverts a figurative mainstay of the beautiful in the play.

Unlike Rivers, the character of Mortimer is split: he is one part eighteenth-century man of feeling and one part sublime bandit or philosophic villain. The values that impel the first part are pre-eminently social: the beauty and sublimity of nature are occasions for fellow-feeling. This equation, imported from the eighteenth-century code of sensibility, is an ethical land-mine. Whatever else they are, sublime nature and characters are antithetical to the code of beauty, sociability, and representability. Mortimer's political program mirrors this aesthetic ambivalence. He is a rebel who seeks no revolution and has no desire to establish a new political order. He only wants to hold the Border until its rightful lord returns. A similar program motivates the autobiographical speaker's revolutionary compatriots in *The Prelude*, who hope to guard the innocent and aid the weak by restoring the true spirit of chivalry.[43] In *The Borderers* the irony of Mortimer's effort to hold the Border for its rightful lord is of course that he is responsible for the death of the man he has been waiting for. A deeper Words-worthian irony is the discrepancy between Mortimer's "outlaw" status and his hope to restore an aristocrat to power. In this political arena the values of the sublime and the beautiful must inevitably clash.

In Rivers Mortimer sees the qualities of a sublime hero: price, action, and "strong feelings," the characteristic pathos of the sublime (33–38, p. 75). He exhibits a subtler internalization of sublime values when he chastizes his band for asserting Herbert is their rightful lord:

> We look
> But at the surfaces of things, we hear
> Of towns in flames, fields ravaged, young and old
> Driven out in flocks to want and nakedness,
> Then grasp our swords and rush upon a cure
> That flatters us, because it asks not thought.
> The deeper malady is better hid –
> The world is poisoned at the heart.   (2.3.337–44, p. 172)

The legislating values of this speech – its scorn for surface interpretations and its attention to hidden, deeper ones – belong to the sublime. Its dramatic irony reflects the doubleness and deception of sublime speech. For the reader knows that in one sense (not the one Mortimer intends) he is right: the world he inhabits is poisoned at the heart because Rivers has poisoned Mortimer's heart.

Matilda inadvertently reveals Mortimer's ambivalent nature when she describes him to her father:

> O could you hear his voice –
> Alas! you do not know him. He is one
> (I guess not what bad tongue has wronged him with you),
> All gentleness and love. His face bespeaks
> A deep and simple meekness; and that soul,
> Which with the motion of a glorious act
> Flashes a terror-mingled look of sweetness,
> Is, after conflict, silent as the ocean
> By a miraculous finger stilled at once.   (1.1.133–41, p. 86)

Voice and face both insist on traits that Matilda and her father value – social virtues and domestic safety. But hidden beneath these surfaces is, as Matilda is obliged to notice, another temperament, one she uses sublime figures to portray. Although she wants her father to see Mortimer as a Christ figure, her image of him as a soul that "flashes a terror-mingled look of sweetness" and is then "silent," even as the ocean might be miraculously "stilled" by Christ, presents a different view of his character. As attributes of sublime feeling and landscape, "terror" and "ocean" image the aesthetic beneath the benevolent surface of Mortimer's expression. Thus if his face "bespeaks / A deep and simple meekness," other powers operate beneath that easily read surface, even as great powers beneath the surface of the ocean may terrify those who rely on that surface for safe passage. In the complex plot relations among tale-telling, speech, and deception that permeate both versions, the reader may, like Herbert, receive Matilda's repeated enthusiastic conditional "O could you hear his voice" (or read his face) with nothing like her conviction.

Speaking to Rivers early in the play of the deeds that lie ahead, Mortimer predicts that they "will be my ruin" (2.1.182–83, p. 122). In the 1842 version he is more specific:

> these strange discoveries –
> Looked at from every point of fear or hope,
> Duty, or love – involve, I feel, my ruin.   (548–50, p. 123)

With the exception of fear, which belongs to the sublime, these "points of view" belong to the Wordsworthian beautiful. Unlike the 1797–99 text, which recognizes Mortimer's aesthetic ambivalence but emphasizes his attraction to the sublime, the later version insists that the values of the beautiful exist in the midst of his attempts to imitate –

more thoroughly than he knows – the trajectory of sublime action which Rivers advises.

In both versions the scene where the two lead Herbert to a gothic dungeon is punctuated by Mortimer's declarations of sympathy for Herbert, to which Rivers responds by telling Mortimer more tales of the old man's supposed treachery (1.3.5–157, pp. 104–18). On the heath where he is finally abandoned, Herbert tries to make peace by reminding Mortimer of tales Matilda told. This "ploy" is, even from Mortimer's deluded perspective, momentarily efficacious. In an aside, he admits that he could "weep too," largely because he hears Matilda's voice in her father's (3.3.63, p. 196). But he immediately rejects this potential union in sympathy:

> I am cut off from man,
> No more shall I be man, no more shall I
> Have human feelings!   (3.3.70–72, p. 196)

This recognition of the consequences of murdering Herbert reveals how thoroughly Mortimer assents to the opposition between the sublime – powerful, vaunting, heroic, and often deceptive, and the beautiful – social, human-hearted, and enmeshed in a network of ethical values that issue from these attributes. Mortimer is in this regard undeluded: to choose a sublime nature and conduct unequivocally, he must alienate himself from the code of human feeling and social conduct which the beautiful upholds.

Yet so deep is Mortimer's commitment to the sublime that landscape becomes a persistent sign of the isolation which that commitment will eventually require of him. As they approach the dungeon, he tells Herbert: "this is a place to make one fearful without knowing why." Herbert disagrees, arguing that "any shelter was a comfort, bewildered as we were, and such a storm bursting over our heads" (2.3.96–98, p. 150). Their disagreement about what the dungeon represents is only partly explained by the fact of Herbert's blindness. For Mortimer, sublime landscapes are uneasy mirrors of his compulsion to behave like an outlaw in what he is told is an heroic cause. Herbert's matter-of-fact response to the dungeon is more emphatic in the 1842 text. He half-reproves Mortimer's assessment of the fearfulness of the scene: "Why so? a roofless rock had been a Comfort,/ Storm-beaten and bewildered as we were" (814–15, p. 151). Herbert does not associate the gothic dungeon with fear because he has no inner fear and guilt that require this scene as their objective correlative.[44]

Because the sublime style or, more precisely, the power that style has to "move" its hearers, is the crux of the struggle between Mortimer and Rivers, Mortimer's disavowal of Rivers's sublime speech is essential to his final tragic and heroic recognition of what he has done. After abandoning Herbert, Mortimer explains that he has crossed over to another level of being, one of "remembered terror" beyond "human thought." In the 1797–99 version he describes this state as a place of "love and peace" (3.5.1–4, p. 208), but in the revised version this phrase is omitted; what is left is "peace and rest." Having punished Herbert outside the laws of society, Mortimer puts himself beyond human affection (1469, p. 209). Eager to define this state as Mortimer's personal hell, Rivers predicts Mortimer's future despair in speeches heavy with allusions to *Paradise Lost* and Schiller's *Die Rauber*.[45] And in the famous lines Wordsworth later adapts for the epigraph of *The White Doe of Rylstone*, Rivers promotes suffering as a sublime agony:

> Action is transitory, a step, a blow –
> The motion of a muscle – this way or that –
> 'Tis done – and in the after vacancy
> We wonder at ourselves like men betray'd.
> Suffering is permanent, obscure and dark,
> And has the measure of infinity.   (3.5.60–65, p. 214)

The speech is a masterful demonstration of the sublime style. Its elevated tone is imperative, God-like, and its diction achieves a parallel elevation by making action and suffering universal qualities. Its argument that suffering "has the measure of infinity" neatly declares the paradoxical nature of the sublime style. But when Rivers argues that remorse and responsibility are illusory by-products of a false belief that actions have consequences, Mortimer becomes suspicious not, as yet, of what Rivers has done, but of the ethical contradictions in what he says. In the later version Mortimer charges him with inconsistency. To argue on the one hand that "suffering is permanent" and "has the nature of infinity" and on the other that "remorse . . . cannot live with thought" is, Mortimer objects, a "wandering" or erring among contradictory meanings (1568–71, p. 217). So let loose of rational and ethical moorings, Rivers's voice betrays its own duplicity.

In the final scene of *The Borderers*, Mortimer declares himself a sublime outcast, but his assumption of this persona is now governed by a diction and perspective that belong to the beautiful. To be sure, other scenes in both versions register the difficulty of sustaining beauty's precepts. Yet in a second meeting with Matilda after he has abandoned her father, Mortimer's sympathy for Herbert and admission of guilt reinstate the beautiful as the norm of conduct. Whereas both versions show us Matilda and Mortimer in sympathetic dialogue about Herbert's abandonment and lonely death, the earlier text presents Mortimer as self-excusing. He tells himself that had Matilda never lived, he would not have committed this act. The Rivers-like casuistry of this disavowal of responsibility is muffled in the later version where, instead of arguing "the fault's not mine" (5.3.38, p. 270), he exclaims, "Mysterious God, / If she had never lived I had not done it" (2124–25, p. 241). In both versions the conditional statement is the same, but in the second its rhetorical import is altered by what precedes it. The exclamation "Mysterious God" is subtly uncommitted about who is responsible for Herbert's death. In the earlier version, Mortimer implies that God is responsible. But the revised context of the second version makes it possible to read his exclamation as a recognition of the mysterious complexity of moral impulse and deception.

A similar revision alters the scene where Mortimer confesses to Matilda. In the earlier version he blurts out, "I am the murderer of thy father" and she runs away, leaving him to soliloquize Rivers-like about his deed:

> (*Alone*) Three words have such a power! This mighty burden
> All off at once! 'Tis done, and so done too
> That I have cased her heart in adamant.
> This little scrip when I first found it here –
> I sunk ten thousand fathoms into hell.
> I was a coward then – but now am schooled
> To firmer purposes. There doth not lie
> Within the compass of a mortal thought
> A deed that I would shrink from – and I can endure.
>
> (5.3.100–8, p. 276)

Like Milton's Satan, Mortimer is fallen yet prideful still. In part his pride is motivated by what he believes to be the efficacy of his "three words" (in the earliest extant version of the scene they are "thy father's murderer"). His claim that these words have power, together with their stylized presentation as a soliloquy, signals the vaunting speech of the satanic rebel. Yet in subsequent lines he is reluctant to celebrate his crime. He abandoned Herbert without food out of carelessness and cowardice: he says in retrospect that had he done the deed "with a mind resolved," he would have had "strength to bear the recollection." But because he did not, he lacks the requisite (sublime) strength to recall his action. The admission signals Mortimer's increasingly troubled allegiance to the code of sublime villainy.

In the 1842 version a short speech to Matilda replaces the blunt confession and long soliloquy of the earlier text. The diction of the revised text and the fact that Matilda remains to hear the whole speech suggest a more equivocal aesthetic perspective. Mortimer tells her:

> It must be told, and borne. I am the man,
> (Abused, betrayed, but how it matters not)
> Presumptuous above all that ever breathed,
> Who, casting as I thought a guilty Person
> Upon Heaven's righteous judgment, did become
> An instrument of Fiends. Through me, through me,
> Thy Father perished. (2177–83, p. 277)

Mortimer's specular relation to Rivers and the cult of the sublime hero/villain is still evident. As Rivers once was, he too has been "abused, betrayed," and like Milton's Satan, he has been "presumptuous above all that ever breathed." But if Mortimer remains Satan-like in his pride, he eschews satanic self-deception. That he speaks to Matilda rather than to himself is a slight yet crucial recognition of the values which will increasingly propel his voice and action, especially in the 1842 version. By having her as his auditor, Mortimer asserts that he is answerable to her and to the human, social values that she and Herbert represent.

Other changes in the 1842 version emphasize Mortimer's new regard for the beautiful as the aesthetic basis for his moral being. The guilt, near-hysteria, and imitations of Rivers which he obsessively declares in the 1797–99 version give way in the revised text to a cooler presentation of Mortimer's gradual disengagement from the man whose shadow he has been. He asks Rivers to "endure" and "feed remorse" with him – a curiously social declaration of their parallel though separate futures as sublime outcasts (2273–78, p. 291). Unlike Rivers, who has tried to recreate Mortimer as "a shadow of my former self," Mortimer denies the mutual isolation that is Rivers's goal. Like a Blakean specter, the "shadow" Rivers hopes to make of Mortimer would be a separate projection of a Rivers who no longer exists. This is the destiny of Romantic satans, set apart from their own "families" of specters and emanations. Mortimer argues instead that however far apart they are – and he hopes that the distance between them is great – they will be united by a rivalship that will spur them on to "peaceful ends." This socialization of their future existence as outcasts registers an implicit reliance on the ethos of the beautiful.

In the final scene of the play, Mortimer requests that a monument be "raise[d] on this lonely Heath" to "record my story for warning" (5.3.262–63, p. 294). Unlike Penrith Beacon, the scene of sublime disclosures about the past and the present, this monument projects the figurative topography of the play forward to future generations, including Wordsworth's, who might learn from Mortimer's story. As an inscribed surface whose message is intended for present and future auditors, this monument re-inscribes the figurative topography of the play with the values of the beautiful. The 1842 version specifies those values:

> Raise on that dreary Waste a monument
> That may record my story: nor let words –
> Few must they be, and delicate in their touch
> As light itself – be there withheld from Her
> Who, through most wicked arts, was made an orphan
> By One who would have died a thousand times,
> To shield her from a moment's harm. To you,
> Wallace and Wilfred, I commend the Lady,
> By lowly nature reared, as if to make her
> In all things worthier of that noble birth,
> Whose long-suspended rights are now on the eve
> Of restoration: with your tenderest care
> Watch over her, I pray – sustain her.   (2294–2306, p. 295)

The assumption behind this commendation is that society and language should, or must, be party to the care he owes Matilda. And in both versions of Mortimer's final speech, the beautiful exercises a subtle control over the final images of sublime isolation. Although he declares his intention to become an exile from society in both versions, the 1842 text domesticates his banishment to a landscape of sublime isolation by identifying its purpose as expiation:

>   Over waste and wild,
> In search of nothing, that this earth can give,
> But expiation, will I wander on –
> A Man by pain and thought compelled to live,
> Yet loathing life – till anger is appeased
> In Heaven, and Mercy gives me leave to die.   (2316–21, p. 295)

This desire for expiation assumes the existence of values which a wrongdoer has transgressed, and someone – a god or a community – to whom remorse is due. By contrast, the 1797–99 version presents Mortimer's suffering not as a response to values beyond himself but as pain that is self-induced, and self-sustaining: "and I will wander on / Living by mere intensity of thought" (5.3.271–72, p. 294). Like Byron's Manfred, whose heroic stature derives less from his crime than from his capacity to suffer and will himself to live, the Mortimer of the earlier *Borderers* is heroic because he wills his suffering. Attentive to how Romantic wilfulness appropriates the vaunting ambition of the sublime, in the 1842 version Wordsworth excises the line in question so that Mortimer suffers according to God's will, not his own.

Whereas in the earlier version he announces, "I will go forth a wanderer on this earth" (265, p. 294), in the later version he asserts that he is driven: "a wanderer *must* I go" (2312, p. 295). The emphatic syntactic inversion of the revised line asserts that Mortimer is now subject to powers beyond himself. This refashioning resolves an ambivalence toward the sublime that troubles the early version and much of the 1842 text as well. If the older Wordsworth is more anxious to diminish the range of influence permitted the sublime, the younger poet agrees that the sublime is hazardous because it lies outside the norms of human society and discourse. Despite these differences, the early *Borderers*, like the versions of *Guilt and Sorrow* that Wordsworth composed in the 1790s, dramatizes the conflict between sublime and beautiful figures that marks a critical turn in Wordsworth's emergence as a major poet.

5

Revisionary aesthetics in The Prelude

I go into the grounds, the extended mansions of remembrance, where is stored the endless import of my senses. There, too, is record kept of thoughts added to the sensual imprints, or subtracted from them, or varying them in combination. Indeed everything ever committed to remembrance is still laid up there, unless long decayed or sunk beyond retrieval. On visits there I make request for what I would withdraw, and some are issued instantly, while others must be sought for at some length in deeper vaults. Still others, clamorous, pour out unbidden and, while a different thing was asked for and is being sought, they dance as it were before me, saying, "Wasn't it us you were wanting?" And I banish them, with a hand's brush of the heart, from the presence of my memory, until what I seek is brought from its cobwebs and restored to light.   Augustine, *Confessions* 10:8

READERS who prefer the two-part *Prelude* of 1798–99 to the expanded versions of 1805 and 1832–1850 frequently explain their preference by pointing out that the early version develops a theme of "single and determined bounds."[1] They argue, quite rightly, that although the speaker of the expanded *Prelude* claims to be looking for just such a theme in Book I, he never finds it. Or, if he does, he seems to lose it by Book v.[2] Even readers who have no special animus against the expanded poem tend to read it as though its "spots of time" were that theme "of single and determined bounds" which the speaker adroitly avoids in the rest of the poem.[3] In some measure, readers could hardly be expected to do otherwise, both because *The Prelude* is long, and because the visionary experience recorded in its "spots" appears to structure or at least dominate the narrative. Yet in the revisionary aesthetics of the expanded *Prelude*, these moments are no more (if no less) than sublime "outcroppings" in a poetic texture that frames or subdues them. More clearly than any of Wordsworth's poems, the 1805 and, to a lesser extent, the 1832–50 *Preludes* present an aesthetic topography or map of individual *topoi*, those scenes of instruction where sublime disruptions take place.

As such, the mental space of the poem resembles that of Augustine's "mansions of remembrance," with one telling difference. Unlike Augustine, Wordsworth's speaker is troubled by unbidden, sublime recollections that refuse to be banished, except temporarily. Ultimately the speaker is the author of this refusal since he wants to find a place for the sublime in the poem and yet limit its powers. Beginning in Book I, the boy's early education "by beauty and by fear" turns into a rhetorical contest between the two. This conflict becomes more pressing in each book, as sublime figures rise up to disrupt the shelters in memory that the Wordsworthian beautiful creates. Critics who prefer the two-part *Prelude* (where sublime outcroppings do dominate the argument) and those who emphasize sublime, visionary moments in later versions tend to neglect the rhetorical (and aesthetic) occasion that prompted Wordsworth's decision to expand the poem on his life – his experience in revolutionary France. Seen retrospectively through the lens of this experience, as I will argue Wordsworth's speaker does see them, the sublime or visionary encounters gathered together in the 1798–99 poem had to be scattered in the expanded poem, where they are joined by troubling figures of revolutionary sublimity. Not surprisingly, the speaker delays and displaces his account of revolutionary France as long and as much as he can, largely because its sublimity retrospectively discredits the sublimity of his early education "by fear." The aesthetic that directs this rearguard action against the sublime is the beautiful.

In a broader sense, the speaker of the expanded *Prelude* repeatedly exchanges one aesthetic perspective for another, either by turning from the sublime to the beautiful or by turning back to the sublime. After reviewing his initial education "by beauty and by fear" in Book I, he emphasizes the values of the beautiful. From this aesthetic perspective, the "possible sublimity" described in Book II is put aside as something prior or at best prospective. Near the end of Book IV he turns again to a sublime figure whose appearance summarizes the most disturbing aspects of similar figures in the books that follow. The new symbolic freight which the speaker now attaches to such figures is elaborated in Book V, the book Wordsworth hurriedly assembled in March, 1804, within two weeks of deciding to expand the poem on his life. The Alpine crossings of Book VI dramatize a range of aesthetic "crossings." In Book VII, the speaker forecasts the chaos of revolutionary France by mapping its Biblical and Miltonic figures onto London. To the hazards of this urban sublime he turns back to the topography of the beautiful in Book VIII, where love of nature leads as much away from the sublime as it does toward the love of humankind. In Books IX and X the long delayed account of revolutionary France reiterates the sublime figures introduced in earlier books, but now in contexts that question the speaker's attraction to the sublime. And in Books XI, XII, and XIII he revisits sublime experiences and topographies to revise their aesthetic focus.

The most dramatic instances of this revisionary aesthetics are those passages in the expanded poem which Wordsworth revised to supplement a sublime perspective or figure with ones that belong to the beautiful, including the Drowned Man episode of Book V, the Book VI sequence that ends with the Ravine of Arve, and the Book XI "spots of time." Of these, the text that offers the most succinct account of this aesthetic pattern is the story of the drowned man whose return to the surface of a lake literalizes a more troubling return of sublime figures to the surface of the speaker's discourse.[4] In the boy of Winander passage that precedes it, the speaker indicates the aesthetic enclosure he seeks. In the 1832–50 texts he makes the place where the "boy" is buried beautiful twice over: "Fair is the Spot, most beautiful the Vale" (1832, 393, p. 104). This placement of beauty at the center as well as the periphery anticipates a more dramatic process of aesthetic enclosure in Wordsworth's revisions of the Drowned Man episode. In the 1799 and 1805 texts, the place where the body resurfaces is variously designated by an adverbial "there." But in the 1832–50 texts the speaker has more to say:

> Those unclaimed garments, telling a plain tale,
> Drew to the spot an anxious Crowd; some looked
> In passive expectation from the shore,
> While from a boat others hung o'er the deep,
> Sounding with grappling irons and long poles.
>
> (1832, 445–49, p. 105)

The substitution of "spot" for "there" tells an even plainer tale than the garments on the shore. In this version the speaker projects his fears onto an "anxious Crowd" whose activity and inactivity dramatize his ambivalent desire to find the body and not find the body. By redefining the "company" of the 1799 text as a "Crowd" and giving it more activities to keep it and him busy, he (re)distributes the shock of discovery. None of these revisions is drastic, yet they signal his recognition that the episode is no longer simply one of many "tragic facts / Of rural history," as it had been in the 1799 poem (*Prel. 1798*, 282–83, p. 50). Rather it is a fact which troubles the speaker's presentation of his history. These displacements clear the way for the retrieval of other aspects of the episode which are not included in the 1799 text.

The 1805 version acknowledges that the drowned man's "ghastly face" is "a spectre shape – / Of terror even" in the midst of a "beauteous scene." Eighteenth-century discussions of *terror* are curiously divided. The term refers either to gothic *frissons*, those thrills which Wordsworth claimed to have put aside in *The Vale of Esthwaite*, or to sublime fear. In the 1832–50 texts, the speaker says that his fear was not "soul-debasing," a phrase which echoes the judgment of those writers, including Wordsworth in his essay on aesthetics, who argued that sublime fear should not include fear for one's life.[5] Yet the phrases "ghastly face" and "spectre shape" imply that the scene provokes a fear which is indeed "vulgar" and "soul-debasing." In the coda Wordsworth added in 1805, the speaker applies a conventional surface to the re-surfaced horror and increases the rhetorical distance which other revisions put between the speaker and the event. Where sublime fears lie buried in Wordsworth's poetry, the beautiful is never far behind. As the speaker says for the first time in 1805,

> And yet no vulgar fear,
> Young as I was, a child not nine years old,
> Possessed me, for my inner eye had seen
> Such sights before among the shining streams
> Of fairyland, the forests of romance –
> Thence came a spirit hallowing what I saw
> With decoration and ideal grace,
> A dignity, a smoothness, like the words
> Of Grecian art and purest poesy.   (473–81, p. 176)

More explicit in 1832–50 about the kind of fear and about "what I saw," revised in this version to read "the sad spectacle" (1832, 458, p. 106), in both versions Wordsworth summarizes beauty's task in his revisionary aesthetics. Because it seeks manageable limits not unmanageable figures, it suppresses some aspects of the sublime even as others are admitted into the text. By these means, the beautiful hallows harrowing scenes.

As an episode which is literally and figuratively concerned with hidden depths and disrupted surfaces, the Drowned Man offers a singular image of Wordsworth's antithesis between the sublime and the beautiful. Disturbing the beauteous scene as it does, the reappearance of a once-submerged dead man threatens the speaker's ability to manage his discourse. His stronger 1805, 1832, and 1850 recognitions of the drowned man as a figure of death and the sublime grant that what has been submerged or denied tends to float back up to the surface. This he cannot prevent, but he can put a prettier face on re-surfaced horrors. If this tale and others like it in the expanded

Prelude threaten death, including, as Cynthia Chase has argued, the death of figures,[6] were they not framed and distanced as they are, their sublime figures would be too threatening for the speaker to do anything other than banish them.

The story of the Drowned Man is exemplary for another reason. Situated as it is in the book Wordsworth composed immediately after he decided to expand the poem on his life, it assists the more complex poetic argument of the new poem by thickening its figurative texture. At least since the Book IV simile which compares what a man "down-bending" from a boat can see in the water to what the speaker has been able to see (or not see) in his own past, images of surfaces and depths have been part of his reflections on the kind of poetic history he writes. In oblique ways their appearance in Book IV calls our attention to other figures in Books I to V that belong to the same "overtone series." For example, the Book IV simile echoes, however slightly, the image of the boy in Book I as he hangs over a cliff. Both suggest that leaning over an edge or depth may endanger either one's life or a speaker's ability to preserve or record his history. These hazards objectify the sublime fear which Kant tried to exclude by insisting that reason rescues the mind from the fear of losing one's life (or speech) before nature's magnitude or might. In Book V of the expanded *Prelude*, sublime fear is on all sides from the beginning, when the speaker queries whether and how to preserve human knowledge from cataclysm. And in the Arab dream and the Drowned Man episodes, deluge and drowning explicitly threaten his life and speech. In his instructive analysis of Longinus's sublime figures, Neil Hertz suggests one reason for this density of figures:

at certain points one becomes aware of a thickening of texture. These are pages where, challenged by an aspect of his theme or by the strength of a quotation, Longinus seems to be working harder at locating his discourse close in to the energies of his authors. At those moments, he too is drawn into the sublime turning, and what he is moved to produce is not merely an analysis illustrative of the sublime but further figures for it.[7]

In Wordsworth's *Prelude* the act of being "drawn into the sublime turning" of figures often turns into the beautiful, as it does in the story of the Drowned Man. Yet not always. In Book IV, for example, a similar "thickening of texture" indicates the speaker's reluctant turn back to the sublime from his preoccupation since Book I with beauty's aesthetic education.

The first unequivocal sign of this new aesthetic control occurs in Book I, when the speaker reviews his progress thus far by recalling "how Nature by extrinsic passion first / Peopled my mind with beauteous forms or grand / And made me love them" (1:572–74, p. 58). In the 1832–50 texts, the same forms are "sublime or fair." None of these versions chooses to recognize the "pain and fear" (1:440, p. 50) critical to this aesthetic progress. Indeed, the speaker presents this suppression as a natural outcome: from pain and fear we learn to "recognize / A grandeur in the beatings of the heart." This argument worked well in the 1798–99 poem, but it cannot account for the sublime fear he feels in revolutionary France. Yet the speaker's intention in Books I to IV is clear enough. Much as he emphasizes the "beauty" in the "forms" of the Lake District (1:590, p. 60 and in 1832, but in 1850: "beauty / Old as creation," 562–63, pp. 59, 61), so does he imply that beauty is somehow prior or stronger when he previews his education "by *beauty* and by fear" (my emphasis).

However, warnings about the hazards of sublime figures appear even in Book II. The speaker asks rhetorically near the beginning of this book, "Ah, is there one who ever has been young / And needs a monitory voice to tame / The pride of virtue and of intellect?" (19–21, p. 66). In the 1832–50 texts these faults are more sharply identified as "pride of Intellect" and "virtue's self-esteem" (1832, 20–21, p. 47). Even the form of the question, which echoes the Book IV invocation of *Paradise Lost* ("O for that warning voice, which he who saw / Th' Apocalypse hear cry in Heaven aloud"), implies that the answer must be "yes." With the characteristic secrecy of sublime figures, this Miltonic allusion implies a parallel between Wordsworth's speaker, who is tempted by pride, and Satan's temptation of Adam and Eve. As Milton's invocation goes on to explain, had they been similarly "warned" about the approach of Satan, their "secret foe," they might have escaped his snare.[8] For Wordsworth's speaker, who compares himself to the fallen Adam in the opening lines of the poem, the implied parallel may conceal his attraction to the sublime, here presented in the thoroughly satanic form of "pride of virtue and of intellect." In the same book the sands of Leven, which in Book X he associates with hearing news of Robespierre's death, are one of many scenes where he recalls the "joyous time" of his childhood. Similarly, Furness Abbey, whose "gloom" and "sobbings" might make it a possible "haunt" for the sublime, is instead a "shelter," a "safeguard for repose and quietness" where the speaker could have made his "dwelling-place" forever (2:120–21, 134, p. 72; in 1832–50, "deep shelter"). This domestication of a potentially fearful place demonstrates the filial and maternal locus of Book II. It also registers a prominent trait of the Wordsworthian beautiful – its capacity to provide *in*habitations for a world whose spectral character the boy has already encountered. From this aesthetic perspective, the speaker of the 1805 poem argues, maternal affection gives a strength that remains "powerful in all sentiments of grief, / Of exultation, fear and joy" (2:270–71, p. 78).

After his mother's death, her love is replaced by a "most watchful power of love" that encourages him to recognize a "register / Of permanent relations" in nature and society (2:310–12, p. 82). Although "beauty" and a "sublimer joy" are included in this register, its aesthetic significance is the speaker's enlarged conception of what the beautiful accomplishes once it becomes more than simply a counter-aesthetic to the sublime. Despite this and subsequent efforts to enlarge his conception of the beautiful, he also admits that by placing value on visible, permanent registers, his life gradually became preoccupied with surfaces. As such, it is like "A floating island, an amphibious thing, / Unsound, of spungy texture, yet withal / Not wanting a fair face of water-weeds / And pleasant flowers" (3:340–43, p. 108). The 1832–50 texts emphasize the analogy and give it a characteristically Wordsworthian topography: "such a life might not inaptly be compared / To a floating island, an amphibious Spot / Unsound" (1832, 335–37, p. 70). Thus however successful beauty's invitation and the mind's acceptance of it are in these books, the speaker retains some consciousness of what they have cost him.

In Book IV these isolated strands of aesthetic difference begin to converge when the speaker compares his record of his past to the figure of "one who hangs down-bending from the side / Of a slow-moving boat" (247–48, p. 136). Although the simile does not describe a conflict between sublimity and beauty, its account of depths and surfaces clarifies their figurative task in Wordsworth's aesthetics:

> As one who hangs down-bending from the side
> Of a slow-moving boat upon the breast
> Of a still water, solacing himself
> With such discoveries as his eye can make
> Beneath him in the bottom of the deeps,
> Sees many beauteous sights – weeds, fishes, flowers,
> Grots, pebbles, roots of trees – and fancies more,
> Yet often is perplexed, and cannot part
> The shadow from the substance, rocks and sky,
> Mountains and clouds, from that which is indeed
> The region, and the things which there abide
> In their true dwelling; now is crossed by gleam
> Of his own image, by a sunbeam now,
> And motions that are sent he knows not whence,

> Impediments that make his task more sweet;
> Such pleasant office have we long pursued
> Incumbent o'er the surface of past time –
> With like success.   (247–64, pp. 136–38)

In 1832–50 the representational crux of the simile is made more precise: the speaker cannot distinguish "mountains and clouds reflected in the depth / Of the clear flood, from things which abide there" (1832, 265–66, p. 86). Since Book I, the speaker has frequently claimed that depths can be grasped or read through a transparent surface. But now he admits that he can discern little in the "the bottom of the deeps" except his own image. As a figure for the "impediments" of surfaces, this simile redirects his attention back to the depths of his history and, in his meeting with the Discharged Soldier, back to those sublime figures that reside below its surface.

The story of the Discharged Soldier begins with the speaker's recollection of a "steep ascent" up a road whose "wat'ry surface" appears to crest the top, where it becomes "another stream" descending to the valley. This image, taken not from Wordsworth's experience of the ascent upon Briars Brow but from Dorothy Wordsworth's description of a different road that "glittered like another stream," suggests the character of the episode that lies ahead. It will be, as the road appears to be, a double crossing. Much as the road that crosses the ridge suggests another crossing from literal road to figurative stream,[9] so will the speaker's actual encounter with a soldier become an aesthetic crossing. Before it occurs in the 1805 text, he offers a last, fit emblem of the beautiful:

> What beauteous pictures now
> Rose in harmonious imagery; they rose
> As from some distant region of my soul
> And came along like dreams – yet such as left
> Obscurely mingled with their passing forms
> A consciousness of animal delight,
> A self-possession felt in every pause
> And every gentle movement of my frame.   (4:392–99, p. 144)

This passage, which Wordsworth excised from the 1832–50 versions, repeats what the beautiful has offered for nearly three books – figures that frame landscape and discourse into "beauteous pictures" and "harmonious imagery." Yet precisely because it emphasizes aesthetic control, it shows how the beautiful is in 1805 a prerequisite to the sublime disruption that lies ahead. Once delight and self-possession make the text safe, the speaker re-admits the sublime.

The meeting with the Discharged Soldier is a visionary encounter

unlike any other in earlier books of the expanded poem. Composed at
Alfoxden in 1798 but never included in the two-part *Prelude* of 1799,
the early version of this episode, like the contemporary poem "A
Night-Piece," presents its narrator as a solitary figure who gazes
fixedly on the ground as he travels beneath a "vault" of "stars."[10] But
the *Prelude* versions call more attention to the sublimity of the soldier
and the scene. They also present a virtual checklist of the elements of
sublime experience in later books: its unexpectedness; the spectral,
unhoused, and abandoned condition (a doubly *unheimlich* appearance) of the soldier; his schizophrenic aspect, indicated by the
speaker's separate notice of him and the shadow that "lay, and moved
not" at his feet; the speaker's urgent inquiry about the man's history –
propelled in part by a wish to "house" what cannot be housed – and
his querulous reproach that a man in this condition ought to ask for
shelter; and, most resonantly, the insufficiency of the soldier's speech
and figure as a fit emblem of what the speaker wants to designate as
"solemn and sublime." Even the trust in God "and in the eye of him
that passes me" (4:495, p. 150), which the soldier claims as *his*
sustenance, are insufficient for the speaker. All of these elements signal
the intransigence of the sublime before the speaker's desire to domesticate it. However, the fact that this narrative has a place in the 1805
Prelude indicates his complex intention to recognize, more fully than
he had in the 1799 poem, the aesthetic which he will continue to resist
with all the craft which the beautiful can supply him as one who tells a
tale he half-wishes not to hear.

The addition of the Discharged Soldier to Book IV, both in the lost
five-book poem of 1804[11] and in the thirteen-book poem to which
Wordsworth committed himself in March of 1804, realigns the
aesthetic argument of *The Prelude*. The outcome of this realignment is
Book V, whose retrograde and projective "drift" takes up where Book
IV ends. As he leaves the soldier at a nearby cottage, the speaker
concludes, "Back I cast a look, / And lingered near the door a little
space, / Then sought with quiet heart my distant home" (502–4,
p. 150). In the 1832–50 texts Wordsworth's speaker rather testily
responds to those who might regard the conclusion of this book as
curiously inconclusive with this defensive coda:

> This passed, and He who deigns to mark with care
> By what rules governed, with what end in view
> This Work proceeds, *he* will not wish for more.

> (1832, 470–72, p. 92)

W. J. B. Owen indicates that Ms. D, transcribed by Mary Wordsworth
beginning in 1832, includes a query about "the omission of these three

last lines" (Owen, ed., *Fourteen-Book Prelude*, 92). This query, and more particularly the lines themselves, suggest that the older Wordsworth was uneasy about the poem's apparently unsteady line of argument thus far. Here the speaker's assertion about "rules" and the "end in view" insist that the poem possesses a coherence which it does not at this stage exhibit. In aesthetic terms, the Book IV narrative about an unsheltered human figure and a speaker seeking shelter for and from that figure functions as a preface to the diverse narrative strands of Book V. These in turn unshelter the Wordsworthian sublime even as they seek new textual and contextual means for re-sheltering it.

In Book V the speaker inscribes this aesthetic conflict in the allusive matrix of figures that gain prominence in this book – deluge, drowning, and tears. The most important of these, deluge, is implicit in the opening lines, where the speaker's query about how to preserve the "products" of intellect from some future cataclysm alludes obliquely to the first cataclysmic event in human history – the Deluge:

> Thou also, man, hast wrought,
> For commerce of thy nature with itself,
> Things worthy of unconquerable life;
> And yet we feel – we cannot chuse but feel –
> That these must perish. Tremblings of the heart
> It gives, to think that the immortal being
> No more shall need such garments; and yet man,
> As long as he shall be the child on earth,
> Might almost 'weep to have' what he may lose –
> Nor be himself extinguished, but survive
> Abject, depressed, forlorn, disconsolate. (17–27, p. 152)

This citation of the phrase "weep to have" from Shakespeare's Sonnet 64 calls attention to other, implicit links between the sonnet and Wordsworth's text.[12] The speaker of the sonnet compares "time's ravages" to the "ruine" that results when "the hungry Ocean gaine[s] / Advantage on the kingdome of the shoare." Both the idea of an inundation and the word *ruine*, which Thomas Burnet had used to characterize the post-diluvial earth,[13] prefigure the deluge that is "imminent" in the Arab dream. Wordsworth's citation of Shakespeare's sonnet may also echo the prophecy of how Adam will respond to the Deluge which Michael offers in *Paradise Lost*:

> How didst thou grieve then, *Adam*, to behold
> The end of all thy Offspring, end so sad,
> Depopulation; thee another Floud,
> Of tears and sorrow a Floud thee also drownd,

> And sunk thee as thy Sons; till gently reard
> By th'Angel, on thy feet thou stoodst at last,
> Though comfortless, as when a Father mourns
> His children, all in view destroyd at once.[14]

Much as Wordsworth's speaker had presented himself in Book I as a new, post-edenic Adam by echoing the last lines of Milton's poem, in Book v he "grieves" (3, p. 152) as Milton's Adam had. And in the Arab dream, he is, like Adam according to Josephus's Deluge narrative, troubled by a prophecy of deluge.[15] The theological rationale for Michael's use of a past tense to convey an event which lies in the future is of course that for the archangel "time" is eternity. Like Michael, Wordsworth's speaker / dreamer[16] seems to transcend time when he dreams that a deluge is "now at hand" (99, p. 156). Yet he too submits, as Shakespeare's sonnet argues human desire must submit, to "time's ravages." Caught between his earlier fear of some future, apocalyptic cataclysm − either earthquake or fire (29–32, p. 154) − and his present fear of an ancient cataclysm come back to engulf him, he is embedded in the strata of human history and of Wordsworth's text. Thus in Book v his initial lament for "the child of earth" who weeps for what he may lose is a prior figure for the Arab's prophecy that a deluge will bring "destruction" to "the children of the earth" (98, p. 156), and for the satiric account later in Book v of how "the children of the land" (228, p. 162) are miseducated, a practice which the speaker compares to the bridge which Sin and Death build so that Satan can transgress Chaos,[17] another Miltonic allusion which assists Wordsworth's claim that the beginnings of time are folded into the speaker's present.

Wordsworth's remarks on tears and deluge in the second *Essay upon Epitaphs* suggest the figurative logic at issue here. Observing that the epitaph which the Marquis of Montrose wrote when he learned that Charles I was dead reads in part: "I'd weep the world to such a strain / As it should deluge once again," Wordsworth comments: "the most tremendous event in the history of the Planet, namely, the Deluge, is brought before [the reader's] imagination by the physical image of tears" (*Prose*, 2:71). In *The Prelude*, v, this conjunction of images does not occur on the surface of the text, although it is brought near that surface by the pressure of allied figures. This difference implies another. In the second *Essay upon Epitaphs*, the political occasion for the epitaph in which the figures of deluge and tears are joined is the regicide of Charles I. As the poem Wordsworth redesigned and expanded to include his experience in revolutionary France, the 1805 *Prelude* must eventually confront the

French regicide of Louis XVI. For Wordsworth and his contemporaries, the similarity between this regicide and that of Charles I was apparent, despite (or because of) Burke's insistence to the contrary.[18] I note Wordsworth's later comment on deluge in a revolutionary context to emphasize the hiddenness of this sublime figure in the early books of the expanded *Prelude*. In Books IX and X, the deluge is a reiterated figure for revolutionary chaos and terror. But in earlier books this history is delayed so that the speaker may create a shelter for it. As the aesthetic correlatives of deluge and its containment, the sublime and the beautiful aid this invention of a space within the poem where history can take its place.

The opening lines of the Arab dream insist that the sublime is on all sides of the speaker's history. The 1832 text emphasizes the sublimity of the dream landscape:

> I saw before me stretched a boundless plain,
> Of sandy wilderness, all blank and void;
> And as I looked around, distress and fear
> Came creeping over me, when at my side,
> Close at my side, an uncouth Shape appeared.

> (1832, 71–75, p. 95)

As Addison had argued and as Wordsworth implies in the first *Essay upon Epitaphs*, a boundless plain, whether desert or ocean, evokes the idea of infinity that is fundamental to sublime experience.[19] In *The Prelude*, V, this aesthetic reversibility is prominent in other Deluge narratives to which the dream alludes. In Ovid's *Metamorphoses*, Deucalion and Pyrrha despair after the waters recede because the waste that remains is no less desolate than the sight of an endless ocean had been.[20] And in *Paradise Lost*, Chaos is depicted as "a dark / illimitable Ocean without bound," a "wasteful deep," an "abyss," and a "darksome Desert." Finally, Burnet's insistence that the Deluge is Chaos come again declares the identity which Milton implies.[21] Collectively these allusions suggest how texts represent sublime figures like the Arab, whose "uncouth Shape" is itself an uncanny double of the Discharged Soldier in Book IV (402, p. 144). As an aesthetic which remains hidden and implicit or at least obscured by the beautiful, the sublime must find its way into texts through rhetorical figures that hide as much as they disclose their contents.

The double aesthetic binding of these figures is made clear in the conclusion of Book V, where words are an "abode," a "mansion," a "proper home" – terms that indicate the presence of the beautiful. But like the sublime "haunt" of the 1800 "Prospectus," words are also spectral habitations whose "turnings intricate" illuminate "objects, forms, and substances" (625–29, p. 184). This shift from a reliance on Nature's endless supply of objects to a reliance on words as collective, transmuting shelters articulates the new direction of the poem. It also suggests how the authority of the beautiful is subtly challenged by words whose "glory" threatens to escape its poetic "home" for some other place.

Book VI revises the account of the 1790 Alpine tour that Wordsworth had offered in *Descriptive Sketches* to acknowledge aesthetic "disappointments" at Mont Blanc and Simplon Pass, scenes whose identification with Alpine sublimity was a commonplace among contemporary travellers. The 1805 *Prelude* corrects its speaker's tourist expectations by surveying a range of possible responses to the sublime and the beautiful – including a null set, a sublime *manqué*.[22] When the speaker calls the "coverts" or narrow valleys of "pastoral life" in the Swiss Alps the "sanctified abodes of peaceful man," he identifies them as beautiful landscapes. Yet by calling them "deep haunts" and "an aboriginal vale" in the 1805 version, he suggests that they are also sublime (428, 437–8, p. 212). The earlier version witnesses a singular (and short-lived) aesthetic cooperation – Swiss mountain society exhibits the composure of the beautiful in the midst of a sublime, primeval landscape.

But in 1818 and 1819 Wordsworth inserted a passage just before this description of Swiss life which casts its uneasy shadow on the narratives that follow.[23] Deploring the 1792 French expulsion of the Carthusians from the monastery of the Grande Chartreuse, the speaker identifies the consequence of revolutionary turmoil for traditional institutions without having to assign that consequence directly to Napoleon, who had no part in this action. Yet retrospectively the removal of the Carthusians prefigured later French "interventions" in Switzerland and elsewhere on the Continent, to which Wordsworth responded in 1806 by composing several sonnets denouncing the subversion of liberty by the Napoleonic code. In *The Prelude* as in *Descriptive Sketches*,[24] the speaker's reaction to the expulsion of the monks is divided between his hopes for revolutionary France and his mature sense that this event "subvert[s] / That frame of social being" (1832, 427–28, p. 124) which the Carthusian rule symbolized. In both versions the "awful solitude" (also described as a "soul-affecting Solitude" in 1832–50) of the scene evokes a reverential sublime, not the "soul-debasing" sublime terror of Book v. In the 1832–50 texts the speaker binds this version of the sublime to an aesthetic of "social being" and "perpetual calm" (1832, 428–30, p. 124). This aesthetic cooperation is not merely destroyed by the arrival of "a military glare /

Of riotous men commissioned to expel / The blameless Inmates"
(1832, 425–27, p. 124); it is preempted by the narrative sequence of
the text, which announces the arrival of the military first.

As it does in the 1802 sonnet "Nuns Fret Not Their Convent's
Narrow Room," the monastic life of these "inmates" illustrates the
spiritual and artistic values of enclosure. Here Wordsworth's speaker
values what a personified "Nature" argues the scene itself will preserve
– man's capacity

> To think, to hope, to worship, and to feel,
> To struggle, to be lost within himself
> In trepidation; from the blank abyss
> To look with bodily eyes, and be consoled.
>
> (1832, 469–72, p. 125)

These preemptive allusions to scenes later in this book, where abysses
or soulless images do not console, ask to be noticed. This scene of
consolation, including the cross which stands erect "as if / Hands of
angelic Powers had fixed it there" (1832, 485–86, p. 126), is "from
the undiscriminating sweep / And rage of one State-whirlwind,
insecure" (488–89). As the last word of the interpolated passage in the
1832–50 texts, "insecure" opens up the unstable aesthetic center
which the discussion of the Grande Chartreuse had briefly stabilized.
And as a scene that "grieve[s]" the speaker because it imposes a
"soulless image on the eye" (453–54, p. 212), Mont Blanc is a
disappointment because nature's sublime usurps the mind's prior
aesthetic education about how well-known sublime scenes would look
to the traveller. In Simplon Pass, which Wordsworth renames generi-
cally as the place where he "crossed the Alps," the speaker recovers lost
aesthetic ground, so to speak, by re-presenting a second aesthetic
disappointment as an occasion for the mind's recognition of its own
sublimity.

This is hardly news for readers of the poem, who rightly argue that
the passage which registers this aesthetic recognition is the famous
apostrophe to the Imagination. And, as many have suggested, this
passage and the narrative that precedes it echo or anticipate what
Kant, Schiller, and Hegel identified as key features of sublime experience. Having crossed the Alps unwittingly by continuing up along a
stream instead of crossing it lower down, Wordsworth's speaker is
shocked, but then exhilarated by his recognition of the discontinuity
between nature's sublime Alpine crossing and his own. This species of
action and reaction recalls Kant's analysis of the dynamically sublime,
refracted through Schiller's suggestion that nature is a precipitating
agent in the mind's sublime. Like Kant, Wordsworth's account of this

recognition substitutes the mind's sublimity for natural sublimity and perhaps, as Alan Liu has argued, for Napoleon as well.[25] The diction of the Book VI apostrophe anticipates Hegel's definition of the sublime as a *via negativa* to the world beyond the appearances of phenomenal reality. The speaker notes how the claims of sense experience are usurped by his recognition of an "invisible world" ("the Mind's abyss" in 1832) that signals "destiny" and "infinitude" (530–39, p. 216; 1832, 595, p. 129). In 1832–50, the insufficiency of human language ("sad incompetence of human speech"; 1832, 594, p. 129) emphasizes the negative relation between the sublimity of the experience and the human, phenomenal terms the speaker must use to represent it.

And yet, as the compositional history of Wordsworth's apostrophe suggests, even so exemplary a sublime text is already subject to a species of aesthetic management. Composed in 1804 and inserted between the Crossing of the Alps and Ravine of Arve narratives after Wordsworth had experimented with using two other passages in the same place, the Book VI apostrophe shows how sublime intrusions (including those Wordsworth does not wish to entertain) are placed and then managed by their surroundings.[26] The text begins to slide toward an aesthetic that domesticates the sublime Imagination even as it is being represented. To make of infinitude an end-point or a "home" or an "abode" as well as a "destiny" is to give it shelter and a slight mark of closure (536–38, p. 216). In the lines that follow, the speaker compares his experience to the annual, revitalizing flood of the Nile. Now yoked to the Imagination, the image of deluge assumes a less threatening visage than it had in Book V:

> The mind beneath such banners militant
> Thinks not of spoils or trophies, nor of aught
> That may attest its prowess, blest in thoughts
> That are their own perfection and reward –
> Strong in itself, and in the access of joy
> Which hides it like the overflowing Nile.
>
> (543–48, pp. 216–18)

Wordsworthian deluges are rarely so subtly contained. As an illustration of how the beautiful can supplant the sublime, the annual but temporary flood of the Nile is a remarkable simile, perhaps necessarily so given the images of deluge and death that haunt the speaker in the preceding book. As a gloss on what the beautiful does to or for the sublime, the simile is as critical as it is elusive. The beautiful domesticates the sublime even as the figure of an overflowing Nile domesticates that of a deluge. Yet the speaker claims something more. The "banners militant" – which, as Liu points out, echo and thus subvert Napoleon's military rhetoric in the Alps – help the mind discover its power. It resides not in spoils or trophies but in an "access of joy" in 1805 (547, p. 218), or the "beatitude" that "hides" this power in 1832–50 (1832, 614–15, p. 130). Here the sublime figure of deluge is transformed into a beautiful flood that nourishes hidden terrain.

In the Ravine of Arve, this terrain is made the geological and lexical surface of the scene:

> The immeasurable heights
> Of woods decaying, never to be decayed,
> The stationary blasts of waterfalls,
> And everywhere along the hollow rent
> Winds thwarting winds, bewildered and forlorn,
> The torrents shooting from the clear blue sky,
> The rocks that muttered close upon our ears –
> Black drizzling crags that spake by the wayside
> As if a voice were in them – the sick sight
> And giddy prospect of the raving stream,
> The unfettered clouds and region of the heavens,
> Tumult and peace, the darkness and the light,
> Were all like workings of one mind, the features
> Of the same face, blossoms upon one tree,
> Characters of the great apocalypse,
> The types and symbols of eternity,
> Of first, and last, and midst, and without end.
>
> (556–72, p. 218)

In lines Wordsworth briefly inserted into the text and later excised, the speaker describes the scene as a "primeval mountain" whose fragments are "powerless ruin" (*Prel.*, p. 211). But in the 1805, 1832 and 1850 texts he excised this allusion to the temporal priority of the sublime to present a power that is exerted against the current of geological time and erosion. Here too the idea of deluge may be implied by the phrase "characters of the great apocalypse," which David Pirie reads as a figure for the ages of geological formation inscribed in the strata of Gondo Gorge. Contemporary geologists, whose hypotheses Ramond de Carbonnières reported in the Swiss guidebook Wordsworth first used in 1790, argued that a deluge (not necessarily the Biblical deluge) had formed the lower mountains that surround the highest Alpine peaks.[27]

What interests me is the way Wordsworth uses *chiasmus* to structure his representation of this geological process as though it were not decay but re-inscription. That is to say, like Blake's relief engravings, Wordsworth's "characters" are what is left and what is to come. The chiastic pattern is made explicit in figures like "winds thwarting winds," which organize the speaker's perception of the scene. With so many superscriptions, these figures harness a sublime tenor (in the past and in the future) to their equilibrium and poetic closure. The effect of this aesthetic subversion (or cooperation) is, as the Miltonic echoes of the closing lines imply, to reunite the sublime "book" of Nature to an Apocalyptic and Miltonic text which describes God. Together these books assign a legible surface to a sublime scene.[28] If the "Pauline ground" of the passage is, as M. H. Abrams has suggested, that Nature is truly God's second book and thus capable of assuming the characters, types, and symbols of eternity,[29] the highly structured oxymoronic oppositions of the text show how much the speaker must do to make these scriptural and natural apocalypses fit together. Fittedness is not a given, as it had been for the speaker of the 1800 "Prospectus." In later poems Wordsworth insisted that only some sublime scenes are appropriate figures of God, a departure from the Pauline confidence of eighteenth-century writers for whom natural sublimity was an image of God.

The descent into the Ravine of Arve thus re-engages earlier debates about the role of "figures of passion" in the sublime style. Kames asserted that such figures are necessary to the sublime, whereas Burke implied that only obscure figures and scenes are appropriate.[30] The figures Wordsworth uses to represent the Ravine of Arve display the "heightened" diction of sublime pathos, yet their syntax is highly crafted and paradoxical rather than obscure. For example, the phrase "woods decaying, never to be decayed" confines "woods" between two inflections of the verb "decay" — one designating continuous action in the present; the other, completed action in a never-to-be-reached future. The figurative power of "woods" depends, then, on its place in a designated poetic context. As the agent that assists the speaker's re-invention of the Ravine of Arve as a *topos* of his aesthetic argument, the beautiful gives the sublime the words it needs to speak of what it is.

Yet the Shelleyan hesitancy that haunts the prosopopoeia of the passage (the scene is *like* a face and *like* a voice)[31] is arresting, particularly so because it is more hesitant about visual semblances. Whereas rocks "muttered" and crags "spake" "as if a voice were in them," and thus are doubly invested with the semblance of a human voice, the "face" of the scene keeps slipping from figure to figure, much as the visual perspective is now up, now down. If the beautiful momentarily holds the surface of the scene and text, this "hold" requires letting one figure go to take up another and another. The implied relation between the beautiful and the visual (and between the sublime and the aural) turns here on the relative fixity or fixedness of the visual, whose "despotism" Wordsworth and his contemporaries acknowledged even as it seduced their vision. As the aesthetic of proportion, known limits, and present time, the beautiful is susceptible to the lure of the visual. The aesthetic counterpointing in Book VI displays the speaker's double allegiance to sublimity and beauty. When the figurative power of the sublime threatens to dominate, as it briefly does in the Crossing of the Alps and the 1804 apostrophe, the speaker turns toward the beautiful. But in the Ravine of Arve, where the figurative pattern is orchestrated by the beautiful, it is checked by his insistence on multiple images for the scene.

The Book VI experience on the upper, more Alpine, Como parodies earlier sublime encounters. The lake sheds its "beauty" and "Abyssinian privacy" to assume "a sterner character" (592, 608, 521, pp. 220–22). Misled by the quarter chime of an Italian clock, they start out earlier in the night than they had intended and are soon "lost, bewildered among woods immense" (622–31, p. 222). Though "doubting not" that daybreak is near, that the "plain track" in the moonlight will guide them (625–29), they are as thoroughly lost as the dreamer of Book V, also described as "doubting not" that the Arab will "guide" him (1850, 5:81, p. 157). In Book VI, when the moon finally rises, its reflection in Lake Como parodies the light that the travellers have waited for:

> An open place it was and overlooked
> From high the sullen water underneath,
> On which a dull red image of the moon
> Lay bedded, changing often times its form
> Like an uneasy snake.　　　　　　　　(6:635–38, p. 222)

The double passivity of the image of a reflection that "lay bedded" transforms what was to have been a pleasant walk by moonlight into an ominous one. The travellers' "error" is now allowed to have been twofold – they erred in direction and starting time (6:640, p. 222). To this the speaker adds other disturbances – insects, the cries of "unknown birds," and the mountains visible against the darkness. Although they can hear the Italian clock at Gravedona, they cannot "read" the meaning of its bells any more than they can find their way by reading the topography. The experience borders on the sublime, but a sense of exaltation is missing. Like children who are strangers in a mountainous landscape, these travellers are not "free from personal fear," but here the similarity between the child's education by sublime fear and the adult speaker's aesthetic education ends.

All the usual Wordsworthian signs of the sublime are present — lostness, error, and fear — but none leads the speaker to feel anything more than plain uneasiness and fear. Neither beautiful, as the lower portions of the Como had been, nor sublime, the episode chastizes the speaker's earlier success in reading sublime "characters" too completely. In the narrative frame of Book VI, which opens and closes with discussions of the progress of liberty in France and Switzerland in 1790, the lesson received above Gravedona "not without personal fear" applies to the aesthetic education in this book and in those that deal with revolutionary France.

In the opening lines of Book VII, the speaker describes himself as a "casual dweller," one who sets up a "vagrant tent" as he travels from one place to the next (60–62, p. 228), a "transient visitant" in London (74, p. 230; "idler" in 1832–50). Unlike beauty's "tents" in the 1800 "Prospectus," these temporary shelters are more spectral than sheltering. This subversion of the beautiful provides a clearing (or temporary encampment) for the speaker's reluctant examination of London as a place whose inhabitants challenge the managed sublime of Book VI. Unlike the "characters of the great apocalypse," which he inscribes in the Ravine of Arve, London is full of "characters" and "faces" he cannot read.

What he attempts but cannot achieve in this book without making himself monstrous is a manageable perspective on London, one that would allow him to read what he sees. Instead, London offers an "endless stream of men and moving things," which he can at best catalogue. At last he retreats, in thoroughly Wordsworthian fashion, to "some sequestered nook" whose relative quiet he compares to "a sheltered place when winds blow loud" (186–87, p. 236). As his rhetoric assumes a Miltonic and Biblical texture, the sublimity of London becomes explicit. Its "thickening hubbub" (227, p. 238) echoes the universal "hubbub wild" of Chaos in *Paradise Lost*.[32] The crowd is a "stream," a "tide" that must be held back, and a "Babel din" (157–58, 206, pp. 234–36). The last image is functionally equivalent to the Deluge in Genesis and in *The Prelude*. Whereas the latter destroys the "face" of the earth so that no familiar signs and landscape remain, Babel destroys the common, edenic language of universal signs which had survived the Deluge.

Tired of his own catalogues, Wordsworth's speaker attempts to impose order on London by familiar aesthetic means. Offering a painting and a prospect as possible models, he describes the coherent vision each creates:

Whether the painter – fashioning a work
To Nature's circumambient scenery,
And with his greedy pencil taking in
A whole horizon on all sides – with power
Like that of angels or commissioned spirits,
Plant as upon some lofty pinnacle
Or in a ship on waters, with a world
Of life and lifelike mockery to east,
To west, beneath, behind us, and before,
Or more mechanic artist represent
By scale exact, in model, wood or clay,
From shading colours also borrowing help,
Some miniature of famous spots and things,
Domestic, or the boast of foreign realms.

(256–69, pp. 238, 240)

These models are both attractive and problematic. Explicitly imitative, they require the superior, even heavenly point of view Wordsworth emphasizes in 1832–50 by presenting the painter as someone "whose ambitious skill / Submits to nothing less than taking in / A whole horizon's circuit" (1832, 240–42, p. 143).[33] For human spirits differently commissioned, this imaginary "bird's eye" view of London must encompass all that the speaker has thus far been unable to survey as a whole. And, like the imagined model of the Lakes with which Wordsworth begins his *Guide*, this "raree-show" establishes relations between its parts and whole that recall the perspectival control of the beautiful. Yet the "absolute presence of reality" in the city resists such fantasies. More troubling still is the fact that this reality is itself theatrical, as the speaker admits when he describes a series of impersonators, "clowns, conjurors, posture-masters, harlequins" (295, p. 242), and finally "Jack the Giant-killer." The most theatrical of all, this figure adopts a delusive disguise – a "coat of darkness" with the word *invisible* written on it (303–10, p. 242) to conjure up the idea of invisibility in the minds of spectators. As an allegoric or emblematic representation of the act of representation, "Jack" queries the project of Book VII – to represent a humanscape of sublime energy and chaos.

The speaker hastily retreats from so negative a reading of his efforts by a familiar route. He humanizes the theatrical image of Mary of Buttermere by invoking her life and character in the North of England, and by burying her permanently there, far from the London stage. Only while viewing tragic suffering on the stage can he recognize – as at the suburbs of his mind – glimpses of "real grandeur." Yet his assessment emphasizes how difficult it is to represent those sublime actions or passions which earlier writers associated with the terms *grandeur* and *tragedy*:[34]

> If aught there were of real grandeur here
> 'Twas only then when gross realities,
> The incarnation of the spirits that moved
> Amid the poet's beauteous world – called forth
> With that distinctness which a contrast gives,
> Or opposition – made me recognise
> As by a glimpse, the things which I had shaped
> And yet not shaped, had seen and scarcely seen,
> Had felt, and thought of in my solitude.   (508–16, p. 252)

In his retrospective comparison between the ghostly, "second-sight procession" of London inhabitants and a Lakes superstition about spectral horsemen (602, p. 258),[35] he rediscovers in London the sublime spectral presence which the boy Wordsworth felt in Book I. Against this shifting of text and context in the poem, the speaker's encounter with the blind beggar is in a sense pre-ordained, for it binds previously separate strands of argument concerning the sublime and its representation. Invoking the sublime figure of inadvertency, the speaker comes upon the blind man by chance and therefore has no time to defend himself against the image of someone who cannot see, can barely hold himself up, but who holds up a paper explaining "the story of the man, and who he was." This "spectacle" demands to be distinguished from the "moving pageant" of Book VII. Because the blind beggar presents a surface of "fixèd face and sightless eyes" that seem to admonish the speaker "from another world" (609–23, p. 260), he signals the disjunction between sublime ideas and their representation. Yet, unlike the "characters" of the Apocalypse in Book VI, the old man's face and paper call the speaker's attention to what he cannot name. In Book VI words and figures are a transparent medium; in Book VII, they resist transparency. The speaker's response is not that of a boy who fears spectral mountain forms, but that of an adult who recognizes that words may evoke, but not "incarnate," sublime figures. One psychological measure of the adult speaker's experience of the sublime is the lack of projection which characterizes this encounter. In Lacanian terms, Wordsworth's speaker exchanges an imaginary, self-reflecting response to the sublime for a symbolic representation of sublime otherness.[36]

In the phrase he uses to declare this exchange ("My mind did at this spectacle turn round / As with the might of waters," 616–17, p. 260), the figure of deluge begins to resurface in the text. Its revolutionary aura emerges in his account of London in a violent mood "when half the city shall break out / Full of one passion – vengeance, rage or fear – / To executions, to a street on fire, / Mobs, riots, or rejoicings" (646–49, p. 262). Wordsworth's use of the future tense to describe events that also occur in revolutionary Paris implies a parallel that becomes more marked in his description of Bartholomew Fair. There the difference between a revolution and a fair is insignificant – both display a chaotic, bursting "parliament of monsters." To describe the scene at Smithfield, the speaker becomes its barker as he surveys it from a showman's platform "above the press and danger of the crowd." The bravura of his catalogue of the animal-like human figures below[37] implicates him in a sublime he has taken pains not to acknowledge – the chaotic destruction and human sublime of revolutionary France and London. It is, he recognizes, a scene that mocks "all Promethean thoughts of man" – including his. The scene is indeed a "blank confusion," but it is not, for once, falsely catalogued (656–96, pp. 262, 264). The distant vantage point and seemingly random catalogue of numerous, often dramatic details anticipate the "urban vista" favored by nineteenth-century realist painters. Like them, Wordsworth's speaker surveys the scene without appearing to compose it as the "painter" described earlier in this book appears to do.[38]

At the end of Book VII, he asserts that although this is "an unmanageable sight, / It is not wholly so to him who looks / In steadiness, who hath among least things / An under-sense of greatest, sees the parts / As parts, but with a feeling of the whole" (709–13, p. 264). To regain this sense of proportion, parts, and wholes, the 1805 speaker invokes the topography of the Lake District, where

> The mountain's outline and its steady form
> Gives a pure grandeur, and its presence shapes
> The measure and the prospect of the soul
> To majesty: such virtue have the forms
> Perennial of the ancient hills – nor less
> The changeful language of their countenances
> Gives movement to the thoughts, and multitude,
> With order and relation.   (723–30, p. 266)

This shift in aesthetic perspective from the sublime to the beautiful declares what the speaker fears about the sublime and values in the beautiful. In 1832–50 even the shift disappears. Now "grandeur" and "beauty" are together the kind of aesthetic pleasure the "sun-burnt Arab" derives from "desart sands," a sublime landscape in the Book V dream of another Arab (1832, 7:746–48, p. 157). Although the duration of the sublime is never explicitly presented in Book VII, it is implied by his repeated notice of the primitive, chaotic, and apparently endless spectacle of strange beings inside theaters and in the streets. In the closing comparison between the "blank confusion" of London and the natural harmony of a mountainous topography, the speaker dismisses London as a place dominated by "self-destroying, transitory things" and offers the "pure grandeur" of the "mountain's outline and steady form" with a compensatory vision of sublime duration. To this he adds the "changeful language" and sense of "order and relation" which the beautiful brings to surfaces as legible "countenances."[39]

In Book VIII, the shortcomings of the London fair are retrospectively viewed through the conservative, Burkean lens of the fair below Helvellyn.[40] The most obvious difference between the two passages is the speaker's rhetorical vantage point. In Book VII, the scene is out "there," although he indicates that he is at first in the midst and then (for safety) above the crowd; in Book VIII, the scene is "this secluded glen" (17, p. 268). This adoption of the formal, yet familiar tone of a pastoral poet's address to the landscape he inhabits secures its familiarity and its status as a fictional arena where this poet may sing. Like Bartholomew Fair, the Grasmere Fair includes beggars, strangers, itinerants, hawkers, a lame man, and a blind man. But these, like the people who dwell in the valley, belong here. They come each year to participate in pastoral and georgic activities from sheep-shearing to selling quack medicines. All these the speaker places in a wide-angle, miniaturizing perspective:

> Immense
> Is the recess, the circumambient world
> Magnificent, by which they are embraced.
> They move about upon the soft green field;
> How little they, they and their doings, seem,
> Their herds and flocks about them, they themselves,
> And all which they can further or obstruct –
> Through utter weakness pitiably dear,
> As tender infants are – and yet how great,
> For all things serve them: them the morning light
> Loves as it glistens on the silent rocks,
> And them the silent rocks, which now from high
> Look down upon them, the reposing clouds,
> The lurking brooks from their invisible haunts,
> And old Helvellyn, conscious of the stir,
> And the blue sky that roofs their calm abode.   (47–62, p. 270)

By focusing on pastoral harmony in the North of England, Book VII resettles the narrative argument of the poem much as the Helvellyn Fair narrative resettles the disturbing elements in the St. Bartholomew Fair. Toward this end, the speaker offers tales of danger and distress ("speaking monuments" in the 1832–50 poem, 172, p. 164) that recognize the pre-eminence of the beautiful in this landscape and society.

In the 1805 poem a covert pattern of suppression and allusion assists this aesthetic resettlement. To illustrate how Nature first taught him "love human," the speaker recalls having once seen a shepherd and his dog high in the mountains, surrounded by "mists and steam-like fogs" that created an "aerial island" on which the two figures seemed to float "with that abode in which they were, / A little pendant area of grey rocks, / By the soft wind breathed forward" (77, 85, 98–101, p. 272). Noting in this passage echoes of Claudio's speech on death in *Measure for Measure* ("imprisoned in the viewless winds, / And blow with restless violence round about / The pendent world"), Jonathan Wordsworth astutely observes: "terror has been replaced by comforting beauty; but the echo is there."[41] Wordsworth's speaker specifies the aesthetic project of scenes like this one when he declares, "beauteous the domain / Where to the sense of beauty first my heart / Was opened – tract more exquisitely fair / Than is that paradise of ten thousand trees" (119–22, p. 274), and later adds that this pattern of life is, in the clarified expression of the 1832–50 text, "rich in beauty, beauty that was felt" (1832, 163, p. 164). Pastoral care on the heights and in the valleys is a human equivalent (along with crops and settlements) to the "order and relation" of beautiful landscapes. As a highly self-conscious poetic genre about the moral perspective which *rus* gives to *urbs*, pastoral calls attention to its status as a poetic fiction. In Wordsworth's poem its speaker retreats from urban cares that have been in some measure a screen fiction for revolutionary fears. True, he assures us that the scenes and episodes he describes are not peopled by a Colin or a Phyllis, yet the versions of pastoral presented in the expanded *Prelude* offer a stage against which the chaotic spectacles of Books VII, IX, and X can be measured.[42]

The speaker himself challenges the aesthetic perspective he asserts at the beginning of Book VIII in the last epic simile in the poem to consider the relation between shadow or delusion and the real. As the traveller of this simile goes from daylight into a dark cave, appearances mingle in "a canopy / Of shapes, and forms, and tendencies to shape / That shift and vanish, change and interchange / Like spectres – ferment quiet and sublime" (720–23, p. 304). As an image of how the sublime manifests itself as an attribute of such "ferment," what the traveller sees suggests why Wordsworth is at once attracted to the sublime and disturbed by it. Once this "ferment" settles, "The scene before him lies in perfect view / Exposed and lifeless as a written book" (726–27, p. 304). The speaker's reaction to the second view is not to recuperate the sublime, but to imagine a visual surface full of distinct images:

> the senseless mass,
> In all its projections, wrinkles, cavities,
> Through all its surfaces, with all colours streaming,
> Like a magician's airy pageant, parts,
> Unites, embodying everywhere some pressure
> Or image, recognised or new, some type
> Or picture of the world – forests and lakes,
> Ships, rivers, towers, the warrior clad in mail,
> The prancing steed, the pilgrim with his staff,
> The mitred bishop and the thronèd king –
> A spectacle to which there is no end.   (731–41, p. 304)

One crucial difference between the first and third views of the scene inside the cave is that the third presents forms and images which in the first resisted incorporation into a system of representation. The advantage of having such a system is that it supplies a picture after the vision instead of "a blank sense of greatness passed away" (744, p. 304). To correct the "blankness" that succeeds the "ferment" of "shapes and tendencies to shape," the speaker turns, as with the might of images, toward the beautiful.

Using the language of a Miltonic beautiful, he turns back to London to see it with the eyes of Adam while he was

> yet in Paradise
> Though fallen from bliss, when in the East he saw
> Darkness ere day's mid course, and morning light
> More orient in the western cloud, that drew
> 'O'er the blue firmament a radiant white,
> Descending slow with something heavenly fraught.'
>   (818–23, p. 308)

The Miltonic indebtedness of these lines,[43] but especially their ornate diction of color and light and their use of noun modifiers, emphasize the speaker's adequate representation of the scene. Wordsworth's point (and Milton's) is that even fallen beings – including those fallen from sublime visions into discourse about the sublime – can and do develop new, more insistently human vocabularies to describe what they see. As the aesthetic of this new seeing in *The Prelude*, the beautiful finds a human scale in scenes which were before barely human. Back in London, now presented as "that vast abiding-place of human creatures," the speaker finds a man holding a sick child. This scene of domestic love and suffering retroactively "settles" the undomesticated images of Book VII by reimagining their location as a domestic shelter whose values are those of the Wordsworthian beautiful.

If the "motions retrograde" (9:1–9, p. 312) of Books VII and VIII deliberately obscure a narrative thread which binds Book VI to Book IX, they also preview the aesthetic terrain which the speaker finally scrutinizes in Books IX and X. In these books the speaker is the *spectator ab extra* whom Coleridge admired.[44] Although his motive for going to France had been, the 1805 speaker admits, "to speak the language more familiarly" (9:35–37, p. 312), his speech is alien. A foreign observer, he hears the sounds of Paris (like those of London in Book VII) as a "hubbub wild." The reiterated echo of Milton's description of Chaos secures a second link between the revolutionary turmoil of mass demonstrations, pamphleteering, and political caucuses in Paris and the crowds (or "parliament of monsters") whose "blank confusion" stupefied the speaker in Book VII. This time, however, he is resolved not to yield but to review the personal and public conflicts which are the reasons for his eventual despair.

In the relatively peaceful (i.e., bloodless) early stages of the Revolution, the speaker establishes a kinship with several young military officers, and with Michel Beaupuy. Aristocratic and French, they accept him as an equal despite his evident foreignness to them in speech as well as birth (9:191–200, p. 322). Their advocacy of traditional chivalric values in a revolutionary context makes them singular representatives of Wordsworth's effort to see the French Revolution as a chilvalric righting of human wrongs and not, as he later came to regard it, as a chaotic upheaval with scant promise of a future peace. What Beaupuy says they are fighting against – the suffering and poverty of the French (especially the female French), the use of *lettres de cachet*, and the absence of a principle of *habeas corpus* – are all misuses of power practiced by the *ancien régime*, whose authority derives from the chivalric past (9:481–520, pp. 336, 338). In allying these men with the heroes of chivalric romance, the speaker faces (or initially doesn't face) an irremedial conflict. Those tales of romance, which had neutralized then transformed his childhood fear of a drowned man's "ghostly face," can have no efficacy here, marked as they are by the course of French history.

In the 1805 version of the story of Vaudracour and Julia – briefly summarized in 1832 and omitted in 1850 – he alters the task he had given to romance in Book V in ways that indicate some recognition of this conflict. Whereas in the earlier book romance was a vehicle for revising ghastly or sublime scenes, now romance places those scenes in a foreground that calls attention to their scandalous sublimity.[45] The "terror" (9:670, p. 344) Vaudracour feels before he kills his would-be captor suggests why neither the speaker nor the French people can be roused by the "voice of freedom" and "public hope" of these times

(9:931–32, p. 356). All are, like Vaudracour, guilty of infanticide – whether accidental or deliberate – and of disobedience to patriarchs.[46]

In Book X revolutionary and sublime images which are separate in other books converge. The hope that the September massacres of 1792 would be only "ephemeral monsters, to be seen but once" is questioned by the speaker's premonition that the "fear gone by / Pressed on me almost like a fear to come" (10:36, 62–63, p. 360). Because sublime fear is on all sides, it cannot be sequestered even momentarily by the beautiful, which briefly "overspread the countenance of the earth" as Book X begins with the speaker's departure from Orleans and Annette Vallon (1–8, p. 358). Here the diction recalls that established for the beautiful in the Ravine of Arve passage of Book VI, but without the same effect. That is to say, so preoccupied is this book with a stern "under"-countenance – the fear and terror of revolutionary France – that it cannot appropriate the language of the beautiful for a temporary, expressive shelter. Instead, the speaker is caught up, as he had been in Book VII, with the sight of human beings as surfaces that cannot be read. Near the "square of the Carousel," beside the Louvre and other architectural and political monuments to the *ancien régime*, Wordsworth sees "the dead and dying" as a "volume whose contents he knows / Are memorable but from him locked up, / Being written in a tongue he cannot read" (46–52, p. 360). What he can do later that night is feel "most deeply in what world I was" (56, p. 360) and what he feels is fear.

The "admonishments" that assisted the boy's education by fear in Book I now warn the adult speaker about the cyclic nature of revolt (10:68–69, p. 360). The 1832–50 texts extend the aesthetic resonances of this warning by adding a suggestion of deluge to the 1805 image of the retreating tide: "the tide retreats / But to return out of its hiding-place / In the great Deep" (1832, 81–83, p. 198).[47] In both versions, the speaker implies that such cataclysms tend to recur when he observes, "the earthquake is not satisfied at once" (74, p. 362). This image, which recalls one of the cataclysms feared by the speaker in Book V, retrospectively identifies this earlier book as a major pre-text for the speaker's Book X recognition that human achievements like those of France prior to the Revolution survive total destruction only if they submit to being changed by forces that envelop them. For the speaker of the 1805 poem, the lesson is no easier for him now than it had been for the dreamer in Book V. No wonder the scene is, in the fullest aesthetic nuance available to the phrase in Wordsworth's poetry, "a place of fear / Unfit for the repose of night, / Defenceless as a wood where tigers roam" (10:80–82, p. 362).[48]

Despite his fear he hopes that someone's speeches or speech – preferably his own – be adequate to the occasion. Turning to the scene in Paris following the September massacres, he proposes to report events, "seeing with my proper eyes" (10:107, p. 364). As a French word imported into English *proper* signals his effort to overcome the linguistic barrier which stands between his "own" speech and that of the French people. Placed before the noun, *propre* means "own," as it does in Wordsworth's text. Placed after the noun, it means "proper." In short, he presents himself as though he were a native Frenchman whose unidiomatic English negatively indicates his command of idiomatic French. Like Louvet, whose "J'accuse" he translates in the preceding lines (10:100, p. 362), he too would like to accuse Robespierre of crimes against the French people. To this end, he generalizes his desire to include others. Now chivalric aspirations take on a specific dimension – that of speech-acts as a "work of honour" in that "place of fear" (10:117–26, p. 364).

Although the speaker has no fear about "the end of things," his fears as well as hopes about what might occur before the end invoke the Biblical register of the Wordsworthian sublime. The "gift of tongues" which he hopes for is the gift lost at Babel. Two other allusions in Book x map the chronology of Genesis onto that of the French Revolution. Back in England, the speaker learns of Robespierre's death while walking along the treacherous sands of Leven. In the context of allusions in Books v and vi to the Deluge and the overflowing Nile, as well as the speaker's association of deluge with revolutionary bloodshed earlier in this book, his remark that the sea was then "at a safe distance, far retired" (529, p. 386) invokes precisely those fears which it is intended to revoke. In his commentary on this passage, DeQuincey describes the scene at Leven as "a perilous waste of sands" where travellers and even guides often perish, either because they misjudge the time when tides are low enough to permit their passage or because they are misled by "the intricacy of the pathless track."[49]

In Wordsworth's text the absence of these dangers (which De Quincey presents as sublime figures) objectifies the speaker's relief that the architect of the Reign of Terror is dead and, less overtly, his recognition that other, similar dangers may reappear, even as the sea will not always be "at a safe distance" from the sands of Leven. Even so negatively presented, the possibility of a deluge or flood assists the Biblical chronology of this book. After Robespierre's death, the speaker comments on how participants and non-participants responded to France's "milder" authority:

> I could see
> How Babel-like the employment was of those
> Who, by the recent deluge stupefied,
> With their whole souls went culling from the day
> Its petty promises to build a tower
> For their own safety.   (617–22, p. 392)

Here as in Genesis, if deluge comes, babel will not be far behind. For this reason, the speaker fails to report revolutionary events in his own voice and thus fails to bring them within safe, linguistic bounds.

Precisely because he cannot successfully displace sublime fear in its various revolutionary and Biblical guises, in Book XI Wordsworth's speaker seeks refuge in reason, the agent of the beautiful.[50] Addressing "breezes" and "soft airs" as "ye motions of delight," and then "ye brooks" and "ye groves" (11:10–22, p. 416), he echoes the pastoral gestures of *Lycidas* and "Tintern Abbey" to restore an aesthetic progress and conflict which the revolutionary sublime had displaced. Having found little solace in reason and abstraction, he presents another, less theoretical, view of the beautiful as benevolent, domestic, female, and allied to a spirit of blessedness in spring (25–28, p. 416). In *The Prelude* the origin of this figure is maternal and equally sheltering – for a time. Outside the poem, an obvious precedent is Burke, whose lingering analysis of female beauty Wordsworth may echo in "She Was a Phantom of Delight," where the figure of Mary Wordsworth insures the bond between spirit and humanity that is for Wordsworth essential to the beautiful.[51]

The currency of the sublime – its elevation, its gaze into futurity, and its claim that the speaker is and has been "one" with great men – is now offered as false coinage. Portraying himself to Coleridge as an Odysseus who has revisited the enticements of the shore – not Circe's but those of "blessèd sentiment and fearless love" – the speaker indicates that he is now willing to give up a "business" which has kept him "upon the barren seas" and, like Odysseus, bound on an "errand ... to sail to other coasts." Here the word "errand" in the 1805 text invokes less admirable resonances than it had in Book V. Odysseus's goal is not an epic mission but an aimless wandering in search of great deeds which are, in the speaker's case – as readers of Books IX and X are by now well aware – never performed. The heroic task is thus reduced to a "business," and a curiously unfocused one at that since all that is apparently required is to stay on "barren seas" and "sail to other coasts." Even the speaker's resolve to avoid the "elevation" he might have achieved by joining the "great family" of the past, which in 1805 includes "sage, patriot, lover, hero" (42–67, p. 418), is mocked by its narrative context, for the speaker has unsuccessfully tried all of these roles in Books IX and X.

At this stage two delusions afflict the speaker in succession: a belief in reason abstracted from feeling, and an absorption in knowledge gained from the eye, named here "the most despotic of our senses" (173, p. 424). These afflictions record, and in recording question, the most rigid traits of the beautiful – its imposition of rational symmetries, and its basis in the known, perceptual world – traits which he is eager to displace because they provide no counterpoise to sublime fear. Instead he seeks the blessedness that Dorothy Wordsworth and Mary Hutchinson offer. In the 1805 and 1832–50 poems, their presence on a return visit to Penrith Beacon revises the aesthetic progress traced in earlier books of the expanded *Prelude*. In Book XI, the pattern of suppression and retrieval which primarily assists the Wordsworthian beautiful in Book V serves both aesthetic responses.

The first suppression concerns the location of the gibbet which the boy Wordsworth supposedly encountered. In "An Unpublished Tour," one of several manuscripts linked to early versions of Wordsworth's *Guide through the District of the Lakes*, he recalls a murderer's gibbet at Gibbet Moss, near Hawkshead. The victim of this crime was the murderer's wife. A late nineteenth-century history of Hawkshead confirms the existence of such a gibbet and crime, but mentions no beacon. Although several beacons were once scattered in the region, there is no record of one near Gibbet Moss. In *The Prelude* Wordsworth locates the gibbet below Penrith Beacon, a well-known marker which had survived the Border Wars between Scotland and England. Some have argued that he saw this gibbet in Cowdrake Quarry, below Penrith Beacon. According to contemporary accounts, cut into the turf near it were some letters or initials, which nineteenth-century commentators could not decipher.[52] The problem, then, is that neither gibbet fully matches the description given in the 1799 poem. At Hawkshead, there was a gibbet, letters, but no crime. The 1799 poem mentions the specific crime, but it does not mention the letters carved in the turf; the 1805 poem suppresses the crime, but mentions the letters.

As Clarke's *A Survey of the Lakes* explains, from Penrith Beacon a visitor looking to the south could survey all the major features of the Lake District. To illustrate the point in the most corporeal manner possible, Clarke included a diagram of what was visible to the south from the beacon (Plate 1).[53] This pictorial representation of a single eye lodged at the beacon dramatizes the tyranny of eyesight in late eighteenth-century discussions of landscape and prospect. In the

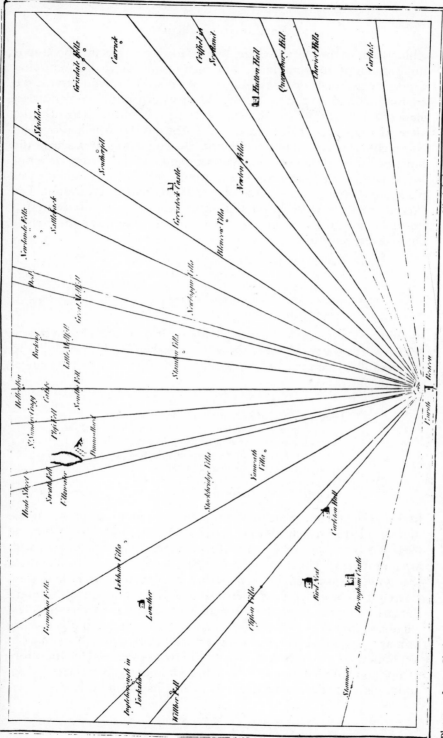

Plate 1   James Clarke. Penrith Beacon. In *A Survey of the Lakes*, 2nd edn (London, 1789).

gibbet scene of the 1805 *Prelude*, Wordsworth subverts the contemporary idiom of topographical and picturesque views by replacing Clarke's corporeal "eye" with the "I" of the speaker, who surveys the continuities and gaps in his history. Much as Penrith Beacon affords a view of the Lakes, so do the "spots of time" that begin here afford a view of the selves, half-hidden and half-exposed, which the poem chronicles. If we recall too that Penrith Beacon marks the scene of the Border Wars between England and Scotland and the hidden center of Wordsworth's *Borderers*, we gain a stronger sense of why he chose this place, not Gibbet Moss, as the place of imaginative restoration. The "spots of time" which begin at Penrith Beacon reveal the contested borderlands of the speaker's aesthetics. In the 1799 text gothic terror controls the narrative:

> A man, the murderer of his wife, was hung
> In irons. Mouldered was the gibbet-mast;
> The bones were gone, the iron and the wood;
> Only a green ridge of turf remained
> Whose shape was like a grave.   (1799, 309–13, p. 9)

By adding "monumental writing" to the turf in the 1805 version, Wordsworth shifts the focus. Now the speaker fears his inability to express fully what the words on the turf and other details of the gibbet scene mean:

> but on the turf
> Hard by, soon after that fell deed was wrought,
> Some unknown hand had carved the murderer's name.
> The monumental writing was engraven
> In times long past, and still from year to year
> By superstition of the neighbourhood
> The grass is cleared away; and to this hour
> The letters are all fresh and visible.   (291–98, p. 430)

In the guise of naming the murderer, the text suppresses his name, the initials or letters which were engraved on the turf, and finally the crime itself. Despite the impediments these changes pose for anyone who attempts to read what the gibbet signifies, the speaker claims that these letters were inscribed to memorialize a dead murderer, and were cleared of debris each year. Here visual and verbal dissonances mark the task of representing the sublime. Because the 1799 version is less enigmatic and thus easier to read, some have argued that it is more primary, or at least closer to what actually existed at Gibbet Moss.[54] Yet both texts suppress and retrieve different evidence. This trajectory of revision calls attention to how the sublime signifies. After 1799, additions complicate the story such that its meaning is overdetermined; more is meant than the speaker can say.[55] Yet specific elements of the gibbet scene – letters, pool, girl, and beacon – are not merely self-referential signs. With a perverseness that he cannot help, the speaker of *The Prelude* re-inscribes words and meanings which he cannot read to mark the difficulty of being lost to himself and of losing others to death. This he acknowledges when he declares that he "should need / Colours and words that are unknown to man / To paint the visionary dreariness" (308–10, p. 432) he encounters near Penrith.

As the sublime encounters of Book I do not, the "spots of time" in Book XI present a childhood experience as a version of the adult speaker's aesthetic education. The boy's lostness, reported as his guide's ("my lost guide") echoes the lostness of the dreamer in Book V and the speaker as he crosses the Alps in Book VI. Like them, the boy is surrounded by objects that ought to show the way, but do not. Even Penrith Beacon, for centuries a guidepost for travellers along the border between Scotland and England, is no help to him. As a scene that cannot be understood simply because it is a well known antiquarian site, it indicates that sublime signs must be known for what they are – primitive and evasive of human expression.

Like the coda added to the Drowned Man episode, Wordsworth's 1805 (and 1850) coda corrects the "visionary dreariness" of the scene, this time by recalling a return visit many years later. Presented as a "blessèd season" and "blessèd time," the 1805 speaker's return in the company of Dorothy Wordsworth and Mary Hutchinson (in 1832–50 Dorothy Wordsworth is not mentioned) casts a different aura over the "naked pool," "dreary crags," and "melancholy beacon." Seen through the lens of this second visit, these sublime features now signify "the spirit of pleasure and youth's golden gleam" (315–27, p. 432). These revisions replace a lost boy's lonely discovery of a gibbet with a group excursion in the company of women who brought domestic happiness to Wordsworth even as their presence domesticates the scene and the boy who saw it. And in 1832–50, this aesthetic revisionism authorizes a domesticated sublime. The speaker asks rhetorically, "and think ye not with radiance more sublime / For these remembrances, and for the power / They had left behind?" (1832, 267–69, p. 241).

DeQuincey indicates the autobiographical pattern suggested by this coda in his account of how Dorothy Wordsworth modified her brother's "ascetic harsh sublimity." "She it was," DeQuincey suggests, "that first *couched* his eye to the sense of beauty, humanized him by the gentler charities, and engrafted with her delicate female touch, those graces upon the ruder growths of his nature, which have since clothed the forest of his genius with a foliage corresponding in a loveliness and beauty to the strength of its boughs and the massiveness of its trunks" (my emphasis).[56] Much as Wordsworth's revision of the Penrith "spot of time" does, this elaborate portrait of sexual complementarity insists that beauty clothes or couches an original sublimity. In *The Prelude*, XI, this aesthetic enclosure makes the narrative safe for yet another sublime intrusion – Wordsworth's troubled recollection of his father's death.

This narrative, which begins with the speaker's hopes for a family reunion during the Christmas holidays and ends with his father's death ten days later, repeats the larger strategy of suppression and retrieval which characterizes the revisions of the Penrith sequence. In "Waiting for the Horses," he describes what he could see from the hilltop where he and his companions waited to go home. He declares that because the day was stormy, he had only an "intermitting prospect" of the scene below (355–63, p. 434). His inability to do more than list the elements of the scene emphasizes the visual gaps in his perception and the verbal gaps in his response. Yet once he tells the story of the death that occurred soon afterward, he can recall numerous details of the earlier scene. These are not manageable portents to which he can easily assign meaning, but portents of a life which can lay no claim to beauty, though it be the heart's desire to do so. To them – the weather, the single sheep and tree, the noise, and the mist – the speaker returns as to emblems of the realm beyond beauty's habitations (376–84, p. 436). Having first suppressed the retrospective significance of his wait at the head of two roads, he then retrieves it when he is able to acknowledge the sublime vision and human loss which are the uneasy contents of his past.

By a progress everywhere marked with suppressions and retrievals, he has come to the place that so frequently lies unacknowledged beneath beautiful surfaces. Like Freud, who urged himself down through the layers of mind ("I must come to the place where that was"),[57] here Wordsworth's speaker seeks that place within the mind's progress where human expression approaches the sublime. To have retrieved this much is the signal achievement of the expanded *Prelude*. Wordsworth's revisions of the Book XI "spots of time" reveals the partial settlements the heart must make and remake in order to meet what it knows and what it has been. Like Wordsworth, we come hither with some strengths and as many terrors. All these demand their place in the mind.

The 1805 tag Wordsworth appended to the end of this book and later omitted is a frank, if awkward, effort to swerve away from this aesthetic crossroads. Telling Coleridge that he won't allow him to "languish ... in these dim uncertain ways," the speaker tries to extricate them both by proclaiming himself "once more in Nature's presence, thus restored, / Or otherwise" (389–94, p. 436). The ambiguous restoration which this formulation betrays is more flexibly allowed in 1832–50. Here too its "place" in the "workings of [his] spirit" (388, p. 436) may assimilate the death of his father to that of his brother:

> Down to this *very* time, when storm and rain
> Beat on my roof, or haply at noon-day,
> While in a grove I walk whose lofty trees,
> Laden with summer's thickest foliage, rock
> In a strong wind, some working of the spirit,
> Some inward agitations, thence are brought,
> Whate'er their office, whether to beguile
> Thoughts over-busy in the course they took,
> Or animate an hour of vacant ease.   (1832, 327–35, p. 243)

The grove where the speaker walks may be "John's grove," so named because John Wordsworth preferred to walk there.[58] If so, his legacy included a place, within as well as without, from which his brother's discourse can proceed. If much is suppressed in the concluding books of the poem, which seek to domesticate the terrors and losses admitted in Books v to xi, much is retrieved in the 1805 text and in subsequent revisions.

Instead of being the prime agent in an education "by beauty and by fear," in Book xii Nature is credited with having offered a "twofold" gift, the "sister horns" of "emotion" and "calmness" or "peace and excitation." Fear is notable for its absence here, displaced by "emotion" or "excitation" (1–10, p. 438). Having replaced sublime fear with emotions which might or might not belong to the sublime, the speaker offers a reason that has been rehabilitated since its last appearance in Books x and xi, where an impaired reason and beauty were momentarily discarded so that he could approach the "visionary dreariness" of the sublime. Now "right reason" again displays "steady laws" (26–27, p. 438) and he dismisses revolutionary or sublime heroes as "the pompous names / Of power and action" which are "little worthy or sublime" (47–49, p. 440). When the sublime returns in the final book, it is under the aegis of the beautiful. He also forges the strongest possible link between the beautiful and the imagination. Turning to "man" and "the frame of life / Social and individual" (39–40, p. 440), he makes these, and "the beauteous world" which they inhabit, the focus of his poetic attention. The knowledge gained from this point of view is cast in terms that are uniquely appropriate to the mental and natural landscapes of the beautiful: an enlarged "horizon" and a sense of "true proportion" about hopes which had once exceeded his rational expectations about the future of society. Now the speaker seeks "good in the familiar face of life" (53–67, p. 440); he also opposes the "natural abodes" of rural existence to the "wearisome abode" and "heart-depressing wilderness" of the city. Wordsworth's exclusion of "visionary dreariness" from this antithesis diminishes the sublime by portraying it as urban and soul-destroying. Finally, the diction of the speaker's regard for the "dignity of man" (83, p. 442) shows how far he has travelled since Books IX and X, when he hoped to capture the very inflections of the Revolution in France by appropriating the French term *propre* to declare his ability to see revolutionary Paris "with my proper eyes." Now he puts this Gallicism aside to emphasize his new focus on "the man / Of whom we read, the man whom we behold / With our own eyes" (85–87, p. 442).

This shift in perspective replaces the global, quasi-heroic perspective of sublime figures and speakers with a more ordinary regard for individuals and cultures. Like Hazlitt and Byron, writers whose ideologies could hardly have been more unlike Wordsworth's after 1800, he recognizes the dubiousness of the *grande geste* and the inapplicability, as Byron perceived it, of Homeric postures to modern epic materials. By avoiding or domesticating the sublime in these books, Wordsworth hardly betrays the Romantic imagination. Instead he inaugurates the Romantic effort to re-define the imagination as something more than sublime vision.[59]

In the final books of *The Prelude*, Wordsworth casts the shadow of the beautiful over landscapes and narratives which in earlier books belonged to the sublime. Walking with his beloved and stopping "by cottage bench, / Or well-spring" (143–44, p. 444) to speak with passers-by, the speaker offers this meditation about the "public road" before him:

> such object hath had power
> O'er my imagination since the dawn
> Of childhood, when its disappearing line
> Seen daily afar off, on one bare steep
> Beyond the limits which my feet had trod,
> Was like a guide into eternity,
> At least to things unknown and without bound.
> Even something of the grandeur which invests
> The mariner who sails the roaring sea
> Through storm and darkness, early in my mind

> Surrounded too the wanderers of the earth –
> Grandeur as much, and loveliness far more.
> Awed have I been by strolling bedlamites;
> From many other uncouth vagrants, passed
> In fear, have walked with quicker step – but why
> Take note of this?   (12:146–61, pp. 444, 446)

If the scenes and incidents attached to this road are the unbounded landscapes and "things unknown" of the sublime and Milton's sublime style, the text closely monitors their sublime intrusion.[60] Thus a sea voyage during "storm and darkness" is celebrated for its "grandeur" and "loveliness far more," yet none of its destructive power is admitted into the text. And although he admits that madmen and vagrants evoke fear and awe, responses traditionally allied to the sublime, the speaker also argues that he was able to dispel his fear by questioning those he met and thus transform the "lonely roads" of such encounters into legible texts concerning "the passions of mankind" (163–68, p. 446).

This code of representability, which assumes that mysterious signs whose origins lie hidden in the past or in the mind can be read, must consider how a power which proceeds from "the depth of untaught things" (310, p. 452) can be made manifest on the surface of a text or a topography. Obliquely and with no little craft, the speaker addresses this paradox at the center of Wordsworth's aesthetics by recollecting another landscape from the past – the plain of Sarum. There he was "raised" to the sublime by a scene, a meditation, and hieroglyphic signs that reiterate the difficult semiotic project of this aesthetics. Wandering in a waste without a track or other guide, he "ranged" over Salisbury Plain in 1794 as he had in Paris in 1792 during the September massacres (10:39, p. 360).

This slight echo marks their shared theme: both dramatize efforts to find words to represent a sacrificial slaughter. The "monumental hillocks" or burial mounds on Sarum's plain are, like the September massacres in Paris, figures for the monumental significance which the speaker seeks to express. But whereas words, even French words, seemed inadequate to the task in Paris, the "Druid" shapes which the speaker interprets are mysterious yet decipherable (12:340–53, pp. 454–56). On the strength of this "antiquarian's dream" ("waking dream" in 1832–50), he asserts that he too can interpret "the vulgar form of present things / And actual world of our familiar days" as visible signs of a "new world" distinct from that of "life's everyday appearances." Here the well-known doctrine of "a balance, an ennobling interchange ... / Both of the object seen, and the eye that sees"

(361–79, p. 456) assumes that "action from within and from without" accurately describes the way that the mind represents reality. The test of this claim occurs in Book XIII, where a sublime landscape and experience are affixed to the rhetoric of the beautiful.

The Ascent of Snowdon recapitulates the revisionary aesthetics of *The Prelude*. Articulating a motif in the Scawfell excursion of Wordsworth's *Guide*, the speaker insists that he relied on a trustworthy "guide" for this ascent. Unlike the Arab of Book v, this guide is a "tried pilot" who casts no doubt on the speaker's faith in his ability to show them how to reach the summit. Moreover, this guide is no visionary desert wanderer, but well known to travellers as the stranger's "usual guide." If being a stranger insures one's response to the potential sublimity of the place, being well guided insures a degree of aesthetic containment. Even as the travellers will not get lost this time, so will the speaker not be subject to those elements of the sublime which cannot be managed by his discourse. However climactic their arrival at the summit, the progress toward this moment is painstakingly ordinary. They engage in "ordinary travellers' chat" with the guide. Little else occurs along the way, except for the "small adventure" of watching the shepherd-guide's dog chase a hedgehog. In brief, the scene should be fearful, for it is a "wild place" and the travel "at the dead of night" (1–27, p. 458). The fear assigned to a similar scene in "Fidelity" is missing here.[61] An intriguing pattern of half-resemblances between this poem and the Snowdon scene calls attention to their differences. In "Fidelity" the dog's faithfulness to his dead master and the shepherd who "reads" this fact obliquely echo the shepherd-guide to dog relation in *The Prelude*, XIII. But here no extraordinary claim for the dog's domestic affection is made because none is needed, since the Snowdon *topos* is, as a figurative and a literal place, wild yet safe.

If the speaker's account of his ascent "With forehead bent / Earthward, as if in opposition set / Against an enemy" (29–31, p. 458) recalls a similar opposition between him and Nature in earlier books, here that theme is presented as a figure of speech. That is to say, what matters is its surface value as a figure whose visual suggestiveness indicates how the speaker's body *looks* as he climbs. Because he makes it clear he knows there is no enemy, the effect of this curious echo of his boyhood encounters with Nature is to foreground the *absence* of fear on Snowdon. Finally, the inadvertence or suddenness of the sublime recurs in this episode, but it serves the speaker's thoroughly "un-sublime" ability to lead the group without getting lost:

And I, as chanced, the foremost of the band –
When at my feet the ground appeared to brighten,
And with a step or two seemed brighter still;
Nor had I time to ask the cause of this;
For instantly a light upon the turf
Fell like a flash.   (13:35–40, p. 460)

Whereas "chance" encounters elsewhere in the poem are vehicles for unexpected revelations which the speaker understands very little or not at all, now he guides the shepherd who had been their "conductor" as the ascent began and declares the meaning of what he sees. The scene includes well-known figures of the Wordsworthian sublime, yet they are immediately legible. The "sea of mist" that usurps "the real sea" by imitating its typical shorelines along the edges of "headlands, tongues and promontory shapes" (43–48, p. 460) is a case in point. It replaces the sea, a traditional sublime landscape, with an image of the sea which the speaker constructs "out of air." As Kant himself might have done, the speaker transforms the sublime by making it serve the human capacity to create images for those "deep truths" that Shelley's Demogorgon insists are "imageless."[62] Turning from this "sea of mist" to an abyss, the speaker appropriates another natural type of the sublime. This "chasm" is a "deep and gloomy breathing-place" whose "innumerable" streams and torrents are collectively "one voice" (56–59, p. 460).

As "a universal spectacle ... shaped for admiration and delight," this scene is in the 1805 poem – unlike the Alpine abyss of Book VI – part of a larger whole. Here, the speaker insists, "Nature lodged, / The soul, the imagination of the whole." This placement of the scene within a larger framework restores the aesthetic perspective absent in Books VII and X, where London and revolutionary Paris present unmanageable spectacles. Now the speaker is a full participant who can make something of what he sees. The "meditation" which he offers is a "perfect image" (60–70, p. 460) not only of the scene at hand, but also of how the Wordsworthian beautiful ventriloquizes the sublime. Echoing Milton's account of creation in *Paradise Lost*, the speaker notes how "a hundred hills their dusky backs upheaved" above the mist (45, p. 460). A vestige of Milton's God brooding over the abyss of chaos may also infect Wordsworth's "perfect image of a mighty mind, / Of one that feeds upon infinity" (70, p. 460).[63] These Miltonic pre-texts – one evident, the other probable – reiterate Wordsworth's association of the sublime with chaos and pre-history. They also show just how unoriginal sublime figures are.

On Snowdon the uncreated and the unknown are lodged at last, fixed in the speaker's discourse as "perfect" images, that is to say, as vehicles perfectly matched to their tenors. Here the tenor remains "sublime" in all its attributes – "awful," "dim," "vast," embued perhaps with a "sense of God" (72–76, p. 462). But his presentation of this vehicle is shot through with assertions about its adequacy: its "strength" is "made visible," it is a "genuine counterpart" to a similar but "higher faculty" in "higher minds" (including the speaker's). Thus the "domination" which "[Nature] exerts upon the outward face of things" (78, p. 462) finds a perfect match in the speaker's ability to do likewise.

Omitted from the 1805 text is a passage about travellers which Wordsworth had included in the five-book version abandoned in March, 1804. The excised material offers "analogies" for the relation between mind and Nature that is the subject of the speaker's exegesis of his ascent of Snowdon. But the collective weight of these analogies endangers the "perfect image" which the final text advances. In brief, they compare the speaker's narrative to the voyages of several travellers, including a rider who fearfully watches a storm over Coniston Lake, and various explorers. The last among them are Mungo Park and William Dampier, who lose their lives. A mediating figure for all these is a horse which is "a Borderer dwelling betwixt life and death" (*Prelude*, 624). This is precisely the problem. All these are endangered species whose fears about death in storms, at sea, or in Africa reintroduce the sublime fear which the speaker finally excludes from the Snowdon episode and his commentary on it. Moreover, because they are figures who have been or might be killed in the sublime landscapes they temporarily inhabit (Park was killed on the River Niger early in 1806),[64] they are unstable "border" images in a text that stabilizes its sublime encounters.

Toward this end, Book XIII secures the ascendancy of values that belong to the beautiful over those of the sublime. Asserting that minds which can make of experience what he has made of the scene of Snowdon are also capable of experiencing "emotion which best foresight need not fear" (115, p. 464), the speaker succinctly displays the sense of control and absence of fear which "foresight" permits. In reviewing "fear and love," the aesthetic coordinates of his imaginative progress, he declares that "to love [is] first and chief, for there fear ends" (143–44, p. 466). This displacement of the dynamic on which much of the poem depends uses a slight, but effective slippage in the meaning of "first." Now love, the aspect of the beautiful which Book XIII emphasizes, is "first" or principal, whereas the sublime had been "first" in the double register of priority and consequence. From this displacement derive others. Thus a "higher love ... comes into the heart / With awe and a diffusive sentiment" (161–63, p. 466) together to pre-empt the sublime.

More telling still is the speaker's use of Milton to describe his early preoccupation with the sublime: "I too exclusively esteemed that love, / And sought that beauty, which as Milton sings / Hath terror in it" (224–26, p. 470). Milton indeed. The-beauty-plus-terror formula is the sublime, still attractive to the speaker despite his inability to manage it in earlier books. In the context of this self-criticism, the Miltonic echo is instructive. In *Paradise Lost* the speaker who sings of beauty which has terror in it is not Milton but Satan, who describes the kind of love and destructive hate which Eve's beauty inspires:

> Shee fair, divinely fair, fit Love for Gods,
> Not terrible, though terrour be in Love
> And beautie, not approacht by stronger hate,
> Hate stronger, under shew of Love well feign'd
> The way which to her ruin now I tend.
> So spake the enemy of mankind.[65]

The allusion identifies Milton's Satan with preference for the sublime which is here, as it will be again in the 1817 ode "On Her First Ascent of Helvellyn," satanic because it belongs to the "enemy of mankind." To neutralize the sublime in the concluding section of the poem, the 1805 speaker redefines it to mean little more than Johnsonian elevation:

> Yes, having tracked the main essential power –
> Imagination – up her way sublime,
> In turn might fancy also be pursued
> Through all her transmigrations, till she too
> Was purified, had learned to ply her craft
> By judgement steadied.   (289–94, p. 474)

This recapitulation – omitted in 1832–50 – signals one last transformation of Wordsworth's errant speaker, who was once unable to capture appearances except as shadows or border images. He retrospectively characterizes his time in France as an "undomestic, wanderer's life" (343, p. 426) and in surveying the "vast prospect of the world which I had been, / And was" (379–80, p. 478) recognizes the figurative topography of the poem and his new control over it. And, like Wordsworth's wheel survey in his *Guide*, this overview makes it possible to see the sublime and beautiful features of this topography as a pattern. By "centring all in love," he makes the beautiful the arbiter of this pattern. In the closing lines he specifies what will be left out when he claims that he and Coleridge will teach

> how the mind of man becomes
> A thousand times more beautiful than the earth
> On which he dwells, above this frame of things
> (Which, 'mid all revolutions in the hopes
> And fears of men, doth still remain unchanged)
> In beauty, exalted, as it is itself
> Of substance and of fabric more divine.   (446–52, p. 482)

Reduced to a parenthetical appearance as the aesthetic of "revolutions in the hopes / And fears of men," the sublime is now circumscribed by the language of the beautiful. No longer the sublime "haunt" of Wordsworth's song, the mind is instead beauty's permanent dwelling-place.

Because the expanded *Prelude* so often sustains the conflict between its sublime and beautiful figures, its revisionary aesthetics is a remarkable achievement. In later poems, the same conflict is more often presented under the aegis of the beautiful. Two very different poems, the 1808 manuscript verse "St. Paul's" and the 1814 *Excursion* indicate the outer limits of the revisionary aesthetics at work in the 1805 *Prelude*. *The Excursion* suggests further how Wordsworth's conception of the beautiful broadened in the early decades of the nineteenth century.

"St. Paul's" and *The Excursion*

Unlike *The Prelude*, "St. Paul's" describes a sublime experience which the beautiful thoroughly, rather than intermittently, contains. The opening lines specify the aesthetic register Wordsworth assigned to his vision of St. Paul's after a difficult meeting with Coleridge, to whom this poem is also addressed: "Press'd with conflicting thoughts of love and fear / I parted from thee, Friend, and took my way" (*PW*, 4:374, ll. 1–2). The speaker's vision of St. Paul's as something "deep," "vacant," "hollow," "shadowy," and "awful" displays the usual signs for the Wordsworthian sublime. To them he predictably responds with a sudden recognition of the scene's "visionary" aspect, calling it "Imagination's holy power." Unlike the apostrophe to the Imagination in *The Prelude*, VI, however, here the speaker's "feet masterless" are a sufficient guide and the vision brings with it "an anchor of stability" whose home-thoughtedness is declared in a manuscript variant which substitutes "security" for "stability" (*PW*, 4:374–75, 374n.). This is no *unheimlich* place that makes the familiar unfamiliar, but a "familiar spot / A visionary scene." This syntactic containment of sublime vision within the familiar assists the aesthetic control announced in the concluding lines:

Pure, silent, solemn, beautiful, was seen
The huge majestic Temple of St. Paul
In awful sequestration, through a veil,
Through its own sacred veil of falling snow.

(PW, 4:375, ll. 25–28)

"St. Paul's" illuminates and domesticates an expressly personal range of concerns that Wordsworth described in a letter written from Grasmere shortly after his return from London. Whether this letter to Beaumont preceded the composition of the poem is difficult to know, although the fact that both describe the scene in similar terms suggests that they are probably contemporary.[66] In the letter Wordsworth explains that he was leaving London and an unwell Coleridge to return to Grasmere, where Sarah Hutchinson was seriously ill, when he saw the vision that became the subject of the poem. Writing about it from Grasmere, he told Beaumont, "the imagery of London has, since my return hither, been more present to my mind than that of this 'noble vale'." The comparison shows that much has happened since the 1800 "Prospectus," initially composed as part of *Home at Grasmere*, to alter Wordsworth's earlier assurance about where beauty's tents could be found. In other words, were this *Home at Grasmere* and were it yet 1800, Wordsworth might have found his "noble vale" shelter and comfort enough. Instead he finds both in an urban setting (to be sure, it is an uncharacteristically deserted London) by imposing the values of the beautiful on a sublime vision. His letter to Beaumont, which describes the vision in some detail without using the adjectives "fair" and "beautiful" (both appear in manuscripts of the poem), suggests that this act of aesthetic revision may have occurred gradually, as Wordsworth considered why "the imagery of London" seemed present to him even after he returned home. Whatever the pre-history of this poem, its aesthetic outcome is clear enough. It comforts the "sorrow" and "uneasiness of mind" mentioned in Wordsworth's letter by offering a sublime vision well supervised by the beautiful.

Like "St. Paul's," *The Excursion* subdues aesthetic conflict in the name of the beautiful. But unlike both "St. Paul's" and the expanded *Prelude*, its revisionary aesthetics was from the first directed toward a larger, public audience whose ambivalent response to revolutionary and Napoleonic France mirrored Wordsworth's earlier reception and rejection of the sublime.[67] Given this ideological pressure, it is hardly surprising that the speakers in *The Excursion* are very nearly unrelenting in their management of sublime figures and values. The difference between the revisionary aesthetics of this poem and that of the expanded *Prelude* is succinctly illustrated by Wordsworth's revisions of a passage he composed for the poem on his life but published in *The Excursion*. In the earlier of two *Prelude* manuscript variants, the speaker declares:

> Two feelings have we also from the first
> [?] of grandeur and of tenderness;
> We live by admiration and by love
> And ev'n as these are well and wisely fixed
> In dignity of being we ascend.   (*Prelude*, 571)

In a second variant "admiration," a synonym for the sublime, is made subject to specific controls. As long as he who seeks "eternal and unchanged" principles

>   regulates
> His notions of the beautiful and grand,
> In him will admiration be no weak
> Fantastic quality that doth betray
> Its owner, but a firm support.   (*Prelude*, 613)

Although the speaker does not say what will happen if the "he" in question does not adequately regulate "his notions of the beautiful and grand," I suspect that without such regulation sublime or revolutionary terror becomes one of those notions. In the *Excursion* versions of the same passage, the potential for aesthetic conflict among versions of the sublime disappears. In the manuscript the operative terms are "Admiration and Love"; in the 1814 published text even this muted aesthetic duality gives way to the aesthetic triumvirate of "Admiration, Hope, and Love" (*PW*, 5:133–133n., IV, l. 763). In short, the opposition between grandeur and tenderness which Pirie argues is critical to Wordsworth's poetry[68] is already subverted in the *Prelude* variants because they exclude sublime fear and its revolutionary context. This exclusion is even more marked in *The Excursion*, where it assists a rhetorical bias toward the beautiful.

The Solitary's allusions to revolutionary France illustrate the strength of this bias. Echoing the Snowdon episode in *The Prelude*, XIII, he gives this account of his first response to the Fall of the Bastille:

> As marvellously seized as in that moment
> When, from the blind mist issuing, I beheld
> Glory – beyond all glory ever seen,
> Confusion infinite of heaven and earth,
> Dazzling the soul.   (*PW*, 5:101, III, ll. 718–22)

This explicit link between a sublime figure and the French Revolution is precisely what the same figure prevents in the last book of the earlier poem. In *The Excursion* such resemblances are more easily declared because the poem is in general more critical of the sublime and more adept at suppressing its figures.

Only on rare occasions does the sublime exhibit traits which it has in earlier poems. As a boy, the Wanderer explains, he experienced a sense of election "not from terror free" (*PW*, 5:12, I, l. 133). Yet in retrospect sublime fear is alien to the Wanderer, who summarizes his earliest scenes of aesthetic instruction with this declaration: "where Fear sate thus, a cherished visitant, / Was wanting yet the pure delight of love" (*PW*, 5:14, ll. 186–87). If much of what its speakers say about love is presented without aesthetic designations, the Wanderer's praise of the region they visit as they try to "correct" the Solitary's despondency uses the values of the beautiful to represent culture and society in the animal kingdom:

> These craggy regions, these chaotic wilds,
> Does that benignity pervade, that warms
> The mole contented with her darksome walk
> In the cold ground; and to the emmet gives
> Her foresight, and intelligence that makes
> The tiny creatures strong by social league;
> Supports the generations, multiplies
> Their tribes, till we behold a spacious plain
> Or grassy bottom, all, with little hills –
> Their labour, covered, as a lake with waves;
> Thousands of cities, in the desert place
> Built up of life, and food, and means of life!
>
> (*PW*, 5:122, IV, ll. 427–38)

The "love of fellowship," presented as the motive for this "social league," completes the aesthetic topography of a scene that would otherwise be a sublime "waste."

Although the speakers of the poem hope to correct the Solitary's despondency, they do not challenge his suspicion of sublime values, which he illustrates with appropriately sublime figures. He asks "Ah! what avails imagination high / Or question deep?" then replies by arguing that "the senseless grave" is a "better sanctuary / From doubt and sorrow" (*PW*, 5:81, III, ll. 208–24). The Wanderer objects to this longing for death, but he agrees that "wisdom is oftimes nearer when we stoop / Than when we soar" (*PW*, 5:82, ll. 231–32). The antithesis echoes the Solitary's doubt about the value of "image high" or "question deep" and his suspicion of the soul that "soar[s] as far as she finds a yielding element." Instead, the Wanderer approves "the beaten track of life" and its "penetrable bounds."[69]

In the Wanderer's lexicon, the term *sublime* usually means "elevation." Lamenting the disappearance of rural ways, he admires the boy

135

"who, in his very childhood, should appear / Sublime from present purity and joy!" (*PW*, 5:275, VIII, ll. 319–20). He also claims that the "sublime ascent" of old age is marked by "the elevation of our thought" (*PW*, 5:289, IX, ll. 88, 93). And when he celebrates nature, he assimilates the sublime to a world whose fixity and visibility belong to the beautiful, or to a version of the sublime that is virtually indistinguishable from the beautiful:

> The sun is fixed,
> And the infinite magnificence of heaven
> Fixed, within reach of every human eye;
> The sleepless ocean murmurs for all ears;
> The vernal field infuses fresh delight
> Into all ears. Throughout the world of sense,
> Even as an object is sublime or fair,
> That object is laid open to the view
> Without reserve or veil.   (*PW*, 5:293, IX, ll. 209–17)

The Wanderer then asks how we could place any trust in a Deity who hid such truths, leaving us only a world where "truth" and "virtue" were "difficult, abstruse, and dark." Given the rhetorical framework of this question, the answer must be that we could not. In part, the poet of *The Excursion* prefers the beautiful because its preference for legibility and social coherence supports a specific theological vision, or as we might now call it, an ideology.

Once Wordsworthian speakers attach this much value to the beautiful, the conflict between sublimity and beauty loses much of its rhetorical energy. This much is obvious. In *The Excursion* and more insistently in other poems and essays, Wordsworth redirects this energy by developing a version of the beautiful that dramatizes the cultural force of ideology (whether radical or conservative). By undermining those sublime figures or speakers that purport to act outside ideology and thus outside history, the beautiful insists that it structures and is structured by history and culture.

6

The aesthetics of containment

Stone breaks scissors, scissors cut paper, but paper wraps stone.

Children's game

As A BRIEF BUT INSTRUCTIVE LESSON about appropriate counter-measures, the game "paper, scissors, stone" illustrates the aspect of the beautiful that Wordsworth elaborates after 1806: its aesthetics of containment. The beautiful "wraps" the sublime by challenging its claim to exist outside time and outside society. This claim is most obvious and most pernicious when Wordsworth's Rivers makes it in *The Borderers*. Yet it also defines the sublime figures and natures that people Wordsworth's several autobiographical accounts of his boyhood as well as his portrait of revolutionary France. However much the beautiful suppresses in its reading of history and culture, it never insists, as the sublime does, that it exists outside either. In the language of the game, the beautiful wins or ought to win not because it is harder or stronger but because it knows about its relation to history and society as the sublime does not.

Considered in these terms, the beautiful displays Wordsworth's recognition that poetic figures and their speakers necessarily exist within structures of meaning that he would have called society or culture but which recent Marxist critics call ideology. By *ideology* I mean not Marx's notion of "false consciousness" but something like the "strategies of containment" that human beings use to order reality. To paraphrase Louis Althusser's influential definition, ideology describes the way human beings live (and figure) their relation to the real conditions of existence.[1] But whereas Althusser and more recently Frederic Jameson suggest that it may be possible to avoid creating still other ideologies if one thinks from within a genuinely Marxist critique of refining ideologies, Wordsworth's presentation of the beautiful as an aesthetics of containment suggests that there is no escaping ideology, whatever the aesthetic or political occasion.

The ideological force of Wordsworth's mature conception of the beautiful is its Burkean rejection of claims for a natural, original code as the moral basis for human behavior in society,[2] a rejection which challenges the belief that the sublime is connate with the origins of culture and for this reason inherently superior. After 1806, partly in response to Napoleon's apparent invincibility as a sublime figure, Wordsworth more sharply questioned the putative originality and purity of the sublime as a code or ideology that mystifies its inherently ideological nature. Like Rousseau at his most ironic, he questions not only what we can know about sublime origins, but the value of original or primitive ideas. Wordsworth's most acerbic attack on the authority of origins appears in his *Reply to 'Mathetes'*, where he satirizes "primitive" societies and efforts to recover them.

In several poems he published after completing the thirteen-book *Prelude*, notably *Benjamin the Waggoner* and *The White Doe of Rylstone*, Wordsworth's aesthetics of containment presents the revolutionary sublime without displacing or succumbing to it. And in his 1815 classification of his collected poems, he introduces competing strategies for containing disturbing speakers or tales. In the 1815 *Poems* and in later editions, the network of relations within and among categories conditions the reception of individual poems. Such narrative containments show how Wordsworth's ideological commitments inform the poetic experiments of his middle years.

Concerning the Convention of Cintra

One political impetus for Wordsworth's increasing attention to the beautiful after 1806 was almost certainly Napoleon, whose unparalleled military and diplomatic powers dominated the first decade of the nineteenth century. Wordsworth's anxiety on this point is the undeclared (or half-declared) subtext of his 1809 pamphlet *Concerning the Convention of Cintra*. Even in the annals of Wordsworth's prose, the style of this essay is unusually crabbed. In part this is so because he made numerous revisions in the text after he sent it to DeQuincey, who had agreed to supervise its London publication.[3] Yet the very fact that Wordsworth felt compelled to change the text so much and so often suggests another, prior reason for the difficulties of the published version. Its main argument is clear enough: Wordsworth condemns the English command for having given Napoleonic France jurisdiction over Spain and Portugal.[4] But the rhetorical energy of the essay is directed against Napoleon as the underlying cause for which the Convention of Cintra is one important effect. Specifically, the figurative logic of the essay works to persuade English readers to manage their fear of Napoleon.

The aesthetic subplot of this logic emerges as Wordsworth charges that the English naval commander, Sir Hew Dalrymple, failed to act "under the obligation of his human social nature" to defeat "the rapacious and merciless adversary" (*Prose*, 1:225). Here he echoes (and is carried away by) the popular view that Napoleon is like Satan, the great adversary.[5] Elsewhere in the essay, satanic resonances are more pronounced. Wordsworth insists that Napoleon's power is a spurious "measure of right" (*Prose*, 1:266), then later mentions his "outlawed" status (*Prose*, 1:341). Yet what most troubles him is Napoleon's effort to present himself as a benevolent God. Unlike Tamerlane and Attila, who imitate God only insofar as they counter-feit "the terrors of Providence," Napoleon "arrogates to himself the gentle and gracious attributes of the Deity" (*Prose*, 1:242). Words-worth's account of this unlawful impersonation is caught between his unwilling notice of the sublimity of destructive power, whether Napoleonic or divine, and his effort to claim "gentle and gracious attributes" for God and the beautiful:

Through the terrors of the Supreme ruler of things, as set forth by works of destruction and ruin, we see but darkly; we may reverence the chastisement, may fear it with awe, but it is not natural to incline towards it in love: moreover, devastation passes away – a perishing power among things that perish: whereas to found, and to build, to create and to institute, to bless through blessing, this has to do with objects where we trust we can see clearly, – it reminds us of what we love, – it aims at permanence, – and the sorrow is, (as in the present instance the people of Spain feel) that it may last; that if the giddy and intoxicated Being who proclaims that he does these things with the eye and through the might of Providence be not overthrown, it will last; that it needs must last.

(*Prose*, 1:242–43)

From tyrant impersonations of the "terrors of providence," Words-worth goes straight to the real thing. "Fear" and "awe" are the emotions of sublimity, as nineteenth-century readers of this pamphlet and Burke's *Enquiry* would have been well aware. Here Wordsworth's emphasis shifts briefly to engage the aspect of the Deity which accords with the values of the beautiful – its spirit of benevolent preservation ("to found, and to build, to create and to institute, to bless through blessing"). But the opposition between preservation and destruction discloses sublime fear again as the verb "last" undergoes an emphatic progression from a possible "may" to the double imperative "needs must." The aesthetic conflict of the passage concerns whether sublime or beautiful figures will control its surface. This struggle for rhetorical power speaks for a struggle which has broader implications. In brief, its outcome will determine whether satanic, destructive power or divine benevolence and the beautiful will be permanent.

Wordsworth attempts to secure the outcome he hopes for by wresting permanence verbally from Napoleon (who had become consul for life in 1802[6]). Arguing that "the enormity of this power has in it nothing *inherent* or *permanent*" (*Prose*, 1:313), Wordsworth asserts that two major defeats will break him. The figurative logic of this assertion depends on the argument that follows. Agreeing with those who say that Napoleon is a colossus, Wordsworth insists that as such he will easily shatter: "if the trunk be of molten mass, the members are of clay, and would fall to pieces upon a shock which need not be violent" (*Prose*, 1:334). Like Kant's claim that the physical superiority of colossal figures is inferior to the intellectual might of the mind's sublimity,[7] Wordsworth's insistence exposes the sublime fear at issue in this essay.

To explain why the English ought to have supported Spain and Portugal in their efforts to resist Napoleon, Wordsworth recalls the English reaction to the French invasion of Switzerland in 1798, when "our condition savoured too much of a grinding constraint – too much of the vassalage of necessity; – it had too much of fear, and therefore of selfishness" (*Prose*, 1:227). His scornful list of the reasons Dalrymple gave for deciding to negotiate with France makes it clear that fear without resistance is fear without sublime elevation: "fear of an open beach and of equinoctial gales for the shipping: fear that reinforcements could not be landed; fear of famine; – fear of everything but dishonour!" (*Prose*, 1:254).[8]

By contrast, Wordsworth praises those "sublime precepts of justice" which Spain and Portugal "had risen to defend" and hopes for "a sublime movement of deliverance" (*Prose*, 1:265, 306). These declarations urge resistance (which Napoleon advised against, as Wordsworth reminds his readers, 1:313) as the version of the sublime that might displace the revolutionary or Napoleonic sublime. The first hint of this displacement occurs early in the essay, when he characterizes the Spanish revolt against French rule in May 1808 as "a sudden elevation" which brings back the possibility of "inward liberty and choice," then defends the moral superiority of opposition to Napoleon (*Prose*, 1:228, 235). The Kantian optimism of the claim that Spain's moral superiority ought to prevail against the "physical power" of its enemy disallows sublime fear and permits a refuge in "universal reason" as one of two sources that give rise to "the power of popular resistance" which Wordsworth recommends (*Prose*, 1:235, 253).

Yet moral superiority could not in 1809 preserve Spain and Portugal from French imperialism. The second source of popular resistance, "the heart of human nature," implicitly recognizes this difficulty and begins Wordsworth's turn toward the beautiful, linked in this essay to feeling, and to love and "genial grace" (*Prose*, 1:266, 306). The pamphlet concludes with an appeal couched in the language and topography of the beautiful. Urging the value of gaining a perspective on recent events, Wordsworth cites the example of Petrarch as one "who ... retired for wider compass of eye-sight, that he might comprehend and see in just proportions and relations; knowing above all that he, who hath not first made himself master of his own mind, must look beyond it only to be deceived" (*Prose*, 1:342). Seen as a horizon which must be defined before one can hope to look beyond it without risking self-deception, this "wider compass" draws little, if any, attention to the fact that it is the limit of vision. Instead, it emphasizes the benefits of enclosure. Wordsworth uses an allied figure to describe a "circle of benevolence" whose relation to "sublime and disinterested feelings" is anything but disinterested:

> the outermost and all-embracing circle of benevolence has inward concentric circles which, like those of the spider's web, are bound together by links, and rest upon each other; making one frame, and capable of one tremor; circles narrower and narrower, closer and closer, as they lie more near to the centre of self from which they proceeded, and which sustains the whole. The order of life does not require that the sublime and disinterested feelings should have to trust long to their own unassisted power.   (*Prose*, 1:340)

The rhetorical cunning of this declaration serves the beautiful even as it does some disservice to the sublime, here presented as elevated feelings that are unlikely to be sustained without being embraced by benevolence. Wordsworth is still not content to let the matter rest. Reiterating essentially the same point, he declares that those who prefer to "soar in the pure region" of "high precepts" should recognize that such precepts are connected to the "groundnest" of the "practice of life." As it does in *The Excursion* when the Solitary criticizes his earlier allegiance to the *philosophes* and revolutionary France, here the criticism of those who "soar" turns on an implicit distinction between sublime heights (and abstraction) and the domesticated enclosures of ordinary life and the beautiful.

Reply to 'Mathetes'

If Wordsworth questioned sublime values repeatedly after 1793, he tended to question them least when he recalled his early education "by beauty and by fear." But less than a year after *Concerning the*

Convention by Cintra appeared, he used an archeological metaphor to demystify the claim that primitive origins and societies are superior to modern civilization and adulthood. In his *Reply to 'Mathetes'*, published in *The Friend* in December, 1809 and January, 1810,[9] he declared:

> the situation of the Mind may be likened to that of a Traveller in some unpeopled part of America, who is attracted to the burial place of one of the primitive Inhabitants. It is conspicuous upon an eminence, "a mount upon a mount!" He digs into it, and finds that it contains the bones of a Man of mighty stature: and he is tempted to give way to a belief, that as there were Giants in those days, so that all Men were Giants. But a second and wiser thought may suggest to him, that this Tomb would never have forced itself upon his notice, if it had not contained a Body that was distinguished from others, that of a Man who had been selected as a Chieftain or Ruler for the very reason that he had surpassed the rest of his Tribe in stature, and who now lies thus conspicuously inhumed upon the mountain-top, while the bones of his Followers are laid unobtrusively together in their burrows upon the Plain below. (*Prose*, 2:9–10)

This analysis of the "lessons" of burial excavations targets two kinds of naivety. The first is that of the over-eager, amateur archeologist whose enthusiasm for excavating burial mounds leads him to believe that he has discovered a primitive giant race. A second naivety, that of primitive races who interpret height as visible evidence of moral or intellectual superiority, makes the cult of sublime genius an avatar of primitive systems of value. The modern parallel to the primitive tribe that chooses its chieftain solely on the basis of stature is the amateur archeologist who, after discovering the burial mound of this chieftain, concludes that all primitive men were giants.

Two other allusions elaborate the aesthetic implications of this analogy. The first is satanic and Miltonic. The "mount upon a mount!" where primitive burials take place is a slight misquotation of Milton's description of Satan enthroned in hell.[10] This allusion points toward a second, buried one – Kant's claim that sublimity exists in the mind's reason, not in physical size or might. Even if Wordsworth does not specifically invoke Kant, he addresses the same issue. What is ancient, buried and primitive – all attributes of the Wordsworthian sublime – is demoted as soon as it is brought to the surface and into present time. According to the aesthetic perspective of the *Reply to 'Mathetes'*, reason, feeling, and beauty are appropriately prized by modern civilization and the adult mind.

Wordsworth applies this archeological lesson to a familiar theme, Nature's education, to argue the irrelevance of his youthful struggle with the sublime:

we have made no mention of fear, shame, sorrow, nor of ungovernable and vexing thoughts; because although these have been and have done mighty service, they are overlooked in that stage of life when Youth is passing into Manhood, – overlooked, or forgotten. *(Prose, 2:17)*

In adult life, he explains, the mind seeks "reason" as the faculty which "works by thought, through feeling" to teach "that beauty which unfolds itself, not to his eye as it sees carelessly the things which cannot possibly go unseen and are remembered or not as accident shall decide, but to the thinking mind" *(Prose, 2:17–18)*. This perceptual analogy argues a new aspect of the beautiful – its capacity to "see" true relations, not simply those which are accessible because they are apparent. Now "objects" gain "intellectual life" from mental communication with reason's beauty.

The Pedlar and *The Ruined Cottage*

We can observe the difference between Wordsworth's earlier narrative experiments and those that reveal his mature aesthetics of containment by comparing the *The Ruined Cottage* and *The Pedlar* as versions of the story of Margaret to the aesthetic management of *Benjamin the Waggoner* and *The White Doe of Rylstone*. Because it dramatizes a gradual emptying of meaning and the insufficiency of natural symbols, Margaret's story illustrates the most negative features of the sublime. In the changing narrative fortunes of her story – at first told separately, then made part of the Pedlar's history, and finally inserted into Book I of *The Excursion*, the rhetoric of the beautiful shapes one of Wordsworth's most poignant early representations of human loss. With something like the furor that has marked debates about the relative merits of versions of *The Prelude*, readers of *The Ruined Cottage* and *The Pedlar* have frequently praised one version to dispraise another. Does the Pedlar impose a comforting buffer between the poet and human suffering by making Margaret the occasion for a display of his philosophic mind? Is his attitude toward Margaret ethical, is it poetic, can it be both? Rehearsing such questions is, I suggest, precisely what Wordsworth did as he told, then retold, her story.[11] As a story about losses for which the beautiful can offer no adequate compensation, it clearly calls for some species of aesthetic containment, however partial. Initially industrious, loving, and domestic, Margaret becomes a resonant, perhaps narcissistic image of how, in the Pedlar's words, "that which each man loved / And prized in his peculiar nook of earth / Dies with him or is changed, and very soon / Even of the good is no memorial left" *(RC, Ms. D, 69–72, p. 49)*.

More damaging still, it is Margaret who gradually despairs and becomes careless of the shelter she inhabits and provides. Beauty's habitations gradually disappear for her as she waits for her husband to return, then loses him to death, and finally lets go of what might be called mimetic faith: the conviction that the things of this world reflect the comforting, domestic hold that human beings would have on them and on each other.

The Pedlar's task in the 1798 version, and more insistently in 1799, is to recuperate Margaret's loss for language and poetry. He does so in 1799 by reading her story through natural emblems of loss – the empty cottage, its abandoned livestock, the spear-grass – and by putting aside the temptation to shut out "natural wisdom" and "natural comfort" (*RC*, Ms. B, 253–54, p. 56). Thus while the Pedlar's narrative reports the loss of meaning, it also identifies natural emblems as signifiers of such loss. The speaker makes this representational strategy explicit:

> He had rehearsed
> Her homely tale with such familiar power,
> With such countenance of love, an eye
> So busy, that the things of which he spake
> Seemed present, and, attention now relaxed,
> There was a heartfelt chillness in my veins.
> (*RC*, Ms. B, 266–71, p. 56)

No poet could ask for more evidence of his mimetic powers. In the 1799 text the Pedlar's concluding speech is more explicit about the aesthetic which supports those powers. Speaking of the spear-grass, formerly an image of the lack of human care for the cottage wall it had overgrown, he now insists:

> I well remember that those very plumes,
> Those weeds, and the high spear-grass on that wall,
> By mist and silent rain-drops silver'd o'er,
> As once I passed did to my heart convey
> So still an image of tranquillity,
> So calm and still, and looked so beautiful
> Amid the uneasy thoughts which filled my mind,
> That what we feel of sorrow and despair
> From ruin and from change, and all the grief
> The passing shews of being leave behind,
> Appeared an idle dream that could not live
> Where meditation was. (*RC*, Ms. D, 513–24, p. 75)

This association of beauty with a stillness beyond change rehearses one of the most emphatic refuges of the Wordsworthian beautiful. Stasis and "tranquillity" turn the mind and eye away from "ruin and change," whose natural signs the Pedlar has domesticated by making them the point of departure for his narrative. By echoing the end of *Lycidas*, the last lines of this version secure narrative and aesthetic closure. Bird melodies "peopled the air" and the speaker and Pedlar "attained[ ] / A rustic inn, our evening resting-place" (*RS*, Ms. D, 531–38, p. 75).

Wordsworth's revisions of Margaret's story show his early interest in the narrative consequences of what I have called his aesthetics of containment. In *Benjamin the Waggoner* (1819) and *The White Doe of Rylstone* (1815), poems he drafted between 1802 and 1808 then revised in manuscript, the hold of the Wordsworthian beautiful is more secure. To put this difference another way: the critical debate about Margaret's story accurately registers a tension that exists in all versions. In aesthetic terms, the reader's perspective on Margaret and the Pedlar's use (or misuse) of her story is divided between the ethos of coherence offered by the beautiful and its sublime negations. But in *Benjamin the Waggoner* and the *White Doe*, the beautiful successfully contains not only the tales these poems tell, but readers' response to them.

Benjamin the Waggoner

Benjamin the Waggoner succinctly demonstrates how much authority the beautiful gradually acquired in poems Wordsworth composed after the 1790s. Like all versions (including those written before 1800) of the poem Wordsworth published as *Guilt and Sorrow* in 1842, *Benjamin the Waggoner*[12] presents similar characters in similar straits – a discharged sailor, his wife, and child – to whom Benjamin gives the shelter of his wagon. But unlike the characters in all versions of *Guilt and Sorrow*, who either find no shelter or a temporary one where visions of the murdered dead trouble their rest, the family that Benjamin rescues does not have to spend the night at the top of Dunmail Raise, where the sailor's wife calls out "this storm that beats so furiously – / This dreadful place! oh pity me!" (223–24, p. 61). Her plea and the place, said to be the burial site of King Dunmail, echo the "female vagrant's" cry from her temporary refuge in "lonely spital" (where a murdered man is said to be buried) on Salisbury Plain. In the conclusion of the poem, the narrator emphasizes the shelter which Benjamin and his wagon once offered:

> The lame, the sickly and the old;
> Men, Women, heartless with the cold;
> And Babes in wet and starv'ling plight;

Which once, be weather as it might,
Had still a nest within a nest,
Thy shelter – and their Mother's breast.   (836–41, pp. 113, 115)

These images of shelter and rest for those otherwise bereft of them evoke familiar resonances in Wordsworth's aesthetics. Benjamin insures, or once insured, the "safety net" of human care that is a reiterated trait of the beautiful.

Were this all, the poem would simply reiterate aesthetic values already well established in earlier poems. But its tone and mock-heroic diction inaugurate a new degree of aesthetic containment with specific consequences for its reception. Charles Lamb's letter to Wordsworth on the occasion of the poem's publication in 1819 (Wordsworth dedicated it to Lamb) suggests what is at issue. Recalling his delight in the version he and other members of Wordsworth's immediate circle read in 1806, he praises its "spirit of beautiful tolerance." Others in this circle of family and friends later reiterate the key terms of Lamb's praise. Crabb Robinson notes in his diary that the tale is told with "grace" and "elegant playfulness."[13] However much Byron disliked the tale and Wordsworth's way of telling it,[14] Lamb and Crabb Robinson rightly call attention to the private climate of reception in which it was created. In doing so, they also indicate the public reception Wordsworth hoped the poem would have when he finally published it in 1819. The bridge between these two audiences is surely the printed dedication to Lamb, whose fondness for drink as well as those in need may have suggested a model for the character of Benjamin. If Wordsworth learned anything from the poor reception of his 1807 *Poems* he learned that how readers respond to a poem is part of its character as a poem. To be sure, he had been experimenting with problems of reception since the *Lyrical Ballads*,[15] yet the signal failure of sympathy among critics of the 1807 *Poems* did more than merely gall Wordsworth; it also spurred him to create a climate of reception for poems and sequences that would allow readers to engage them on his own terms.

The beautiful dominates this climate of reception in two ways. First, *Benjamin the Waggoner* and the *White Doe* emphasize the most obvious values of the beautiful – benevolence (Lamb's "spirit of beautiful tolerance") and social coherence. Second, their narrators shape refractory sublime figures and stories to other aesthetic ends by controlling potential ambivalences in ways that *Lyrical Ballads* speakers frequently do not. These later poems are not less interesting for being less ambivalent. Rather, their narrative control puts the other side of Wordsworth's poetic achievement in high relief. Seeing how these poems manage potential aesthetic conflicts tells us as much about Wordsworth's poetics of aesthetic containment as it does about other poetic occasions where he does not contain disturbing figures.

In *Benjamin the Waggoner* the greatest threat to the Wordsworthian beautiful is the story itself, since Benjamin and the kind of unofficial shelter he gave have disappeared when the poem begins. Yet the speaker makes this tension the place where readers are asked to do what Benjamin once did by adopting his (and the speaker's) "spirit of beautiful tolerance." Thus the images of shelter and rest with which the poem concludes are an invitation to readers to sympathize with what Benjamin was and did. Sympathetic reception is not sympathetic action, but it establishes the climate in which such action can take place.

The poem subtly registers the potential aesthetic conflict it masters in this fashion by having the sailor recall his part in the 1799 Battle of the Nile, Napoleon's spectacular early defeat and a major English naval victory. In 1806, when the poem was circulating in manuscript, only the most optimistic (or most desperate) could have been expected to read this defeat as a portent of Napoleon's ultimate defeat. As Wordsworth's 1806 sonnet on Napoleon's victory in the Battle of Jena ("Another year, another deadly blow") makes clear, this hoped for outcome was at the time anything but certain. Moreover, in 1799, as English observers noted with either chagrin or admiration, in part because Napoleon had astutely diverted public attention from the Nile defeat toward the diplomatic successes of his Egyptian campaign, he was made first consul soon after his return from Egypt.[16] In both versions of Wordsworth's poem, the narrator shows a surprisingly even-handed disregard for military heroics on either side of the Battle of the Nile, which the sailor describes during a drinking bout with Benjamin. By re-presenting this story in this way, the speaker undermines its heroic significance. Instead, mock-heroic values dominate the fictional space created by the sailor's story. As he reels back to Benjamin's wagon, the narrator compares him to "a hero, crown'd with laurel" (435, p. 79). However, the 1819 text also presents the battle itself (not the sailor's account of it) as "dismal conflict, and the might / And terror of that wondrous night!" (419–20, p. 77), making it sound like the battle between God and Satan in *Paradise Lost*. Because this revision admits Miltonic sublimity and "terror," it retrospectively declares the aesthetic containment at work in the earlier version, written at a time when the Battle of the Nile probably seemed little better than a pyrrhic victory against an otherwise invincible strategist. Apart from this revision, both versions minimize the value of the heroic sublime by having a drunken sailor and waggoner claim an heroic stature that neither exhibits. Their aesthetic and human value lies elsewhere.

The aesthetic stability of the poem is especially apparent in the narrator's playful, slightly mocking portrait of Benjamin. Since he represents the values of the beautiful, presenting him as a mock-heroic figure entails risks. By hazarding them, Wordsworth specifies the strength of his aesthetics of containment. Imitating the sailor's heroic self-image, Benjamin insists that he too is a "pilot" beset by many trials:

> I hate a boaster – but to thee
> Will say't, who know'st both land and sea,
> The unluckiest Hulk that sails the brine
> Is hardly worst beset than mine.   (523–26, pp. 87, 89)

To this the narrator wittily assents when he notes that Benjamin ties the sailor's model of Nelson's ship the *Vanguard* to the back of his wagon. He then deflates Benjamin's self-image by presenting his unlucky encounter with the irate owner of the wagon in mock-epic terms. At first, he explains, Benjamin and his companions are protected from discovery because they are hidden in mist:

> Never, surely, old Apollo,
> He, or other God as old,
> Of whom in story we are told,
> Who had a favourite to follow
> Through a battle or elsewhere,
> Round the object of his care,
> In a time of peril, threw
> Veil of such celestial hue;
> Interposed so bright a screen
> Him and his enemies between!   (683–92, p. 103)

The narrator sustains the mock-heroic epic analogy by presenting the owner's arrival as an event dictated by "malicious Fates" who refuse to be turned aside by divine ruses.

These devices, which insist that the story is subject to a light but deft control, ultimately make the narrator rather than Benjamin the figure on whom the aesthetics of the poem and its reception depends. Although the disappearance of Benjamin is the elegiac complaint of its conclusion, delight, not regret, dominates the tone. In the 1819 text several adjustments assist the narrator's invention of a pact with readers that extends the aura of benevolence which is the point of Benjamin's history. In the earliest manuscripts he addresses Benjamin familiarly and directly as "thou." But in the 1819 text, "thou" is changed to "he" to mark the narrator's detachment from the main character. In the conclusion of both texts, however, he calls the wag-goner "thee." In the 1819 version this *new* proximity of address retracts the narrative distance that had existed at the beginning of the poem. The effect of this reversal is to imply that despite Benjamin's absence, the narrator is somehow still close to him, or, more pre-cisely, to the "spirit of beautiful tolerance" his story illustrates. The agent of this new proximity is the text as it conveys the story of Ben-jamin to Wordsworth's reader. What the narrator hopes to achieve is made clear by the terms of his regret:

> In him, while he was wont to trace
> Our roads, through many a long year's space,
> A living Almanack had we;
> We had a speaking Diary,
> That, in this uneventful place,
> Gave to the days a mark and name
> By which we knew them when they came. (796–802, p. 111)

As a visible calendar or almanack, Benjamin insured continuity for the communities he visited. And because the text of this "speaking diary" was the need to care for human beings, its social and Burkean message is what the narrator wishes to transmit. Thus his repeated, stressed use of "we" suggests that as a member of those communities, he communicates values identified with Benjamin to those who never saw him. The full elegiac import of the conclusion is waylaid by this act of transmission, which insists that even though Benjamin is gone, his values remain. They are, moreover, those of the beautiful: dom-estic safety, social regard, and – through the narrator's projection of them into the circle of reception – permanence.

Like the female vagrant in versions of *Guilt and Sorrow*, Benjamin suggests how the Wordsworthian beautiful differs from its Burkean model and possibly corrects Napoleon's efforts to legislate the rights and duties of individuals to their society. As a comic figure whose weaknesses are as apparent in the narrative as his generosity and sociability, Benjamin presents a version of tradition and custom not much emphasized by Burke, who celebrates the intellectual and material inheritance of those best suited to govern. From a Burkean perspective Benjamin is rather someone who serves: he is not a "statesman" in the North of England, nor is the wagon he hauls (or its mastiff) his own. Moreover, the yeomanly service he does is not to his master (who fires him), but to the sailor, his family, and the social and human values which are the subject of the poem. Finally, the character of Benjamin may also suggest a more haphazard, more typically English alternative to the legislated civility of the Napoleonic code.[17]

The White Doe of Rylstone

When it was finally published in 1815, *The White Doe of Rylstone* still exhibited the "faults" which Coleridge had summarized in 1808 as "a disproportion of the Accidents to the spiritual Incidents," by which he meant the poem's lack of action and emphasis on spiritual values. Wordsworth probably chose not to publish the poem in the intervening years because of these objections, and because he feared more criticism from those who had attacked his two-volume *Poems* of 1807.[18] But after the poem appeared, he chose to regard what Coleridge had complained about as its achievement. In 1816 he wrote to Francis Wrangham:

Of the White Doe I have little to say, but that I hope it will be acceptable to the intelligent, for whom alone it is written. – It starts from a high point of imagination, and comes round through various wanderings of that faculty to a still higher, nothing less than the Apotheosis of the Animal, who gives the first of the two titles to the Poem. And as the Poem thus begins and ends, with pure and lofty Imagination, and every motive and impulse that actuates the persons is from the same source, a kindred spirit pervades, and is intended to harmonize, the whole.[19]

Wordsworth's tone is defensive in part because, as Peter Manning has suggested, Byron's slightly earlier (and much cheaper) *Corsair* had by this time outsold the more expensive quarto edition of the *White Doe*.[20] This marketplace rivalry also registers an aesthetic conflict between the values Wordsworth celebrates in the poem and the cult of the sublime outcast/hero which Byron's romances, including *The Corsair*, celebrate. The figure of Napoleon is implicated in this conflict, in part because he so obviously exemplified the traits of the sublime hero, but also because Wordsworth knew that Byron admired Napoleon. These concerns, or a version of them, are the implied context for the letter to Wrangham, which Wordsworth dated "Thanksgiving Day, 1816," that is January 18, the day set aside in national thanksgiving for Napoleon's final overthrow and the publication date for Wordsworth's "Thanksgiving Ode" on this occasion (*PW*, 3:155). As a romance that stubbornly refuses to affirm heroic values, the *White Doe* challenges revolutionary upstarts (and their commercial or military success). And, despite Wordsworth's diffident notice of the limited readership of the poem, one target of his anti-romance is a contemporary audience that was as eager to read about Napoleon's latest exploit as it was to read Byron's latest romance.

Like *The Borderers*, the *White Doe* deals with border rebellion, but its attitude towards the Rising of the North displays none of the ambivalence of the earlier work. Wordsworth insured this difference, in significant measure a difference in aesthetic perspective, by his choice of historical subject. Whereas he might more easily sympathize with the causes of the thirteenth-century Border Wars, his anti-Catholic views made his opposition to a rebellion of Northern Catholics against a Protestant monarch inevitable. Not surprisingly, the later poem echoes the dramatic situation of *The Borderers* to stabilize, if only retrospectively, its more troubled view of rebellion against an established social and political order. For example, like Mortimer's rebellion against Herbert, which expresses oedipal and generational jealousies, Emily's bitter complaint to her one Protestant brother Francis before their Catholic father leads all the sons into battle raises the possibility of a father–son struggle for authority: "might ever son *command* a sire, / The act were justified today" (*PW*, 3:297, ll. 450–51). But because Francis does not "command" his father, the structure of familial authority remains intact. This obedience stabilizes the larger rebellion against authority that Francis calls a threat to not only a "just and gracious queen," but to "a pure religion, and the claim / Of peace on our humanity" as well (*PW*, 3:295, ll. 285–88).

Wordsworth makes the aesthetic relation between the two poems explicit in the first motto for the 1837 edition of the *White Doe*. The first part is extracted from Rivers's *Borderers* speech about suffering, action, and infinity. Wordsworth completes it with a seven-line reply:

> "Action is transitory – a step, a blow,
> The motion of a muscle – this way or that –
> 'Tis done; and in the after-vacancy
> We wonder at ourselves like men betrayed:
> Suffering is permanent, obscure and dark,
> And has the nature of infinity,
> Yet through that darkness (infinite though it seem
> And irremoveable) gracious openings lie,
> By which the soul – with patient steps of thought
> Now toiling, wafted now on wings of prayer –
> May pass in hope, and, though from mortal bonds
> Yet undelivered, rise with sure ascent
> Even to the fountain-head of peace divine."   (*PW*, 3:283)

Like the poem for which it is a preface, the last half of the motto advances the values of the beautiful – its graciousness, peace, and theological authority – as a corrective to Rivers's code of sublime suffering and guilt. As a stratified text, the motto shows in linear fashion how the rhetoric or verbal landscape of the sublime can be transformed into the beautiful.

The pretext for this motto in 1837 and later editions, Wordsworth's dedicatory stanzas to Mary Wordsworth, inaugurates a chinese-box of reception with Rivers's sublime text inside. In effect, this placement subdues his sublime words before they are spoken.[21] The aesthetic stratigraphy of these stanzas goes back to 1808, when the Wordsworths read the story of the doe and Spenser's Una as parallel texts. As Wordsworth implies in these stanzas, between 1808 and 1815 the death of two Wordsworth children made it impossible for them to read either tale. But by 1815, with the added context of this intervening "sorrow," they reread the story of the doe in a climate more receptive to its powers of consolation (*PW*, 3:281–83). In short, because it describes Emily's suffering and eventual consolation, it comforts its family of readers as they had not needed to be comforted in 1808. As agent of this careful orchestration of contexts, the beautiful insures that this tale of border rebellion will be read from its perspective. Wordsworth suggests that this consolation is "needful when o'er wide realms the tempest breaks, / Needful amid life's ordinary woes" (*PW*, 3:282, ll. 53–54).

A similar aesthetic control within the poem insures that it will be read not as an affirmation of heroic romance but as a romance centered on different values. Its account of the Percy uprising is placed "off-stage" and reported to Emily by a family servant, not a returning combatant, after several characters and the narrator have proclaimed the wrong-headed futility of the enterprise. In symbolic terms as well, the uprising is an empty sign, or at least one defined by ironic negation. The Catholic banner which Francis Norton carries into battle is a sign of false, erring hopes, since he carries it to express family loyalty not to affirm the religious and political values it is intended to signify. As a standard bearer who believes the standard and what it signifies are rivals in folly, Francis vitiates a major convention of the chivalric romance. Having hollowed out the sublime, heroic center of this Scottish romance, Wordsworth creates a space which the beautiful gradually inhabits.

In the symbolic center of that space is the white doe, which acquires emblematic significance[22] as the Catholic banner which Francis Norton carries into battle is emptied of value. When she first appears, the narrator says

> White she is as lily of June,
> And beauteous as the silver moon
> When out of sight the clouds are driven
> And she is left alone in heaven;

Or like a ship some gentle day
In sunshine sailing far away,
A glittering ship, that hath the plain
Of ocean for her own domain.   (*PW*, 3:285, ll. 59–66)

The "Apotheosis of the Animal" begins here, as disarmingly conventional love conceits give way to similes which are less conventional. The first indicates that the doe, like the moon shining in a cloudless heaven, is a solitary figure. In the second, this figure displaces a satanic, Miltonic simile.

In the 1815 *Preface* Wordsworth uses Milton's comparison of Satan to the image of a fleet when seen from a distance ("so seem'd far off the flying fiend") to illustrate the powers of the imagination. The doe is uncannily (or cannily) like Milton's Satan. Whereas he is like a fleet seen "far off" (*Prose*, 3:31), she is like a ship "in sunshine sailing far away." Her mastery of the ocean setting is the more remarkable because she is just one ship which "hath the plain / Of ocean for her own domain." By contrast, the figure of Satan masters the landscape of Milton's poem because its size makes it look like an entire fleet.[23] The doe's mastery is subtly displayed by the difference in size. Her singularity is the aesthetic measure of her power to compose landscape and feeling, whereas Satan's absorbs the image of an entire fleet. In other words, he counterfeits a multitude, as one would expect of so Kantian a sublime figure. The aesthetic implication of the difference between Satan and the doe is striking. Whereas a beautiful figure focuses its surroundings, a sublime one absorbs them.

What is obvious and yet crucial about this is the emblematic visibility of the doe, announced early in the poem. "Couchant beside that lonely mound" (*PW*, 3:289, l. 203), she subverts the traditional heraldic significance of "couchant" animals. Unlike the lion's "couchant" posture, which indicates heroic and regal preparedness, the doe's indicates spiritual repose. Her form and actions are the key to her aesthetic value. To counter superstitious fears about why she visits Bolton Priory, the narrator explains "why she duly loves to pace / The circuit of this hallowed place" (*PW*, 3:289, ll. 204–5). The poetic closure of the homophonic end-rhyme emphasizes her value as a sign of the Wordsworthian beautiful. A similar cooperation between meter and rhyme foregrounds her figurative stability as a "beautiful form." She is, the narrator insists, "spotless, and holy, and gentle, and bright; / And glides o'er the earth like an angel of light" (*PW*, 3:290, ll. 236–41). As an emblematic, heraldic figure, she moves *as she is* to signify "a world of fixed remembrances / Which to this mystery belong" (*PW*, 3:290, ll. 209–10). No double-headed guidepost that

points in one direction toward unseen or unknown meanings, she is
Wordsworth's adequate emblem, an expressive container of her own
significance.

The doe's aesthetic office in the poem is to supplant not only
deluded heroic action, but the sublime despair which that action
leaves behind. In his farewell to Emily, Francis declares that the other
side of this rebellion is hopelessness and a "dark abyss" and he
wrongly predicts that the doe will abandon her after the Norton
family falls (*PW*, 3:299–300, ll. 532–65). His judgment of the role he
must perform out of family loyalty and his death exhibit a sublime
affect without a corresponding sublime elevation. Reluctantly taking
up the Norton banner, he feels "blank awe," "vacancy," and "horror
strong" (*PW*, 3:325, ll. 1387–88). After the battle he is mistaken for
a "traitor" and killed. For two days his body lies "unnoticed"
because, the narrator explains, "at that time bewildering fear /
Possessed the country, far and near" (*PW*, 3:329, ll. 1503–4). As that
which "bewilders" human beings such that they are unable to
perform fundamental human acts like burying and mourning the
dead, the sublime is here identified with disorder, and with actions
and signs like the Norton banner that err insofar as they do not or
cannot signify the truth. Wordsworth's anti-Catholic bias is evident
in this portrait of the Rising of the North as the folly of Catholic
renegades from a true state and church. But the irony of Francis's
death, which occurs because he carries a Catholic standard, argues a
more general (and fatal) semiotic disorder.

Sublime imagery also dominates the scene where Emily learns the
outcome of the battle:

> High on a point of rugged ground
> Among the wastes of Rylstone Fell,
> Above the loftiest ridge or mound
> Where foresters or shepherds dwell,
> An edifice of warlike frame
> Stands single – Norton Tower its name.
> It fronts all quarters, and looks around
> O'er path and road, and plain and dell,
> Dark moor, and gleam of pool and stream,
> Upon a prospect without bound.   (*PW*, 3:318, ll. 1163–72)

Offered as an emblem of Emily's inner desolation, the scene is an
accurate, if damning description of a sublime landscape. It is a "waste"
and the perspective from which the narrator describes it is so "high"
that it is "above ... / Where foresters or shepherds dwell." Norton
Tower stands "warlike" and "single," removed from human society
and its concerns. Its visual domination of the scene ("it fronts all

quarters") allows it to survey, in addition to the scene below, its own specular image – "a prospect without bound." The singularity of the tower discloses the dubious ethical perspective of sublime, visionary prospects. Both the setting and the tower's dominion over it signify futile, overweening military machismo. Unlike the singularity of the white doe, which draws others toward her, sublime singularity indicts the tower, the heroic code it represents, and the early nineteenth-century fascination with the sublime "singularity" of geological features or ancient architectural monuments.[24] In Wordsworth's text the association between singularity and the sublime remains, but its value is radically altered. Here it designates an unlawful, prideful rebellion.

The barrenness of sublime landscape and language also afflicts Emily after the rest of the Nortons are dead. She "wander[s]" the narrator suspects, in sublime, desolate places: sea, desert, perhaps an "island which the wild waves beat" (*PW*, 3:331, ll. 1555–65). She finally returns to Rylstone to "seek a haven / Among her native wilds of craven" (*PW*, 3:332, ll. 1617–18). The domesticating force of the "haven/Craven" rhyme makes "native wilds" a scene of refuge, and the proximity between "haven" and "heaven" indicates the theo-logical aura of this shelter. Before her return, the Norton mansion had become "a joyless human Being, / Of aspect such as if the waste / Were under her dominion placed" (*PW*, 3:331, ll. 1580–82). The curious emptiness of this personification indicates the figurative hazards of the sublime, which "wastes" figures by emptying them of meaning. In this instance, the contrary rhythms of the figurative gesture tend to obscure its outcome. In the guise of personifying the Norton mansion – having already de-personified it by noting that it "of its pride / Is stripped" (ll. 1575–76) – the narrator gives human attributes back to it. Yet these are at once negative ("as if a joyless human Being") and, more subtly, "naturalized" and thus literally de-personified, since the "aspect" is its "dominion" over the sur-rounding waste. Unlike the "characters of the great apocalypse" in *The Prelude*, VI, which give a divine "face" to the natural features of Gondo Gorge, the "aspect" of the Norton mansion is a de-humanized reflection of a desolate natural setting.

In Canto VII the return of the white doe reverses the impulse toward despair and vacancy which dominates the middle cantos of the poem. As if to provide a new, human "aspect," the white doe's first action is to lay its head on Emily's knee and give her "a look of pure benignity" (*PW*, 3:333, l. 1656). The narrator emphasizes the communicability of this look by calling the doe "a lovely chronicler of things / Long past"

whose "speaking face" communicates "promise" (*PW*, 3:334, ll.
1674–77). The fact that even after Emily's death the doe continues to
visit Francis's mound suggests precisely where the need for blessing
and comfort remains strongest – with Francis, whose life and death are
emblems of irony and despair. The doe gives Emily courage to visit his
grave and, while there, to return to the "abyss . . . /Of thought" (*PW*,
3:338, ll. 1821–22) that had preoccupied her there. Another revisitation the two make to Norton Tower hallows "the savage spot; /
Which Emily doth sacred hold / For reasons dear and manifold" (*PW*,
3:337, ll. 1798–1800).

The concluding lines of the poem emphasize the emblematic character of the doe as it lies near Francis's grave, a "Calm spectacle, by
earth and sky / In their benignity approved" (*PW*, 3:340, ll. 1903–4).
To the contrast between the doe and the ruin of Bolton Priory, the
narrator assigns a verse motto: "thou art not a child of Time, / But
Daughter of the Eternal Prime!" (*PW*, 3:340, ll. 1909–10). This
ecphrasis offers the doe to the reader as an emblem of the beautiful
whose human, social regard enables consolation. As a "daughter of
the Eternal Prime," the doe also replaces the temporal priority of the
sublime with a lineage that is, paradoxically, first or prime – the first
and yet timeless "hour" that organizes history in this poem. If this
aesthetic subversion saves the beautiful for eternity, it also jeopardizes
the sense of being in history and in time that marks its other
appearances in Wordsworth's poetry. This blurring of aesthetic
distinctions, which is more marked in later poems as Wordsworth
appears to grow less interested in aesthetic oppositions, may register
his uneasiness with the traditional and in 1815 still influential claim
that the sublime is the aesthetic of heroic and universal history. The
White Doe instead promotes an alliance between the beautiful and
history seen from the perspective of eternity.

1815 *Poems*

The aesthetics of reception implied by Wordsworth's classification in
the *Poems* of 1815 is modelled on that created for (and by) early
versions of the *White Doe* and *Benjamin the Waggoner*. Much as the
pre-publication reception of these poems in Wordsworth's immediate
circle secured their meaning as tales that console and unite readers, so
does the 1815 classification seek to engage readers by offering
relations between poems and categories which they interpret. Readers
who do so are double agents of the Wordsworthian beautiful: they
create a network of meaning and reception as they seek out the "order

and relation" between parts and wholes. The classification itself, a version of one Wordsworth described to Coleridge in 1809, is a curious mixture of chronological, political, and faculty-oriented categories. Its critical reception has been nearly as varied. Some editors have used it, others have put it aside. Some critics have dismissed it as inconsistent and clumsy.[25] Others have defended it without being able to agree about its organizing principle or principles.[26] As this reception history implicitly acknowledges, the 1815 classification exhibits no single principle because it has several. Collectively, they provide multiple, stratified contexts for Wordsworth's poems. From edition to edition, as he shuffled categories and poems within categories, their interrelations steadily increase, inviting readers to attend to differences and alliances within and among editions.[27]

As the poem which is last in the 1815 *Poems*, as it is in nearly every later edition in which it appears, the "Intimations Ode" summarizes the principal office of the beautiful in Wordsworth's classification.[28] As Manning observes, Wordsworth revised the ode after its first publication in the 1807 *Poems* because its obscurities had troubled readers, among them Crabb Robinson, who suggested he retitle it "to guide the reader to a perception of its drift." Beginning in 1815, Wordsworth retitled it "Ode: Intimations of Immortality from Recollections in Early Childhood." Manning explains that the new title is itself "an act of interpretation" which, together with the substitution of the three lines from "My Heart Leaps Up" for the ambiguous Virgilian motto (*paulo majora canamus*), "limited the rich equivocation" of the 1807 version.[29]

What interests me is the strategy of limitation. The 1815 epigraph from "My Heart Leaps Up" quells doubts put into textual and readerly play by its Virgilian predecessor. Whereas earlier readers were invited to sample the ode's ambiguities of faith and transcendence through a Virgilian lens which was itself ambiguous, after 1815 readers are "guided" by introductory material that asserts interpretive closure. Yet it is also the poem in the 1815 edition which brings its classification to full circle, as Gene Ruoff argues, by displaying most of the modes and generic shapes (or tendencies to shape) which the rest of the poems exhibit. And as a poem whose most prominent generic antecedent is the sublime ode from Milton to Gray, the "Ode: Intimations of Immortality" complexly enacts the aesthetic work required when the beautiful brings (or imposes) its sense of order and relation on texts which harbor thoughts "too deep for tears."[30] If these thoughts are less equivocally presented in the revised text, this version also shapes the ode to its rhetorical and aesthetic office in the 1815 classification – to "house" in brief compass what comes before. A hidden affiliation between this ode and early manuscripts of "On the Power of Sound" repeats the network of alliances on the surface of the 1815 classification. In 1837 Wordsworth said of the later poem: "when first printed in 'Yarrow Revisited', I placed it at the end of the Volume, and in the last edition of my Poems, at the close of the Poems of the Imagination, indicating thereby my own opinion of it." In several early manuscripts of "On the Power of Sound," its epigraph is *paulo majora canamus*, the epigraph deleted from the 1807 "Ode: Intimations of Immortality," also placed last in several editions.[31]

Within the classification the beautiful serves different categories, among them "Poems of the Affections" and "Poems of the Fancy." Similarly, while the sublime is for the most part sequestered among "Poems of the Imagination," it also emerges in other categories, such as "Epitaphs and Elegiac Poems" or "Inscriptions," and in isolated poems like "Michael," which Wordsworth placed among "Poems Founded on the Affections." The aesthetic implications of these placements (and displacements) tend to be most strongly marked among the "Poems of the Imagination." Here the beautiful may create a number of textual layers to provide a stratified context for a sublime figure, or the sublime may stand alone, with or without indications of its value; or Wordsworth may play one aesthetic against the other.

Few of the 1815 "Poems of the Imagination" are as explicit in their use of topographical differences to illustrate aesthetic values as "View from the Top of Black Comb," composed in 1813.[32] Much like the 1817 "Ode: Pass of Kirkstone," it contrasts sublime ascents with beautiful views. What is intriguing about this familiar Wordsworthian theme is the aesthetic response it triggers at the end of the poem. As a summit that "commands a more extensive view than any other point in Britain" – as Wordsworth tells the reader in a note, Black Comb is topographically sublime. In an early manuscript it is also a sublime goal for the traveller who "entertains a wish / By lofty place to elevate his soul" (*PW*, 3:289n.). By removing this designation from the published text, Wordsworth silences the sublime value he had at first given to this sublime prospect.

The logic of this suppression emerges as the speaker describes what happens to "Mona's Isle" as he climbs. Once a "lofty mount" whose "cultured fields" and "habitable shores" suggest a beautiful landscape, it soon becomes "a dwindled object, and submits." The speaker's use of "and" instead of a subordinate "which" or "that" makes it clear that the island has no control over this alteration in its visual prominence. The perceptual effect to which these lines refer – that views from different heights affect the apparent size of distant objects – is a commonplace in eighteenth-century discussions of landscape. Wordsworth's speaker uses it to mark the tyranny of the sublime eye, whose vistas are highly uncertain, variable perceptions. He asks, "Yon azure ridge, / Is it a perishable cloud? Or there / Do we behold the line of Erin's Coast?" (ll. 23–25). Of several pre-publication variants which de Selincourt does not record, Carl Ketcham notes that one substitutes "perishable" for "transitory."[33] Either adjective registers the instability of the sight; together they call attention to Wordsworth's effort to represent that instability as a sign which the speaker and an implied auditor cannot read unequivocally. When the speaker compares the "line of Erin's Coast" to a "land sometimes by the roving shepherd-swain / (Like the bright confines of another world) / Not doubtfully perceived" (ll. 26–28), he amplifies the uncertainty of sight and representation which sublime prospects encourage. A second 1815 variant, "wandering" for "roving," echoes a larger figurative code in Wordsworth's aesthetics. "Wandering" far from a known world and society is a sublime action, and one which is actionable in the stern regard of the Wordsworthian beautiful. Although the speaker perceives the "*confines* of another world" (my emphasis), this is all he can "not doubtfully" perceive.

I elaborate the hesitancies of these lines because they forecast the aesthetic posture of the last seven, where an infinite, sublime vista is presented in the language of the beautiful:

> Look homeward now!
> In depth, in height, in circuit, how serene
> The spectacle, how pure! – Of Nature's works,
> In earth, and air, and earth-embracing sea,
> A revelation infinite it seems;
> Display august of man's inheritance,
> Of Britain's calm felicity and power! (ll. 28–34)

Sublime limitlessness is notable for its absence from the passage, which emphasizes implied boundaries ("depth," "height, "circuit," and "earth-embracing sea"). The slight hedge of "a revelation infinite it seems" summarizes the aesthetic ambiguity of this sublimity, which projects an aura of enclosure and security that depends on the language of the beautiful. Other phrases ("serene," "calm felicity," and "display august of man's inheritance") which ally this beatified sublime to British imperial power indicate the Burkean stamp of this aesthetic conversion.

In the "French Revolution," the means of aesthetic conversion occupy the borders of the poem, where they urge a specific reception. Its full title, "French Revolution, As It Appeared to Enthusiasts at its Commencement. Reprinted from *The Friend*," and the brief note explaining its relation to the poem on his life transform the poem into a cautionary tale that retrospectively queries its speaker's uncontextualized enthusiasm for revolutionary beginnings (*PW*, 2:264). Framed by its title, note, and finally by the political context for its 1809 publication in *The Friend*, phrases in the poem like "pleasant exercise of hope and joy" and "seemed" echo with implied negations. Looking back through the layers of text and context that Wordsworth added after he composed the poem in 1804 (and through its 1804 text back to its multiple contexts), the reader sees the poem at the center (or at the end) of a series of frames that place the revolutionary sublime inside and in perspective. Much as he does in the *White Doe*, here Wordsworth relies on framing texts and, as Ruoff has observed, its placement among "Poems of the Imagination" to suggest that the values which the poem attaches to the sublime are not affirmed by its contexts.[34] These acts of placement are the work of the beautiful, which orders events and scenes over time to create a permanence different from that of the sublime, whose "duration" belongs to pre-history, not to the annals of recorded history suggested by Wordsworth's subtitle.

The problems sublime speakers create for texts and audiences are dramatized by the critical reception of "Gipsies," first published in 1807 and included among "Poems of the Imagination" in 1815. Since its publication readers have been incensed by its speaker's pompous, self-absorbed point of view. Coleridge indicted the poem as an instance of Wordsworth's "*mental* bombast" and Hazlitt mocked the once and former poet of "wise passiveness" for complaining about indolent gypsies. Half-criticizing Hazlitt's critique, Keats both allowed and disallowed what he assumed to be Wordsworth's crankiness, asserting that Wordsworth would never have written the poem if he had thought "a little deeper."[35] In "Gipsies" the speaker chastizes gypsies for staying in the "self-same spot" for more than a day as though unconscious of the passage of time that he observes in the movements of moon, sun, and stars. His irritation is barely tempered with condescension: "they are what birth / And breeding suffer them to be; / Wild outcasts of society" (*PW*, 2:227, ll. 26–28). Nor does he attach any value to their solidarity. The fact that they have remained in the "same unbroken knot," linked through its end rhyme with "self-same spot" (ll. 1–2), is likewise a target of his scorn. Isolated himself, he looks at a band of gypsies and charges that *they* are isolated from the values of work and community to which he displays no apparent connection.

David Ferry calls his "sublime arrogance." David Simpson observes that the "hyperbole of the sublime moment" in "Gipsies" sounds very much like the "vicious poetic diction" which Wordsworth had criticized in lines from Gray's "Sonnet on the Death of Richard West." The net effect of this rhetoric is, Simpson points out, a Brechtian alienation of speaker from situation, of reader from speaker. Ruoff argues that the speaker is Wordsworth, angry with the gypsies for "spoiling the view," and that the poem displays the "intolerance" of "Wordsworth's imagination."[36] Ruoff's claim makes perfect sense for the 1807 "Gipsies," which appears under the heading "Moods of My Own Mind" (*Poems, 1807,* 211). Wordsworth's relation to the speaker becomes less clear in 1815, when "Gipsies" joins several "Poems of the Imagination" whose speakers are half-refracted, exaggerated self-portraits, among them the captain of "The Thorn" and the revolutionary enthusiast of "French Revolution." For these one can make the case that Wordsworth understood his poetic excesses at least as well as Coleridge did.

By itself, however, "Gipsies" offers no counterforce, aesthetic or otherwise, to its sublime speaker. As wanderers who have no economic or social ties to a place and community, the gypsies show no more relation to the Wordsworthian beautiful than the speaker does. "Gipsies" shows what happens when a sublime speaker gets all the words. Without a title, an accompanying note, or the contextual pressure of a debate about gypsies akin to the one concerning rural poverty invoked by "Alice Fell"[37] – all of which Wordsworth supplies for "French Revolution" – the poem is a raw display of an unfettered sublime rhetoric that leaves neither the reader nor the gypsies any place to stand. By nature exclusive and excluding, the sublime admits neither contexts nor the need for them. "Gipsies" thus illustrates what Keats called the "wordsworthian or egotistical sublime" (although Keats didn't apply the term to this poem). As a critical exposition of sublime egotism, the poem also suggests why Wordsworth found it difficult to distinguish between sublime egotism and the transcendental regard of Kantian self-consciousness. From the perspective of the Wordsworthian beautiful, both look on human affairs as spectators from without.

Wordsworth's placement of "Gipsies" among "Poems of the Imagination" recognizes that sublime arrogance and hyperbole belong to the imagination. Whether these are its only attributes is another matter. Its 1815 placement and Wordsworth's successive instructions to the printer of the 1807 *Poems* for its placement in that edition also register several views of its sublime rhetoric. Wordsworth initially instructed the printer of the 1807 edition to place it before "To the Cuckoo," then decided that it should instead precede "The Sparrow's Nest." Each of these 1807 placements argues a different climate of reception for "Gipsies" as a mood of the poet's mind. Its temporary placement before "To the Cuckoo," the poem Wordsworth cites to illustrate the imaginative power of poetic figures in the 1815 *Preface*, emphasizes the value of sublime figures and vision. But its final 1807 placement implies a different assessment. Whereas the speaker of "Gipsies" categorically dismisses the "knot" of gypsies as insignificant wastrels, the speaker of "The Sparrow's Nest" praises the "simple sight" of a nest whose synonyms ("home," "shelter'd bed," "dwelling") employ figures of the Wordsworthian beautiful (*Poems, 1807, 212–13*). In 1807 the contrast between these moods of the poet's mind is aesthetic: the first offers a sublime perspective, the second a beautiful one.

In 1815 this aesthetic contrast evaporates. "The Sparrow's Nest" joins "Poems of the Affections," where it remained until 1845. In the 1815 "Poems of the Imagination," "Gipsies" precedes "Beggars," another poem about the wandering poor. This new placement invites closer attention to the sublime vision of "Gipsies." In "Beggars" the speaker tells of giving money to a strikingly beautiful woman who begs for help, telling a tale of poverty which he thinks improbable. Later in the same day he meets two of her children, who also beg for money, claiming that their mother is dead. Since their resemblance to the mother is obvious, he scolds them for lying and they run off. In both poems the speaker's relation to his subject is barely a relation, since each sees gypsies or beggars across social and economic barriers that preclude his access to knowledge about his subject. The principal difference between them is not so much that the speaker of "Beggars" *talks* to the beggars (although this effort is one sign of this difference), but that he implicitly acknowledges his lack of knowledge when he wonders about the woman's history and, in a later pendant poem, about what has happened to the boys (*PW*, 2:225). No cloud of unknowing afflicts the speaker of "Gipsies," whose confident dismissal of his subject is made more apparent in 1815 by its difference from the poem that follows it. In short, the circle of reception created by the 1815 classification hems in the sublime vision and rhetoric of "Gipsies" by inviting comparisons between it and other "Poems of the Imagination" and, more proximately, between its view of its subject and that of "Beggars."

Praised by most readers but mentioned by only a few since Coleridge, "Yew-Trees" seems to invite Crabb Robinson's puzzled response to it and "Nutting": "they are fine, but I believe I do not understand in what their excellence consists." Coleridge believed the excellence of "Yew-Trees" is its last half, which he quoted to show Wordsworth's poetic greatness. Several recent critics offer quite different accounts of the poem. Ruoff reads its descriptions of the single yew and the Borrowdale group as signs that refer to "radically discontinuous structures of experience." Michael Riffaterre argues that referential claims about the meaning of its descriptions deny or neglect the "verbal structures" or "codes" that make poems poems. By emphasizing the ghostliness of the poem's figures and speaker, Geoffrey Hartman's reply to Riffaterre suggests why we too may wonder in what the excellence of "Yew-Trees" consists.[38]

Although the referentiality of the poem is not as precarious as Riffaterre contends, "Yew-Trees" is undeniably reticent about what it means and who its speaker is. As Hartman points out, because the impersonal syntax of its opening line ("There is a Yew-tree, pride of Lorton vale") is noncommittal about the speaker's authority for making this statement, readers are tempted to forget the poem has a speaker, much as Riffaterre does in his structuralist reading.[39] I suspect that the poem's odd reticence about its speaker and subject assists two related strategies. The first is its foregrounding of differences between the single yew and the Borrowdale group. This strategy becomes more evident in successive revisions of the poem, from an extant draft Wordsworth probably composed in 1804 to the published version that appeared among "Poems of the Imagination" in 1815. Wordsworth's revisions, particularly those he made after 1811, record beauty's figurative capture of the sublime figure with which the poem begins. As Robert Scholes says of deconstructionist premises about reading texts: "the text cannot say all it means, because its meanings are enabled by its silence on some crucial point."[40] Wordsworth's pre-publication drafts of "Yew-Trees" display then conceal tensions about which the published poem is half-silent. The second strategy is invitational. Because the speaker is reticent about the meaning of the ghostly personifications that haunt the Borrowdale group, the poem invites readers to make their reading of these figures part of the poem's familiar (or fraternal) gesture toward shared meaning.[41] Oddly poised between their traditional names as personified trees of mourning (Fear, Hope, Death, etc.) and their conviviality, they at once encourage and check the reader in the act of reading them.

In the earliest manuscripts the phrase "pride of Lorton Vale," which names the single yew, has pride of place in either the opening lines or the provisional title. This phrase disappears from the first of two drafts composed after 1811, but it reappears in the next draft and in the published text in approximately the same location as before. A parallel series of revisions marks the emergence of the transitional phrase of the final text, "But worthier still of note / Are those fraternal Four of Borrowdale." In the first three manuscripts, the speaker says lamely (and none too clearly), "nor those fraternal Four in Borrowdale." The gist of the sought-after contrast emerges in the next version, which adopts the transition of the published text. In short, although the phrase "pride of Lorton Vale" is at first given prominence in the poem, it disappears briefly and then reappears in the first version to specify the hierarchy of values which subordinates the single yew and its epithet to the Borrowdale group.

The aesthetic logic of this subordination is implied by the structural imbalance of the earliest manuscript, which gives the single yew three lines and the Borrowdale four the rest. The second manuscript adjusts the imbalance by adding lines which explain that the yew has contributed weapons to various wars. In this version, probably the most intriguing of the pre-publication texts, the transitional "nor" (which later gives way to "But worthier still of note . . .") is cluttered with cancelled lines which point back to the solitary yew, followed by an interlinear addition, "joined in the solemn and capacious grove," the line that follows the new transition in the published text. The aesthetic trajectory of these changes is, I suggest, governed by the speaker's initial reluctance to elaborate the meaning of the yew and, when he does, his equal reluctance to turn from that meaning.

Isolated in its own "darkness," the single yew has for centuries furnished weapons to various wars, some of which, like the Percy uprising, are rebellions whose legitimacy Wordsworth questions in *The Borderers* and again in the *White Doe*. DeQuincey makes a similar claim about the "savage grandeur" of trees on the Lonsdale estate in his biographical sketch of Wordsworth's childhood. These trees were, he suggests, "coeval with the feuds of York and Lancaster, yews that possibly had furnished bows to Coeur de Lion."[42] Two buried allusions to Wordsworth's tragedy extend the antithetical relation between the single yew and the Borrowdale grove. Early in *The Borderers* Mortimer tells Rivers that he used to listen to Matilda tell about her father's adventures as they sat near a thorn which had sprouted from the churchyard wall in Lorton. Robert Osborn notes that this thorn is in fact the yew described in "Yew-Trees" (*B*, 80 and 80n.). As a tree which was just six years old at the time of the Border

Wars and one which Mortimer associates with the nexus of love and oedipal rivalry that Rivers later directs to his own purposes, this thorn/yew is thus from its origin identified with rebellion. Its antagonism to the grove is suggested by a second buried allusion. In his early preface "On the Character of Rivers," Wordsworth calls Rivers the kind of villain who "lays waste the groves that should shelter him" (*P. Bord.*, 63). In "Yew-Trees" the aura of antagonism is effaced or minimized to allow the figurative difference between the single yew and the grove to take precedence.

The age and duration of the single yew merit special attention. "Produced too slowly ever to decay," its "form and aspect" are "too magnificent / To be destroyed." So presented, the yew is a sublime figure whose visual surroundings echo its hiddenness and negativity. As he does not in the published text, in later years Wordsworth specifies the aesthetic resonances of the "durability" of the yew. In a Fenwick note he suggests it must be "as old as the Christian era," then reports an old guide's claim that it had without a doubt existed "before the flood" (*PW*, 2:503–4n.). The last remark, safely attributed to a speaker whose authority is equivocal, identifies the yew with Wordsworth's most reiterated sublime landscape and figure. The final text of the poem is more reticent, yet it clearly designates the satanic and Miltonic aura of the yew's sublimity by noting its "vast circumference and gloom profound," its revolutionary past, and its pride (*PW*, 2:210, ll. 4–13).

In the second manuscript the last two of these traits are linked just at the point in the text when its speaker approaches the ungainly transition "nor." Lined out and replaced with the more admiring notice of its magnificence and duration which the published text retains, the phrase "Obdurate and invincible appears this" is followed by notice of its solitary, living nature and this half-completed (and lined out) thought about its origin: "produced, so calculating thought might deem." For what purpose the yew might have been deliberately produced the manuscript does not say, although the implied answer is "to provide weapons of war." This more critical presentation of the yew is minimized in subsequent versions, which give the same history more succinctly and dispassionately. Because brevity and dispassion stabilize the inherent passion and expressiveness of the sublime, they mark the speaker's effort to tell what the yew is without getting absorbed by its sublimity.

In "Yew-Trees" topographical placement is a visible figure for the aesthetic difference between the single yew and four yews of Borrowdale. As Ruoff also observes, the yew is isolated in its place and history, whereas the four yews display a familial proximity to each other and to Borrowdale.[43] Moreover, as the "pride of Lorton Vale," the yew is at once located and unlocated. The synecdoche "pride," the middle term between the yew and Lorton Vale, specifies their relation by a two-step figurative displacement. The vale has pride and the figure of that pride is the yew. Or, the yew belongs to the vale by virtue of its role as an image of the pride of the vale. In either direction the identity of the yew depends on an intervening figure, whereas the parallel phrase "fraternal Four of Borrowdale" has no intervening term. Rather it personifies the four yews by making their location a figure of residence. They are "of Borrowdale," as one might say William Wordsworth was "of Grasmere." That is to say, they belong to a place as human beings might. This attribution of a local habitation and a name depends on a different aesthetic and structure of representation. Whereas the yew is sublimely "other," its meaning displaced metonymically onto other places in the past which it retroactively absorbs, the Borrowdale "Four" are at home. They speak for and of figures that aspire to contain meaning rather than those that work to displace it. In short, they belong to the Wordsworthian beautiful, whose powers they exhibit.

Their principal aspect, to which the text repeatedly refers, is the extent to which they contain the figures that gather there. Like the "huge trunks" themselves, each "a growth / Of intertwisted fibres serpentine / Up-coiling, and inveterately convolved" (ll. 16–18), the ghostly personifications that congregate in the grove of yews collect rather than disperse their meaning. Fear, Hope, Silence, Foresight, Death the Skeleton, and Time the Shadow belong together as participants in the funereal code to which yews belong in the English landscape garden. Their referentiality is important for what it reveals about the figurative enterprise sanctioned by the Borrowdale Four. On this point Riffaterre is quite right: readers of these personifications who have tried to impale them as allegorical presences have overshot the mark,[44] as indeed the contrast between Wordsworth's grove of yews and the one Addison offers in his "Allegoric Vision" implies. As the antechamber to a "Grotto of Grief," Addison's "Grove of Yeugh-Trees" is presented as a generic figure for groves "which love to over-shadow Tombs and flourish in Church-Yards." And in this allegoric vision the "inhabitants" of the place evidently take its identification with grief seriously, wailing and tearing their hair at the feet of the trees. Wordsworth's scrutiny of Addison's views on gardening and landscape suggests that the appearance of Addison's archaic spelling "yeugh-trees" in all but one pre-publication manuscript of Wordsworth's poem is probably not accidental (*Poems, 1807*, 665–67). But the real wit of the allusion is the difference between the two allegoric visions. Wordsworth's "Yew-Trees" loosens the clipped allegorical representation of Addison's vision, much as the clipped yews of the earlier box or knot garden yield to the meditative groves of the English landscape garden.[45]

To the degree to which the allegorical names in Wordsworth's poem matter, they constitute a witty aesthetic turn on both Addison and the sublime. At least one of them, Fear, ought to belong to the sublime. And several of them could belong to the overtone series established in the poem for the revolutionary or warlike sublime. But they do not. Instead they sociably gather in a grove to mark an enabling aesthetic cooperation between figurative meaning and description. In his influential treatise on the "modern" English landscape garden, Thomas Whateley argues that "beauty" is the essential character of a grove because of its "assemblage" of trees.[46] The assembled generosity of Wordsworth's grove and its figures is the subject of the concluding lines. Meeting in a sacred place "to celebrate" in "united worship" is what we might expect of them. But when we read that they may also gather "in mute repose / To lie, and listen to the mountain flood / Murmuring from Glaramara's inmost caves" (ll. 31–33), we discover their remarkable security and volubility *as figures*. Here the tyranny of the sublime eye is banished as visual personifications gather in silence to listen to the personified sound of a "murmuring" flood, secure in their capacity to respond to other figures in the poetic landscape to which they belong. Unlike sublime figures and speakers, who absorb or deny their surroundings so that they may be isolated in their own darkness, beautiful figures are receptive, even sociable. The Borrowdale four are "worthier still of note" precisely because they entertain and contain such figures.

In editions of Wordsworth's poems published after 1815, placement is, like revision and shifts in aesthetic perspective, a way to "stratify" the meaning of poems by embedding them in categories and collections which exert metatextual pressures on the poems which are the "parts" of their "wholes." Such pressures could and often did multiply each time Wordsworth inserted new poems or shifted poems from one category to another. Here one example must suffice. In 1817, Wordsworth composed an "Ode" which he finally titled "Composed upon an Evening of Extraordinary Splendour and Beauty." First published in the 1820 *Poems*, where its title is simply "Evening Ode," it remained among "Poems of the Imagination" until 1837, when it assumed its present title and position among "Evening Voluntaries."

In a note Wordsworth explains that "allusions to the Ode entitled 'Intimations of Immortality' pervade the last stanza" (*PW*, 4:13). In fact, they pervade the poem. Somewhere between a code and a gloss, the "Evening Ode" shapes the reader's reception of the earlier ode – which it *precedes* in all editions – much as Coleridge's gloss to *The Rime of the Ancient Mariner* tries to shape the reader's reception of the mariner's tale.[47] Because Wordsworth's 1817 ode converts images of sight and vision in the earlier ode by revising their aesthetic value, it demonstrates one extension of beauty's offices beyond 1815.

As the poem begins, the speaker explains how he would have reacted if the "effulgence" of the evening had been momentary: "I might have sent, / Among the speechless clouds, a look / Of blank astonishment" (*PW*, 4:10, ll. 1–4). This imagined "look" and the lack of speech attributed to the clouds register the sublimity which might have been had the scene "disappeared with flying haste." Because it does not, it is an enduring spectacle within the fictional space of the poem. As an attribute of the sublime which Wordsworth often transfers to the beautiful after 1800, permanence signals the aesthetic preference of the poem, which banishes the sublime by making it a condition contrary-to-fact. The phrase "speechless clouds," which personifies the clouds even as it takes human speech away, witnesses the anti-figurative impulse which the speaker assigns to the sublime as the aesthetic of "blank" looks and emptied figures. Moreover, the duration of the scene implicitly challenges the transience ("fallings from us, vanishings") which is the double focus of loss and recompense in the "Intimations Ode."

The 1817 ode most explicitly subverts the earlier ode by redefining its principal figures of sight and vision. Now "gleam" (l. 19) is part of what the speaker *sees*, not what has "fled," and "vision" designates remarkable clear-sightedness:

> Far-distant images draw nigh,
> Called forth by wondrous potency
> Of beamy radiance, that imbues
> Whate'er it strikes with gem-like hues!
> In vision exquisitely clear,
> Herds range along the mountain side;
> And glistening antlers are descried;
> And gilded flocks appear.   (*PW*, 4:11, ll. 25–32)

Strikingly unlike the mists and clouds that obscure sight or deceive the perceiver in some Romantic poems,[48] including Wordsworth's, this atmosphere clarifies vision. By a sleight-of-eye, "far-distant images draw nigh," so "nigh" that the speaker can identify details. The scene surpasses imagined "choirs of fervent Angels" which, he insists, "could not move / Sublimer transport, purer love, / Than doth this silent spectacle" (*PW*, 4:10–11, ll. 11–19). However briefly, what is seen challenges what is imagined but not seen. Looking up at a mountain ascent ("those bright steps that heavenward raise / Their practicable way"), he is content to be "rooted here" at "this transcendent hour" (*PW*, 4:12, ll. 50–60). Thus if the experience is visionary and transcendent, it is "rooted" in what can be seen and is known.

The prayer the speaker offers to the "Dread Power! whom peace and calmness serve / No less than Nature's threatening voice" (ll. 69–70) replaces the Biblical echo used in one manuscript variant, where this power is presented as one "whom storms and darkness serve, / thunder or the still small voice." The published text excises this echo of Elijah's description of the coming of the Lord as "a still, small voice," gives precedence to "peace and calmness," and declares their equal status with "Nature's threatening voice" as servants of divine power. The diction of this version occupies an unsettled middle ground between Wordsworth's earlier vocabulary of sublimity and power and his mature identification of beauty and a beautified sublime (i.e. without fear) with God. Years later in a brief "Prelude" to his *Poems, Chiefly of early and late years* (1842), he offers readers a similar "promise of a calm, / Which the unsheltered traveller might receive / With thankful spirit." And, as Wordsworth argues in poems early as well as late, the collective source of this calm is "reason," "love," and "beauty / Lodged within compass of the humblest sight" (*PW*, 4:176–77, ll. 8–10, 29–39).

Other poems and their revisions, among them *Peter Bell*, reiterate Wordsworth's preference for the beautiful and its aesthetics of containment. Buried sublime figures and fears are not just suppressed or displaced; they are thoroughly re-contextualized.[49] This aesthetic strategy extends Wordsworth's earliest experiments in *Lyrical Ballads* with poetic speakers and their hearers. It also shows how readers as well as figures are transformed by the poetic climate of the Wordsworthian beautiful.

7

"Family of Floods"

FROM EARLY TO LATE, in major as well as minor poems, Wordsworth represents the unstable character of the sublime in images of floods, torrents, and waterfalls.[1] Collectively these images and the poems in which they appear summarize the turns and counter-turns of his aesthetics. The last of them, the 1824 sonnet "To the Torrent at Devil's Bridge. North Wales," offers a retrospective reading of these images as a "family of floods." The phrase reveals the aesthetic conversion which this sonnet advances: the beautiful neutralizes the semiotic errancy of the sublime by making it serve a "family" of topographical and finally historicizing resemblances. Three other poems, "Lines composed a few miles above Tintern Abbey," "Composed at Cora Linn in Sight of Wallace's Tower," and "The Jungfrau and the Fall of the Rhine near Schaffhausen," illustrate earlier moments in this history of aesthetic conflict and its containment.

In part Wordsworth's use of floods, torrents, and waterfalls as sublime figures extends an aesthetic and pictorial tradition that begins with Longinus, whose use of *torrent* as an image of uncontrolled passions is allied to Wordsworth's. Longinus argues that a "chain" of metaphors is appropriate to the sublime style precisely because it represents passions which are "so much worked up, as to hurry Like a Torrent, and unavoidably carry along with them a whole crowd of metaphors." Repeating the literal and metaphorical crossings of meaning embedded in this statement, he adds that it is the "nature" of "the pathetic and the sublime . . . to run rapidly along, and carry all before them, so they require the Figures they are worked up in to be strong and forcible."[2] This, I suggest, is the figurative work performed by Wordsworth's images of floods, torrents, and waterfalls. Collectively they assist the aesthetic conversion that hovers in Longinus's statements about the relation between sublime passion and its constraining figures. From the perspective which the sublime authorizes, sublime passions produce sublime figures; but from the perspective of the beautiful, the figures articulate the passion.

In his reading of "Yew-Trees," Michel Riffaterre has argued that in this and other poems these images belong to a recurrent " 'sound of waters' structure" which translates the act of "looking at" into "listening to."[3] I would add that this translation occurs gradually. Earlier poems present looking at and listening to as separate, non-competitive spheres of activity, the first conducive to public discourse and meaning, the second to private or interior contemplation. But in poems such as "Yew-Trees" and "To the Torrent at Devil's Bridge," the activity of "listening to" establishes the poetic powers of sound over sight. I disagree, however, with Riffaterre's further claim that this translation produces mere "noise" or "sound," as though Words-worth's images of sound were a mantra-like hum, or tenors no longer (or never) in search of vehicles. In all the poems that belong to Wordsworth's "family of floods," what is listened to is not an a-referential or self-referential poetic voice, but one whose recurrent naming of images composes the stratified history of his aesthetics. Although their referentiality tends to be masked as long as visual or topographical resemblances take up the foreground of reading, it is widely indexed in these poems.

Among the poems where these images appear, "Tintern Abbey" is the most deliberately personal, more intensive than extensive in its declared range of reference. Yet it exemplifies the relation between scene and revisitation that is the rhetorical occasion for all four poems. As its speaker suggests, and as Wordsworth reminds readers when he quotes lines from the poem to justify his 1815 classification, "Tintern Abbey" partly recalls the "state of mind when 'the sounding cataract / Haunted me like a passion' " (*Prose*, 3:29), when the eye or the pleasures of sight tended to dominate. In later years, both the haunting and the passion altered as waterfalls and floods became "dual signs"[4] of liberty and revolutionary disorder. This turn from sight to sign is mediated by sound, not as an "empty" sign but as one whose resonating properties signify the semiotic project of Wordsworth's aesthetics.

In an 1812 letter to Mary Wordsworth, he adds another layer of private resonance to the 1798 poem. Writing to her just before she visited the Wye scene for the first time, he quotes the earlier poem (without quotation marks): "O Sylvan Wye thou Wanderer through the woods how often has my Spirit turned to thee!" then continues, "I shall now have a thousand added reasons to think of this Stream with tenderness when I know that you are pacing its banks."[5] And in another letter replying to her reply, Wordsworth says that he had been reading "Tintern Abbey" at Lamb's "and repeated a 100 times to myself the passage [this time with quotation marks] 'O Sylvan Wye thou Wanderer through the woods,' thinking of past times, & Dorothy, dear Dorothy, and you my Darling."[6] Here the phrase repeated from the poem and his preceding letter mediates their temporary separation by extending the network of connections which the poem asserts. This strategy of repetition also extends the figure of address in the poem to include Mary as well as Dorothy Wordsworth. Finally, in this passionate love letter to his wife, Wordsworth uses the poem rather than the scene to represent that passion. This assignment of passion to a poetic *topos* whose resonances are prompted but not controlled by recalling the Wye scene and Mary Wordsworth's intended visit is crucial because it displays the figurative intent of this and other Wordsworthian revisitations.

"Composed at Cora Linn in Sight of Wallace's Tower"

Like many other tourists who visited Cora Linn, a famous waterfall in Scotland, Wordsworth commemorated a return visit in 1814 by writing a poem which, he later asserted, expressed "feelings" about the scene which he had had on earlier visits.[7] Some of those feelings probably derive from his second visit to the scene in 1803, in the company of Dorothy Wordsworth and Coleridge. In her *Journal* of this tour, Dorothy Wordsworth recalls that as they returned from a viewpoint below the falls, they stopped higher up to look again, resting on a bench "placed for the sake of one of these views." There they met, she wryly comments, "more expeditious tourists than we," a couple who had proceeded directly to the view above the falls, much like modern tourists who stop briefly to look at the Grand Canyon before going on to Los Angeles. When the two groups met again still farther up the path, the "gentleman" called the waterfall *"majestic."* At first Coleridge was delighted with the accuracy of this epithet because, Dorothy Wordsworth explains, "he had been settling in his own mind the precise meaning of the words grand, majestic, sublime, etc., and had discussed the subject with Wm. at some length the day before." But when the gentleman amiably proposed two more epithets for the scene – "sublime and beautiful" – Coleridge "could make no answer."[8] Either he was plagued by similar encounters, or he altered the story with each retelling. In one version, Coleridge locates the scene at "the celebrated cataract of Lodore" near Keswick. Now the offending tourist is "a lady of no mean rank" who exclaims that the waterfall is "sublimely beautiful, and indeed absolutely pretty."[9]

Wordsworth's silence about an incident that Coleridge and Dorothy Wordsworth both record suggests an important difference in his aesthetic response to this scene and others like it. Whereas Coleridge used the incident to illustrate the need for precise aesthetic terminology, Wordsworth used this kind of scene first to indicate the problematic nature of the sublime and later to specify its competition with the beautiful. Unlike Thomas Campbell's 1837 poem commemorating his return visit to this scene, Wordsworth's "Composed at Cora Linn in Sight of Wallace's Tower" (PW, 3:100) is not primarily concerned with his (or anybody else's) response to the waterfall, but with its visual and figurative relation to Wallace's Tower.[10] The vehicle for the speaker's tentative affiliation between this tower as a sign of sublime rebellion against tyranny and the "flood" of the River Clyde at Cora Linn is the sound of the "flood," which echoes in "caves [that] reply with hollow moan," making Wallace's Tower "vibrate[ ] to its central stone" (ll. 4–6). Other lines that identify Wallace with "sublime" rebels like Leonidas and William Tell (ll. 20, 41, 45) create a slight but important link between floods and sublime revolt. Since Wordsworth uses this figure in other poems to signify sublime tyranny, the motive for his figurative hesitancy in this poem is probably political as well as aesthetic.

"The Jungfrau and the Fall of the Rhine near Schaffhausen"

Wordsworth's several commemorations of the Rhinefall, a Swiss scene that was celebrated among contemporary travellers and artists, elaborate the resonances he gradually attached to this and other "torrents." One modern historian dismisses the return of English travellers to Switzerland after Napoleon's defeat as an event prompted by the romantic taste for "le spectacle des torrents et des cascades".[11] This dismissal neglects an obvious but salient point: English tourists returned to Switzerland in greater numbers *after* Napoleon's final defeat in part because his earlier subjugation of the Swiss had infuriated them.[12] Wordsworth's second visit to the Rhinefall in 1820 is a case in point. Between 1790, when he and Robert Jones visited the scene, and 1820, when he returned with Mary and Dorothy Wordsworth and other companions, the Rhinefall became a major *topos* of the Wordsworthian sublime, signifying both Swiss resistance and French tyranny.

In 1790 Wordsworth wrote to his sister that his first visit to the Rhinefall had disappointed him because, as he put it, "I had raised my thoughts too high."[13] This phrasing reveals how thoroughly his aesthetic expectations were conditioned by contemporary discussions of the sublimity of this scene, including the account in William Coxe's *Travels in Switzerland*, which Wordsworth and Jones frequently consulted during their 1790 tour.[14] Both the verb *raised* and the complement *too high* are commonplace in eighteenth-century definitions of the sublime. So, on his first visit Wordsworth expected to experience sublimity but did not. Yet years later in his essay on aesthetics, he used the Rhinefall – a large rock or rocks which jut up where the waters of the Rhine drop down about 100 feet – to illustrate how the mind experiences the sublime.[15] And in the 1822 edition of his *Guide*, he identifies the same scene as an exception to his general rule that Alpine waterfalls do not usually impress travellers with the idea of sublimity.[16] Between 1790 and 1820, then, his response to the Rhinefall changed from disappointment that he experienced no sublimity to admiration for its capacity to impress him with its sublimity.

If visual cues were the key to Wordsworth's aesthetic response, he need not have been disappointed in 1790. Coxe is quite clear that to get "the most sublime point of view" of the falls travellers should cross the Rhine at Schaffhausen or below the falls and look at it from the right bank. The left bank offers a very different view, one which a much reprinted nineteenth-century guidebook called "disappointing."[17] Of this view, Coxe says:

Hitherto I had only viewed the cataract obliquely; but here it opened by degrees, and displayed another picture, which I enjoyed at my leisure, as I sat down upon the opposite bank.[18]

Whereas from the right bank the falls block out views of the surrounding landscape, from the left they are part of a widened scene which Coxe and later travellers enjoyed at their "leisure," hence without feeling the admiration and qualified fear which Wordsworth and earlier writers identified with the sublime. Wordsworth's 1790 account of his visit suggests that he did not follow Coxe's advice but continued along the left bank of the Rhine from Schaffhausen above the falls to a point several miles beyond them.[19] Although he and Jones could have crossed the river briefly just below the falls – where boats were docked and for hire by the late 1790s – if they did, what Wordsworth saw still disappointed him. If he did not cross the Rhine below the falls, one reason for his disappointment may have been visual. Yet I doubt this, in part because his description of the 1790

Plate 2 S. Alken. *Falls of the Rhine*. 1787. In William Coxe, *Travels in Switzerland* (London, 1796). Sterling Memorial Library, Yale University.

route suggests that he did not cross the Rhine near the falls, but more particularly because thirty years later he chose to cross and re-cross the Rhine just below the falls, as though he wished to be certain to experience what he had not experienced in 1790. As Dorothy Words-worth explains in her *Journal* of the 1820 tour, this time he canvassed all the locations which Coxe mentions, first crossing below the falls with Mary and then returning to the left bank with Dorothy. Like Coxe, Dorothy Wordsworth emphasizes her impression of the subli-mity of the scene from views high on the right bank and in the middle of the river below the falls. As she crossed the Rhine with her brother in "that small unresisting vessel," she felt "helplessness and awe" but "not fear."[20] This reaction, which parallels the one Wordsworth describes for the same scene in "The Sublime and the Beautiful," suggests that both made the 1820 visit an occasion for reading the Rhinefall as a scene for their aesthetic instruction.

The older Wordsworth's wish to experience sublimity at the Rhine-fall probably owes something to paintings and engravings of the scene which he saw between his first and second visits, including J. M. W. Turner's controversial 1806 painting *Falls of the Rhine*. These visual representations are important precisely because they depict stages in a process of representation which this and similar "torrents" undergo in Wordsworth's poetry between 1790 and 1820. According to Dorothy Wordsworth, they looked at "prints" of the Rhinefall before her visit there in 1820. And, as she indicates, eighteenth-century engravings depict the view from the left bank of the Rhine. Although several eighteenth-century artists published engravings, paintings, or draw-ings of this view, the one which would have been easily accessible to the Wordsworths appears in illustrated editions of Coxe's *Travels* after 1796 (Plate 2).[21] Two other engravings by the Basel engraver Christian von Mechel record perspectives which are only slightly different from the one used in the engraving in Coxe's *Travels*. Both are, Mechel notes, "after" drawings by the topographical painter Philippe-Jacques de Loutherbourg. The first print, *La Cataracte du Rhin près de Schaffhause au moment du lever de Soleil*, uses a point of view below Schloss Worth and the inlet which the Rhine creates below the falls. The angle of the engraving omits the inlet entirely and focuses instead on a foreshortened view of the foaming waters of the Rhine just below the falls. In the second print titled, predictably enough, *La Cataracte du Rhin près de Schaffhause au clair de la Lune*, the point of view used is at the midpoint of the inlet, well above Schloss Worth (Plate 3).[22]

If Dorothy Wordsworth's first glimpse of the Rhinefall inspired her

Plate 3 (i)   C. von Mechel. *La Cataracte du Rhin près de Schaffhause au moment du lever du soleil.*

Plate 3 (ii)   *La Cataracte du Rhin près de Schaffhause au clair de la Lune.* 1797. Both plates copyright Helbing & Lichtenhahn Verlag AG, Basle, Switzerland.

Plate 4 Philippe-Jacques de Loutherbourg, *Falls of the Rhine*. 1788. By courtesy of the Board of Trustees of the Victoria and Albert

with reverence for its "mystery,"[23] the view of the "old prints" diminished that sense of mystery by subordinating the Rhinefall and those who come to see it to a larger visual frame. This absorption of viewer and spectacle by a larger series of topographical relations encourages comparisons between and among the various parts of the new visual whole; for this reason, it transforms a sublime scene into something else – perhaps the beautiful, the picturesque, or a Gilpin-esque hybrid like the "picturesquely grand." As Wordsworth argues in his essay on aesthetics, the mind experiences the sublime only if its absorption in the scene is so complete that no comparisons between it and the surrounding landscape are possible.[24]

Unlike eighteenth-century paintings and engravings of the Rhine-fall, Turner's *Falls of the Rhine near Schaffhausen* depicts the view from the right side of the Rhine, just below the viewpoint Coxe judged "the most sublime." Turner's painting was exhibited at the Royal Academy in May 1806, along with Sir George Beaumont's *Peele Castle*, a painting which became the visual occasion for "Elegaic Stanzas," Wordsworth's poem commemorating the death of his brother John. According to Joseph Farington, Wordsworth and Beaumont had tickets to see the exhibition the day after it opened. Soon afterward, members of Beaumont's circle of artists and friends sharply criticized Turner's use of color and paint in the 1806 painting.[25] Wordsworth's initial reception of the painting was probably shaped by this criticism, inasmuch as he admitted two years later in a letter to Beaumont that his patron's pictorial judgment usually guided his own. Yet in the 1822 edition of his *Guide*, Wordsworth offers grudging praise for recent English "experiments" in sketching Alpine scenes.[26] Among those experiments were almost certainly Beaumont's 1819 Swiss sketches and Turner's Swiss watercolors, exhibited in the same year.[27]

By using a view whose "sublimity" Coxe's influential guidebook had ratified, Turner announced a new aesthetic perspective on an old subject. The 1805 painting reflects both his early emulation of Loutherbourg, who had painted the scene in 1788, and his reaction against the topographical tradition which Loutherbourg repre-sented.[28] Loutherbourg depicts the falls from the left bank, using a twisted perspective which makes them seem closer than they could be given the flattened, calm water which occupies the space between the falls and the painter or viewer (Plate 4).[29] This choice of perspective also makes the Rhine appear to flow toward the inlet where the painter or viewer stands. In effect, Loutherbourg tried to have it both ways: the falls are more massively represented and, for this reason, more

Plate 5   J. M. W. Turner. *Falls of the Rhine near Schaffhausen.* 1806. By courtesy of the Museum of Fine Arts, Boston, Bequest of Alice

impressive in their appearance than they are in earlier prints. But the twisted perspective of the painting gives the viewer a sense of security and leisure which amplifies the response which Dorothy Wordsworth, like Coxe, associates with the view from the left bank of the Rhine.[30] Separated from the falls by the inlet, the viewers in the painting watch the spectacle without being caught up in it, much as those who sat inside Loutherbourg's *eidofusikon* – a room where scenes of "storm and stress" were projected onto the walls while spectators "heard" sounds appropriate to what they saw – could feel that they were in the midst of a sublime spectacle like a storm at sea without being there at all.[31]

Turner's selection of a point of view to the right of the falls and below Schloss Laufen places viewers (both those within and those outside the painting) closer to the falls, which dwarf its spectators (Plate 5). Because the waterfall occupies more of the picture space than it does in earlier views, it becomes the commanding center of the painting. Turner heightens this effect by adopting the oblique point of view Coxe describes, making it difficult to locate the Rhinefall in a larger topographical context. Both Wordsworth and Turner create a version of the sublime in which the viewer is so absorbed in and by the spectacle that few other details in the surrounding landscape matter, if indeed they are observed at all. Whatever Wordsworth's initial evaluation of Turner's 1806 painting, the poet who sought out various perspectives on the Rhinefall in 1820 was probably encouraged to do so by Turner's earlier choice of a new, "sublime" perspective.

Incidentally or not, the first stages of this reorientation appear in Wordsworth's poetry in the same year that he saw Turner's 1806 painting. The Wordsworths spent that winter at the Beaumont estate in Leicestershire amid the Beaumonts' extensive art collection. There Wordsworth planned a landscape garden for the estate and composed several political sonnets, including one on the French subjugation of the Swiss. Earlier in the same year, he either discussed his views on the sublime with Coleridge and other visitors, or wrote some of those views down, presumably as part of his manuscript on aesthetics.[32] The timing of the 1806 sonnet on the Swiss is puzzling since the French already had subjugated the Swiss eight years earlier, and Napoleon sent his troops back to do more of the same in 1802.[33] Throughout this period Wordsworth followed the fortunes of the French armies as closely as reports from English intelligence abroad allowed him to do.[34] And on several occasions he dashed off sonnets which were frankly topical. Why then did he wait until 1806 to write the sonnet on the Swiss?

One answer to this question lies, I think, in the imagery of the poem. The speaker argues that the floods and mountain torrents of Switzerland are the "chosen music" of Liberty – music which the French have silenced.[35] The same images appear in the 1805–6 *Prelude*, where they signify not liberty but what the speaker fears about the French Revolution and the sublime: their capacity from a Burkean perspective to overflow and destroy social and political limits that insure civilized government, much as the Biblical deluge effaced all signs of Edenic landscape and civilization.[36] Burke's *Reflections* makes this association explicit: "But let them not break prison to burst like a Levanter, to sweep the earth with their hurricane, and to break up the fountains of the great deep to overwhelm us."[37] And in Wordsworth's sonnet, "September, 1802. Near Dover," the channel between England and France is a "barrier flood" whose "power" and "mightiness for evil and for good" may or may not protect England (*PW*, 3:114–15).

A parallel vocabulary of flood and destruction characterizes French discussions of the Revolution in the 1790s. Napoleon himself uses it in a 1796 address to his troops, reprinted in the *Annual Register* in 1800: "You have precipitated yourselves, like a torrent, from the heights of the Appennines."[38] Camille Desmoulins, who had participated in the storming of the Bastille but was himself sentenced to the guillotine in 1794, described the course of the Revolution as *torrent révolutionnaire* which drowns its actors in its undertow.[39] For Wordsworth and his contemporaries, "le spectacle des torrents et des cascades" could never again be an entirely trivial taste.

By late 1806, then, Wordsworth had recognized that the eighteenth-century identification of sublimity with genius and freedom from constraint had been undermined by the darker energies of revolutionary France. For some years afterward, he kept these two versions of the sublime separate by suppressing his earlier association between liberty and sublimity. In "The Jungfrau and the Falls of the Rhine," one of many poems he composed to commemorate his return to the Continent in 1820, the speaker declares that the Rhine becomes a "flood of madness" when it reaches the Rhinefall. Dorothy Wordsworth's several statements about her aesthetic response to this and other Swiss torrents and waterfalls which the Wordsworths visited during their 1820 tour suggest that the presence or absence of "sublime" emotions was a topic of conversation. She says of the Falls of the Reichenbach, "it gives little of that feeling which may be called *pleasure*: it was astonishment, *and* awe – an overwhelming sense of the powers of nature for the destruction of all things, of the helplessness of man – of the weakness of his will, if prompted to make a momentary effort against such a force." By contrast the Rhinefall impressed her with feelings of helplessness and awe, but not fear, precisely the configuration of emotions Wordsworth identifies with the sublime in his essay on aesthetics.[40]

In Wordsworth's 1822 *Memorials of a Tour of the Continent*, the collection in which the Rhinefall sonnet first appeared, poems on other "torrents" and famous scenes on the Continental circuit are interspersed with poems that commemorate scenes made famous by Napoleon's victories and defeats, including Waterloo, the Swiss war memorial near the lake of Thun, and the fallen column at Simplon Pass, an abandoned monument which Napoleon had intended to place in Milan.[41] In the same year, Wordsworth also published his sonnet on the Rhinefall in *Ecclesiastical Sonnets*, where he retitled it "Illustration: The Jungfrau and the Fall of the Rhine near Schaffhausen" to indicate its thematic and figurative relation to the sonnets on religious persecution that flank it in this collection. This placement, which Wordsworth retained in later editions of his collected poems, makes the destructive power of the Rhinefall a figure for the blood baths of French Huguenots, the theme of the preceding sonnet, and for religious persecution in England during the reign of Charles I, the theme of the third sonnet in the group (*PW*, 3:382–83).

In a note explaining why he reprinted the sonnet on the Rhinefall in *Ecclesiastical Sonnets*, Wordsworth cites an incident recorded in Ramond's French translation of Coxe's *Travels*. Falling on his knees on the scaffolding to the right of the Rhinefall, a German traveller declared: "Voilà un enfer d'eau!"[42] The elliptical character of Wordsworth's "explanation" is worth noting. Intended to suggest an association between the scene and religious persecution that is hellish or deserving of hell-fire, the phrase "a hell of water" also completes an allusive spiral of images that begins in the 1793 *Descriptive Sketches*. In a note appended to the earlier poem, Wordsworth declares that the sublimity of an Alpine sunset derives from the spectator's impression of "a deluge of light, or rather of fire."[43] As Dorothy Wordsworth and other nineteenth-century travellers noted, on the left bank of the Rhine beside the falls was an iron foundry, powered by the falls itself. From the foundry shot columns of fire which Dorothy and William Wordsworth watched until sunset.[44] Thus what they saw in 1820 repeated the configuration of sunset, fire, and deluge which Wordsworth had described in the note appended to *Descriptive Sketches*.

By the time Wordsworth returned to the Continent, this configuration had, to use a visual analogy, greater depth of field. For by then the Rhinefall had become the focus for a network of allusions which had not existed for him when he visited the scene as a young man. During the nearly thirty years which separate his two notes on Alpine sublimity, he wrote numerous poems, including the 1805–6 *Prelude* and the sonnets on Switzerland and the Rhinefall, which examine affinities between cataclysmic destruction on the one hand, and torrents, liberty, waterfalls, and the sublime on the other. A later point of entry into this network is the role Wordsworth assigns to the Rhinefall in his essay on aesthetics, where the scene illustrates the two views of the sublime which he had kept separate for so many years: the mind's capacity to resist revolutionary torrents and remain free; and its parallel capacity to participate in those torrents and in doing so also remain free. Wordsworth explains that the rock's resistance to the waterfall makes them both antagonistic partners in the "intense unity" which he asserts is essential to the sublime (*Prose*, 2:356). In an earlier chapter I suggested that in making this claim Wordsworth himself resists the Kantian sublime, which comes into being when the desire to resist nature's might invites reason to offer a crucial comparison between nature's physical might and the mind's intellectual might. As his use of the same term in *Concerning the Convention of Cintra* suggests, the resistance Wordsworth seeks to demonstrate is political as well.[45]

In Wordsworth's 1806 sonnet on the Swiss, the speaker's association of liberty and resistance with the Swiss is negative: the Swiss have lost their liberty and they cannot resist the French. But by 1820, Napoleon had been defeated (although not by the Swiss) and French troops had withdrawn from Switzerland.[46] Yet as the Wordsworths travelled through France to Switzerland, they were, Dorothy Wordsworth wrote, constantly reminded of Napoleon's earlier military successes.[47] Like other travellers to Europe after Napoleon's defeat, they could still read signs of the force that the Swiss had not been able to resist in the famous scenes they visited, including Schaffhausen, where the French destroyed a bridge over the Rhine in 1799, as they retreated from Switzerland just ahead of the advancing Austrian army.[48] In the 1801 edition of his *Travels in Switzerland*, Coxe lamented the loss of this bridge and Dorothy Wordsworth echoes Coxe in her journal entry for their visit.[49] Because Schaffhausen is the northernmost Swiss canton, and as such separated from the rest of Switzerland by the Rhine, it is the northern gateway to the Alps for invading armies as well as tourists.[50] For this reason, French troops had to defend or destroy any bridge which crossed the Rhine at Schaffhausen if they were to cross the Swiss Alps or retreat from them. By burning this bridge behind them, the French delayed the Austrians long enough to regain the French frontier.

"The Jungfrau and the Fall of the Rhine near Schaffhausen"

From Wordsworth's anti-Jacobin perspective on Swiss history, then, the destruction of the bridge at Schaffhausen may be an image of how the French suppressed Swiss independence from 1798 until the end of the Napoleonic Wars. Likewise, the Rhine itself may have reminded Wordsworth of Napoleon's reorganization of Switzerland, which disregarded the traditional sovereignty of individual Swiss cantons and their frontiers.[51] According to this reading, the Rhine is for Wordsworth a visual reminder of how Swiss frontiers were overrun by revolutionary France. Finally, although the bridge over the Rhine was destroyed, the fact that the Rhinefall remained made it a singularly appropriate image of the enduring, if passive Swiss resistance to revolutionary France. When Wordsworth used the Rhinefall to illustrate resistance to and participation in sublime forces, he was trying to do for the Swiss and the sublime what he could not do for either in 1806 – allow the Swiss to triumph over Napoleon and the sublime to triumph over its own destructive energies. In his (probably much earlier) remarks on the sublimity of "images of duration, [or] impassiveness" in "An Unpublished Tour," he specifies the relation between natural sublimity and scenes of battle that is implicit in his repeated notice of the sublimity of the Rhinefall. Presenting "the sight of rocks of everlasting granite or basaltic columns, a barrier upon which the furious winds or the devouring sea are without injury resisted" as an example of this kind of sublimity, he insists that this image of "duration" or "impassiveness" conveys an idea of permanence in the midst of "decay and change." Such scenes recall, he adds, "the state of a field of battle after a murderous conflict" (*Prose*, 2:317–18).

Wordsworth's allied reading of the Rhinefall as a figure of aesthetic and political resistance ignores an obvious but critical geological fact. In "The Sublime and the Beautiful" he explains that the rock and waterfall together demonstrate a continuous "state of opposition & yet reconcilement" which has endured "for countless ages" (*Prose*, 2:356–57). Reading his own description of the scene as a sublime figure, he concludes that the mind can experience resistance and sensations of sublimity not merely indefinitely but perpetually. Here he contradicts Coxe, who declares that the "height of the falls diminishes every year," and that the "two crags, which now rise in the midst of the river, will in time be undermined and carried away."[52] No doubt Coxe was right on both points. And since Wordsworth was by this time well acquainted with the long-term effects of erosion, he ought to have been persuaded by the logic of Coxe's assertion.[53] In fact, when he stopped to look at the Valais region of Switzerland during the same 1820 tour, he told Crabb Robinson that the Alps were "in a state of decay – crumbling to pieces."[54] The revisionism of his contrary assertion concerning the Rhinefall demonstrates its critical semiotic task in his aesthetics. As a sign of the mind's enduring capacity to sustain sensations of sublimity even as it resists nature's might, the Rhinefall cannot be subject to decay.

The last stages of this revisionism are well marked in poems Wordsworth composed after Napoleon's final defeat. In his "Thanksgiving Ode," published on January 18, 1816, the day England set aside in national thanksgiving for that defeat, Britain's endurance prefigures the relation between rock and waterfall which Wordsworth soon afterward ascribed to the Rhinefall as revolutionary text and image:

> Firm as a rock in stationary fight;
> In motion rapid as the lightning's gleam,
> Fierce as a flood-gate bursting at midnight
> To rouse the wicked from the giddy dream.
>
> (PW, 3:157–58, ll. 77–80)

And in a pre-publication manuscript variant of the "Introduction" to *Ecclesiastical Sonnets*, the speaker compares Freedom to "a torrent combating / In victory found her natural resting-place" (PW, 3:341, ll. 6–7n.). This revival of an association which Wordsworth often suppressed after 1793 seems to have required at least one revisitation and several poems. Thus if in 1818 Wordsworth could still speak retrospectively of Europe during the Napoleonic Wars as "deluged with blood,"[55] by 1822 he had made his peace with this *topos* of the revolutionary sublime.

This cumulative response to the Rhinefall demonstrates the complex revisionary impulse of Wordsworth's aesthetics. Between 1790 and 1820, it was not – because he refused to allow it to be – like a landscape "to a blind man's eye." Yet the stages of this revision were not deliberate recognitions, but stages in a kind of mental travelling which occurred over a thirty-year period. Barred from Switzerland for most of those years, Wordsworth re-imagined the Rhinefall in the midst of other, more evident inquiries in his poetry and prose. By the time of his second visit or soon after, the scene had become a focus for political and aesthetic concerns he had kept separate in the invervening years.

"To the Torrent at Devil's Bridge"

When he returned to the Continent in 1820, Wordsworth pursued a double axis of revisitation, looking at scenes he and Jones had visited in 1790 and at ones Napoleon had conquered or hoped to conquer.

Four years later, when he toured Wales with Mary and Dora Wordsworth, the declared objects of his return were more personal than
public. As the letter he wrote to Beaumont during this tour makes
clear, it was organized around visits to friends and scenes Wordsworth
had first encountered in the 1790s. The friends included Robert Jones
and Uvedale Price; the scenes included at least two exemplary landscapes of the Wordsworthian sublime – Snowdon and Cader Idris. In
part, then, this tour recalled experiences Wordsworth had long
associated with aesthetic concerns. In its Gilpinesque catalogue of
various viewpoints on well-known scenes, Wordsworth's letter to
Beaumont also displays a reflective distance on those concerns.
Included in this letter in part to illustrate Wordsworth's conviction
that scenes like this "cannot be adequately rendered with a pencil," the
sonnet "To the Torrent at Devil's Bridge. North Wales" elaborates the
aesthetic consequences of such distance.

The sonnet marks Wordsworth's effort to memorialize this scene,
which – like others he had visited as a young man – he had not earlier
been able to do. He says: "I had seen these things long ago, but either
my memory or my powers of observation had not done them justice."
Both the sonnet and his account of the circumstances of its composition subtly revise the visual figure implied by the phrase "powers
of observation." For in telling Beaumont that "while Dora was
attempting to make a sketch from the chasm in the rain, I composed by
her side the following address to the torrent,"[56] he recalls his earlier
conviction that scenes like this, whether in Wales or the Alps, could
not be adequately "rendered with a pencil." This conviction is
dramatized by the familial competition implicit in his decision to place
himself next to Dora as he addresses the scene which she *attempts* to
sketch "in the rain." Read as Wordsworth's notice of the different and
unequal powers of sight and sound, the sonnet subordinates the visual
similarities which link this torrent to others in order to convert the
sublime figures inscribed in floods, torrents, and waterfalls into a
collective figure of the beautiful.

As Hartman has observed, "To the Torrent at Devil's Bridge"
domesticates the sublime, but not in the ways or for the reasons he
proposes.[57] Less a poem which exemplifies Wordsworth's later style
than one which calls attention to rhetorical strategies he had used in
much earlier poems, the sonnet makes repeated use of a traditional
figure of the sublime in the octave in order to subvert it in the sestet.
Whereas the octave offers figures that mark the unstable nature of the
sublime, the sestet familiarizes the sublime *topos* of torrents and
waterfalls by (re)naming them "a family of floods."

As sublime tropes on the Longinian apostrophe to a hidden or absent deity, the speaker's questions about the name of the "torrent" identified in the title elaborate a relation between naming and hidden or absent origins that is slightly different from the one Wordsworth offers in the first *Essay upon Epitaphs*, where he describes how a child would "inevitably" answer his own questions about the provenance and issue of a "running stream" (*Prose*, 2:51). Whereas this child's questions are interior and unhistoricized (i.e. their "history" is private and mythic), the speaker's summarize the private and public contexts for the *topos* he invokes, since his questions about the origin of a sublime "force" acknowledge parallels between its British "source" and metonymic "sources" in other lands.

This figurative mapping of a literal "force" ("waterfall" in the North of England dialect) alters the aesthetic preference suggested by the speaker's use of the Longinian figure. The "force" whose name is requested is doubly named: its topographical name is given in the title but its name as a *topos* emerges in the octave (*PW*, 3:43). In this sense the questions are not disingenuous. The figurative name and history of the "torrent" and not its topographical name are what matter. Both the strategy of asking a god's name and the chain of metaphors that follow are Longinian. But their import in Wordsworth's aesthetics is to announce the "pull" which the beautiful exerts in all acts of naming. Once given a name or even asked for one, the sublime begins to move toward, even within, the aura of the beautiful. This domestication of sublime figures of speech is not an avoidance of apocalypse but a consequence of poetic speech. And this aesthetic swerve is in the rhetorical nature of things. In Wordsworth's aesthetics the tension between passion and speech implicit in Longinus's claims about how the figures of the sublime style restrain sublime passion serves to describe the boundary which interior passion and its poetic expression must negotiate. Like most boundaries, this one provokes transgressions from both sides. It is made porous by the beautiful, which speaks first for the sublime and then for [her]self.

The questions of the octave are poised between two tasks: as historicizing sublime figures, they must ask the name of this torrent in ways that indicate other torrents whose association with recent European history makes them appropriate vehicles for the revolutionary sublime; but as figures which will finally assist the beautiful, they cannot answer their own questions. Instead, like those Asia asks Demogorgon in *Prometheus Unbound*, these questions imply answers which, if spoken, would declare that the aesthetic name for this and other torrents is the sublime.

The questions begin innocently enough with a poetic allusion to Pindus, the mountain range in Greece that was sacred to the Muses. This allusion suggests, as Hartman observes, several poetic resonances in Wordsworth's earlier poems, most of them in passages which readers have consistently identified with the Wordsworthian sublime.[58] Yet what is at least as remarkable are the other allusions that proceed from the same antique source. The rhetorical figure which advances this second group is oblique. Read metonymically through the adverbial phrase "where the band / Of Patriots scoop their freedom out" (ll. 4–5) as a figure for the Greek struggle for independence from the Ottoman Empire in which Byron had died in April of 1824,[59] and as a still more refracted figure for the Swiss struggle against Napoleonic France, "Pindus" authorizes another chain of "torrents." In part, one link between the two chains of resonances may be the Pindaric ode form, which late eighteenth-century English poets frequently associated with bards who were rebels against an established order.

The first in this second chain is named. As the source of the Rhine, "Viamala" is, as Wordsworth describes it in the letter to Beaumont in which the sonnet appears, a "narrow chasm through which the Rhine has forced its way." The literal and figurative "crossings" enacted in these and subsequent lines proliferate exponentially. The "evil (or bad) way" of the Rhine leads to an actual force, the Rhinefall at Schaffhausen, whose position on the Swiss frontier nearest to France makes it a troubled image of borders and their transgression. If nineteenth-century travellers used the term "Devil's Bridge" to describe a number of bridges in England, Wales, and on the Continent, including one at Viamala, the Devil's Bridge which Coxe and numerous travellers and artists after him identified was the great stone bridge over the Reuss in St. Gotthard Pass. If, as Hartman also suggests, the resonances suggested by crossing borders and chasms work powerfully on Wordsworth during his return visit to the torrent and bridge in Wales,[60] the Alpine wooded bridge he mentions in the 1793 *Descriptive Sketches*, or the one the French destroyed at Schaffhausen in 1799 may be, if not the same bridge, images of the hazards of trying to negotiate one's passage, in language or in landscape, over a sublime "force."[61]

The political resonances of this hazard figure prominently in what the French army of the Directory did to the Devil's Bridge over the Reuss in 1799. In the 1801 edition of his *Travels*, Coxe says that they destroyed it to delay the retreat of the Russian army under Alexander Suwaroff. In this and earlier editions, Coxe insists that the bridge and chasm are one of those sublime scenes of horror, of which those who have not been spectators, can form no perfect idea; they defy the representations of painting or poetry.[62]

In the same note he quotes Suwaroff's description of the Russian retreat across this gorge and ascent of Mt. Blanc to illustrate just how sublime a passage the French forced upon their enemy. Wordsworth's 1790 route apparently did not include a passage over the Reuss on this Devil's Bridge, but Dorothy Wordsworth makes it clear that they used this route in 1820.[63] The bridge must have been rebuilt soon after the French destroyed it, for in 1802 Turner sketched it for the first time. When Dorothy Wordsworth saw it in 1820, she described it as being covered with masses of bright orange lichens.[64] In short, from "the dread chasm" (l. 10) in the sonnet "To the Torrent" and the scene it represents, Wordsworth's speaker can see a good many others, including several he declines to name. Standing beside Dora Wordsworth at another Devil's Bridge four years after he, Dorothy, and Mary Wordsworth stood on the one over the Reuss, Wordsworth addresses the Welsh torrent so that he may recall others that connect his history to that of Napoleonic Europe.

By gathering these torrents up into a "family of floods," the sestet seeks to prove not which torrents are which, but what their figurative identity is. From this perspective, names do not matter, in fact they cannot matter if the speaker is to be able to acknowledge the power they represent. Whereas the octave refuses to name all the torrents in part to keep their sublime figuration below the surface of poetic speech, the sestet acknowledges the "power" which this "family" has over "Poets, young or old" (ll. 13–14). So explicit a summation of Wordsworth's long fascination with "the sounding cataract" is made possible by the speaker's refusal to allow the visual tyranny of such scenes (remember Coxe on the impossibility of representing the Devil's Bridge over the Reuss in poetry or painting and Wordsworth on the sketching Dora) and his acknowledgment of their resonating power as sound and figure. The absence of torrents from the list of things he is "permitted to behold" (woods, snows, skies) witnesses the enabling catachresis of the sestet. True, the objects of vision are in one sense determined by where the speaker stands: "from the dread chasm" he looks up. But this seems precisely the point: by looking up he places this chasm and torrent in a larger topographical frame whose ability to encompass a sublime scene signals an aesthetic conversion of sublime images which are single and field-dominant. Now a larger temporal and social arena submits sublime images to scale, making them serve a widened perspective and reality. If the beautiful is no more named in the sonnet than the sublime is, its traditional offices are amply represented in the sestet, which gives the sublime not only a home but a "family."

As an aesthetic that assists a widening series of resonances like those spiritual echoes Wordsworth assigns to the ear in the 1828 ode "On the Power of Sound" (PW, 2:323, ll. 1–8), the beautiful addresses the need for echoes which link past to present, private to public meanings. As the speaker of the ode observes, "Voices," "Shadows / And images of voice" (ll. 33–34) project their own history as a series of poetic resonances which the "oracular" (and auricular[65]) cave of the ear authorizes and receives. Wordsworth's figurative turn toward the beautiful advances this extensive rather than intensive view of the poet's task.

For some writers, including Wordsworth, the world beyond the text is implicated in the text. Those who have argued to the contrary have claimed that signs refer only to other signs or to other texts.[66] The first part of this claim is true. The Rhinefall is not simply a place for Wordsworth; it is rather a sign which he encodes and then attempts to decipher. But the second argument – that signs refer only to texts – is misleading less because of what it asserts than what it assumes: that such texts cannot be located in relation to places or events in the world, or in affiliations between these and texts. Wordsworth's response to the Rhinefall and other "torrents" suggests instead that signs exhibit visual and aural resonances that extend beyond the texts in which those signs appear. For this reason, they cannot be read as self-contained, self-consuming artifacts. As vehicles that support several contexts and tenors within and without his poetry and prose, Wordsworth's "family of floods" shows how things in the world are *significant* in the radical sense of this term.

In Wordsworth's later poetry the dizzying, emptying detours and countersigns which are the errant sign language of the sublime yield to the beautiful, which sanctions and extends the task of gathering inferences and echoes from several frames of meaning – in this case, an extensive one which binds the history of Napoleonic Europe to the history of Wordsworth's poetic career. To grant this argument, a reader has to be willing to believe in readings that partly depend on what Umberto Eco has called "inferences by intertextual frames"[67] and to suppose that in Wordsworth's poetry torrents and waterfalls are a *topos* where literal and figurative resonances repeatedly cross each other. In "To the Torrent at Devil's Bridge," this *topos* encodes a set of values Wordsworth had associated with the beautiful for nearly thirty years. The turns and counter-turns of Wordsworth's revisionary aesthetics sanction competing versions of how signs can or should refer. Whereas the sublime makes use of signs whose meanings err, the beautiful creates signs that stabilize families of meaning. Whatever one's semiotic preference, it is crucial to recognize that early and late in his poetic career Wordsworth did both.

8

Conclusion:
aesthetics and poetic language

I WANT TO BEGIN WITH A DISCLAIMER: aesthetic differences do not constitute Wordsworth's understanding of how poetic figures work or how they refer. Yet in essays he wrote on poetics and the poetical character – from the 1800 to 1802 versions of the *Preface* to *Lyrical Ballads* to those published with the 1815 edition of his *Poems* – he frequently illustrates the task of poetic language with figurative oppositions derived from his aesthetics, among them surface vs. depth, hiddenness vs. exposure, and containment vs. unboundedness. Thus in the *Preface* to *Lyrical Ballads* he at first defines poetry as a "spontaneous overflow of powerful feelings," then later completes this definition by inscribing this overflow in a series of re-presentations and re-actions that lead finally to poetic composition. Here too he presents rhyme, meter, and even "ordinary feeling" as elements that temper or restrain excitement or passion that might otherwise "be carried beyond its proper bounds." And his notice of the "formal engagement" between readers and poets which his poetic experiments must inevitably offend assumes that such engagements will not cease, but must be recreated.[1] In the 1815 *Essay, Supplementary to the Preface* he insists that this recreation is the task of any "original Genius." Like Hannibal in the Alps, such a poet is "called upon to clear and often to shape his own road."[2] Even without aesthetic designations, these claims extend the antithetical impulse of his aesthetics to his poetics.

Wordsworth's most radically antithetical claim about poetic language emerges when he defends (and appropriates) the materiality of poetic figures, whether the figure of this materiality is the durability of the language really spoken by men or the epitaphic monument. This defense of poetic figures as "twofold" treasures – at once material and spiritual – is, to be sure, a particular instance of a more general dialectical impulse that allies Wordsworth with Blake and perhaps

193

Hegel.[3] Yet for Wordsworth as for Blake particulars count as generalizations may not. Or, to put this difference another way, although it may not be idiotic to generalize about Wordsworth's poetics, it is probably hazardous to do so without appealing to his poetic practice and, I would argue, those essays in which he variously describes "the business of poetry" (*Prose*, 3:63).[4]

Wordsworth was well aware of the hazard of materiality – the tendency to be "fed / By the dead letter, not the spirit of things," as he says in *The Prelude* (8:431–32, p. 288). In an early manuscript probably composed in 1798 or 1799, he presents this hazard as the poetic delusion he has tried to avoid by choosing to be silent rather than write bad verse:

> nor had my voice
> Been silent often times had I burst forth
> In verse which with a strong and random light
> Touching an object in its prominent parts
> Created a memorial which to me
> Was all sufficient and to my own mind
> Recalling the whole picture seemed to speak
> An universal language: Scattering thus
> In passion many a desultory sound
> I deemed that I had adequately cloathed
> Meanings at which I hardly hinted thoughts
> And forms of which I scarcely had produced
> A monument and arbitrary sign.   (*Prel.* 1798, 163)[5]

As he suggests in lines below these, delusions of poetic grandeur make composition a "considerate and laborious work." If the aspiration of poetic labor is to achieve "a function kindred to organic power / The vital spirit of a perfect form," in practice the poet may end up with little more than "a monument and arbitrary sign" – or silence.

Read with Wordsworth's later praise of epitaphic monuments in mind, this general dismissal of "monuments" is surprising. In the *Essays upon Epitaphs*, written more than a decade later, he presents them as figures for the artifact-ness of poetic figures, the source of their strength and their weakness. I suggest that Wordsworth altered his earlier assessment to harness those arbitrary signs he still hoped to avoid in the *Preface* to *Lyrical Ballads*, where he assigns them to the province of poetic diction (*Prose*, 1:144). If, as he later acknowledges in the 1815 *Essay, Supplementary to the Preface*, language is "a thing subject to endless fluctuations and arbitrary associations" (*Prose*, 3:82), poets must find ways to channel or temporarily suspend otherwise endless fluctuations of tenor and vehicle. To ward off this "counter-spirit," as he calls it in the third *Essay upon Epitaphs*,[6]

Wordsworth tries to make the material letter of poetic figures work for (rather than against) their spirit. In the *Essay, Supplementary to the Preface*, he insists on their cooperation. Like religion, poetry is "transcendent," yet it cannot exist without "sensuous incarnation" (*Prose*, 3:65). As the word made flesh, the figure of incarnation insures an indivisible as well as sacramental relation between poetic figures and meaning. When Wordsworth substituted the figure of incarnation for the more traditional one of language as clothing or dress[7] (which he had used in the 1798 lines about the difficulty of poetic composition), he raised the stakes of his argument, since incarnation still requires "submitting ... to circumstances" or, in other words, becoming human.

The aesthetic resonances that complicate his analysis of "the emotions of the pathetic" in the same essay demonstrate the hazards of submitting transcendent ideas to "circumstances." Initially Wordsworth classifies these emotions by distinguishing those which are simple and direct from those which are complex and revolutionary. Since this classification clearly echoes his own aesthetic conflict between a sublimity against which, as he says, the heart "struggles with pride" and a beauty to which it "yields with gentleness," it is hardly surprising that he soon abandons it for John Dennis's less troublesome distinction between "ordinary" and "enthusiastic" pathos (*Prose*, 3:82–83).[8] As that circumstance to which his aesthetics submits (or against which it rebels), the revolutionary sublime shows the material and figurative hazards of incarnation. This point is, I think, missed by recent critics who offer Schiller's "historical sublime" as a radical model for criticism and politics. For what Schiller took no note of in praising the transcendent freedom of the sublime is the historical circumstances that transformed the promise of sublime freedom into its negations.[9]

Preface to Lyrical Ballads

Wordsworth first explores the arbitrariness of language and poetic figures in the 1800 *Preface to Lyrical Ballads*, where it assists his distinction between the poetic language of his eighteenth-century predecessors and his own (theirs is arbitrary and artificial, his is adapted from the language really used by men). But in the 1802 *Appendix on Poetic Diction*, he presents arbitrariness as the condition of modern poetry, that is, poetry alienated by intervening centuries of poetic practice from its ancient sources, where passion and figurative expression were inextricable. Like similar claims made by Blake and

Shelley, this argument about the origin of poetry compels poets to find a new figurative language, one that revives the ancient bond between passion and expression.[10] What is intriguing about this familiar Romantic argument is the pressure it exerts on Wordsworth's thinking about the epitaph and traditional figures like personification. Initially he says nothing about the first and dismisses the second. But in the revised 1802 *Preface* he is more attentive to the nature and value of personification as a poetic figure whose arbitrariness and artifice made it a useful Romantic scapegoat for neoclassical poetics in general. The 1800 *Preface* declares:

> Except in a very few instances the Reader will find no personifications of abstract ideas in these volumes, not that I mean to censure such personifications: they may be well fitted for certain sorts of composition, but in these Poems I propose myself to imitate, and, as far as is possible, to adopt, the very language of men, and I do not find that such personifications make any regular or natural part of that language. I wish to keep my Reader in the company of flesh and blood.
>
> (*Prose*, 1:130)

Despite his disclaimer on this point, in the context of his polemic about the sources of genuine poetic language, he does censure personification.

In the 1802 text Wordsworth makes essentially the same claim — that personifications "do not make any natural or regular part of that language" (i.e. the very language of men) — but he significantly modifies his earlier censure. This version also includes a new sentence about passion and figuration that discloses the aesthetic logic at work in this revision. Whereas in the first version a qualifying phrase at the beginning ("except in a very few instances") allows Wordsworth to use an absolute negative in the main clause ("the Reader will find no personifications of abstract ideas"), the 1802 version eliminates the qualifying phrase and incorporates its meaning into the main clause — now "personifications of abstract ideas rarely occur in these volumes." Wordsworth reasons in 1802 that this is so because such figures "are utterly rejected, as an ordinary device to elevate the style, and raise it above prose" (*Prose*, 1:131). Taken in part from earlier debates about Longinus and the sublime style,[11] *raise* and *elevate* indicate the pressure of Longinian concerns on Wordsworth's text. The sentence added to the 1802 text admits the old debate about passion and what Longinus called "extravagant" figures:

> they [personifications] are, indeed, a figure of speech occasionally prompted by passion, and I have made use of them as such; but have endeavored utterly to reject them as a mechanical device of style, or as a family language which Writers in metre seem to lay claim to by prescription. (*Prose*, 1:131)

This clarification is, I think, just that. It acknowledges a bond between passion and elaborate figures that echoes traditional arguments about sublime passion as the pre-condition for using such figures. Words-worth makes the same pre-condition for personification – a poetic figure frequently identified with the sublime style in earlier aesthetic theory.[12]

These revisions show Wordsworth willing to deal with personifi-cation and similarly artificed (and potentially arbitrary) figures for the sake of the passion such figures may communicate better (this second point is implicit) than figures that do make a "natural or regular part" of the language spoken by men. Also implicit here but more fully declared in the *Essays upon Epitaphs* is his recognition that such figures are, like extreme expressions of grief, powerful and genuine precisely because they are neither natural nor regular. Unlike his 1798 verse, which ruefully marks the opposition between passion and signs that are "arbitrary" because they bear no relation to passion, later essays reveal Wordsworth's efforts to manage rather than deplore the disjunction between the two.

In the *Preface* to *Lyrical Ballads*, Wordsworth hopes to counter the inherent arbitrariness he later assigns to language by relying on the durability or permanence he finds in rustic language or, as he usually preferred to call it, "a selection of language really spoken by men" (*Prose*, 1:123).[13] Whether or not Wordsworth's ballad experiments do in fact use this language and whether it offered what he said it did, is not I think the reason readers are and have been fascinated by his ballad experiments. Coleridge's criticism tends to waylay our notice of this point.[14] What still attracts readers to these poems and prefaces is in part their conviction that such poetic figures endure. In the radical sense suggested by Wordsworth's later analysis of epitaphic monu-ments as carriers of "the knowledge that endures" (*Prelude*, 5:65, p. 154), these figures are, or purport to be, durable, material – letters that convey spirit by virtue of their materiality.

Essays upon Epitaphs

In the *Essays upon Epitaphs*, composed between 1808 and 1810, Wordsworth returns to the matrix of figures he had earlier assembled in the story of the Drowned Man – death, drowning, burial, and the disruption of surfaces – to examine their material contribution to his analysis of grief and its poetic expression. These essays argue that, if rightly understood, the language of epitaphic monuments fuses depths of feeling with the surfaces of epitaphic inscription. But to make this claim, Wordsworth wrestles with the "counter-spirit" of his own figures – the pressure of their materiality as the dead letter. In the first essay, for example, he uses the word *substance* in two different senses: one minimizes the distance between epitaphic surfaces and the feelings they express; a second emphasizes the distance between them. When he says that the "form and substance" of epitaphic monuments (*Prose*, 2:60) encourage travellers to read their inscriptions as they lean against them or repose in their shade, he claims that the material form of the epitaph assists its meaning by providing readers with shade or a place to lean. But earlier in the essay Wordsworth argues that the epitaphic monument is a "senseless stone" whose "language" is the "benignant" (and ventriloquized) voice Nature puts there (*Prose*, 2:54). Because this distinction between epitaphic form and Nature's voice qualifies the extent to which the "form and substance" of the epitaph might be said to act in concert, it allows Wordsworth to argue that behind the "veil" of the epitaphic form the reader finds "a substance of individual truth" (*Prose*, 2:66). To summarize these different accounts of "substance," we might say that epitaphs transmit a spiritual "substance" even as they are inscribed in a material one. Put this way, the word *substance* marks the difference between the depths and surfaces of epitaphs as inscriptions and monuments.

Yet even as Wordsworth devalues the materiality of epitaphic monuments, he claims it is essential to curb the passion or spiritual substance of the inscription, even as the act of carving an epitaph in stone seems to check its author's expression:

the very form and substance of the monument which has received the inscription, and the appearance of the letters, testifying with what slow and laborious hand they must have been engraven, might seem to reproach the author who had given way upon this occasion to transports of mind, or to quick turns of conflicting passion; though the same might constitute the life and beauty of a funeral oration or elegiac poem. (*Prose*, 2:60)

Here Wordsworth uses explicitly aesthetic designations to illustrate the tension between the spirit and letter of epitaphic inscription. "Transports" and "passion" echo Longinus's terms for the emotions that produce sublime figures. At issue for Wordsworth and Longinus is whether sublime passions sanction figures whose extravagance of hyperbole might be otherwise unacceptable. Longinus urged, sometimes against the grain of his own examples, that sublime passion forges the link between nature and art which is requisite to true sublimity of style.[15] In the *Essays upon Epitaphs* Wordsworth equivocates, arguing at some points that hyperbole or extravagant figures are appropriate in epitaphs and at others that they are not. In this passage he says that they are not, though he allows that they can be the "life and beauty" of other forms of elegiac expression. This claim manages to sequester sublime passions by making them constitutive of beauty in the most formal and conventional modes for expressing grief over death – elegy and oration.

In the second essay the Wordsworthian beautiful is also the subtext for a discussion of the language that is appropriate for epitaphs:

> [they] shall contain thoughts and feelings which are in their substance common-place, and even trite ... grounded upon the universal and intellectual property of man; – sensations which all men have felt and feel in some degree daily and hourly. (*Prose*, 2:78)

The Burkean resonances of "property" indicate the relation between epitaphs and the dead which these essays propose. As containers, epitaphs are the dwelling places whose "common-place"-ness insures the community of feeling which binds the dead and the past to present and future readers. As community property, they create places where grieving and consolation can occur.

Well aware that this community depends on figures to sustain it, Wordsworth for the first time rejects the traditional metaphor for the relation between meaning and expression. According to Longinus, words "cloath composition in the most beautiful Dress, [and] make it shine, like a Picture."[16] Wordsworth now disagrees:

> Words are too awful an instrument for good and evil to be trifled with: they hold above all other external power a dominion over thoughts. If words be not ... an incarnation of thought but only a clothing for it, then surely will they prove an ill gift; such a one as those poisonous vestments, read of in the stories of superstitious times, which had power to consume and to alienate from his right mind the victim who put them on. (*Essays upon Epitaphs 3, Prose*, 2:84–85)

Like the cloak Medea gave Jason out of her heart's bitterness, the words-as-clothing metaphor is hazardous because it does not insist on a sacramental union of words and things modelled on the Pauline (and Wordsworthian) binding of "letter" to "spirit."

However, because sublime passion constantly threatens to disrupt poetic expression, Wordsworth occasionally prefers to hide such passion, even bury it with the bodies of those for or about whom epitaphs speak. Thus in the third essay he advises that the Duke of Ormond's lament for his dead son would have been "unbecoming" had it been "placed in open view over the Son's grave." He argues that "the sublimity of the sentiment (i.e. 'that he preferred his dead Son to any living Son in Christendom') consists in its being the secret possession of the Father" (*Prose*, 2:88). Yet in the second essay he defends the hyperbole of Montrose's epitaph for Charles I as "a mean instrument made mighty because wielded by an afflicted Soul, and strangeness is here the order of Nature" (*Prose*, 2:72). The logic of this justification follows Longinus, who argued that figurative or stylistic excesses are justified by the naturalness and strength of sublime passion.[17] And in the same essay he admires the "fantastic images" used by a Westmoreland husband for his wife's epitaph as sincere expressions of the husband's grief, but not as an epitaph: "these fantastic images, though they stain the writing, stained not his soul" (*Prose*, 2:73). Images that stain the writing but not the soul drive a wedge between the epitaphic surface and what it represents. In the case of Montrose's epitaph, a sublime figure is needed in 1809 to declare Wordsworth's solidarity with those who object to regicide, be the victim Charles I or Louis XVI.

Wordsworth also uses a sublime figure (albeit one without political resonances) in the first essay to argue that a child knows "origin and tendency are notions inseparably co-relative":

Never did a child stand by the side of a running stream, pondering within himself what power was the feeder of the perpetual current, from what never-wearied sources the body of water was supplied, but he must have been inevitably propelled to follow this question by another: "Towards what abyss is it in progress? what receptacle can contain the mighty influx?" And the spirit of the answer must have been, though the word might be sea or ocean, accompanied perhaps with an image gathered from a map, or from the real object in nature – these might have been the *letter*, but the *spirit* of the answer must have been *as* inevitably, – a receptacle without bounds or dimensions; – nothing less than infinity.   (*Prose*, 2:51)

The claim that even a child will understand that infinity is the spirit of this landscape, whose sublimity is declared by the phrase "a receptacle without bounds or dimensions," leads Wordsworth into a semiotic complexity at odds with his main point. The site of complexity is the letter, which may be either "an image gathered from a map," "words," or "the real object in nature." Whereas "an image gathered from a map" assumes a conventional, abstract system of topographical representation, the "real object in nature" assumes a naive perceptualist model of how language refers to things. Between these two kinds of "images" are "words," whose relation to the map image and the "real object" is not specified. Collectively these options subvert the point of the example by indicating how it might not illustrate a simple correspondence between what the child sees and what he thinks.

Why does Wordsworth risk this sublime figure? One answer is supplied by the context for this passage, which readers tend to consider out of context, as the self-aggrandizing isolation of sublime figures invites us to do. According to Wordsworth, the fact that a child will "inevitably" understand that a sublime landscape refers to infinity shows that even children can comprehend the "principle of immortality." Indeed this is the reason for writing epitaphs at all. Without this principle, he explains, death would subvert "the principle of love," of "social feelings," and "the faculty of reason which exists in Man alone" (*Prose*, 2:50). From the perspective of the beautiful, epitaphs are the most difficult acts of naming because they refer to what exists beyond the limits of human life. For this reason, the feeling they represent is inevitably exaggerated, uncomposed, or inexpressible. In short, he risks this sublime figure precisely because he must if epitaphs are to speak to the community of the living about what is buried and past.

1815 *Preface* to *Poems*

The 1815 *Preface* is less troubled, if it is troubled at all, by the power of sublime figures and passion. To argue, as some have, that this essay is reactionary, even conservative, is to neglect its consideration of what Wordsworth calls "the business of poetry." In fact, "too business-like" is the charge that some have levied against it for defining the imagination by explaining how specific poetic figures work. René Wellek dismisses Wordsworth's examples as "curiously inept: they merely cite very ordinary metaphorical transfers." W. J. B. Owen concludes that this method of definition is inferior to the demonstration offered by passages like the "Crossing of the Alps" in *The Prelude*, VI.[18] These dismissals of the 1815 *Preface* assume that transcendence – whether British, German, or American – is the key to Wordsworth and the Romantic imagination. Yet, as Ruoff rightly insists, the value of the 1815 *Preface* is its attention to what seems so "business-like – the "metaphorical transfers" Wellek found so ordinary.[19]

I begin with Wordsworth's analysis of three figures in which the literal meaning of the verb *hang* serves different figurative ends. Cynthia Chase has argued that Wordsworth's language is here duplicitous insofar as his implicit claim – that a literal rather than imaginative use of language is as flatly imitative as a monkey's gestures or a parrot's speech – makes the literality of these activities do the work of metaphor.[20] Yet on this occasion (readers have found others in Wordsworth's prose) I suspect that Wordsworth's polemical distinction between literal and imaginative uses of language leads him almost immediately to specify a more trenchant relation between the literal meaning of the verb *hang* and different figures that employ this verb. As he is drawn into thinking about the pressure of literal meaning on poetic figures, Wordsworth abandons his analysis of the opposition between literal and imaginative language. Noting that parrots and monkeys "hang" from different objects by using beaks and claws, or paws and tail, he quotes similes by Virgil, Shakespeare, and Milton that recapitulate the literal options available for hanging – place and appendage (*Prose*, 3:31). His first example is from Virgil's first Eclogue, where Meliboeus explains that he can see his flock "hanging" from a distant hillside. The second is from the scene in *King Lear* when the disguised Edgar "warns" the blinded Gloucester about approaching the Dover cliffs. Wordsworth cites Edgar's description of what he "sees" on those nonexistent cliffs: "halfway down / Hangs one who gathers samphire."[21] The third is Milton's epic simile comparing Satan on his way to earth to a distant "fleet" which "*hangs* in the clouds."

Simple insofar as it is unextended, Virgil's simile is the closest to the literal meaning of the verb. Had Meliboeus said instead that he could see trees or rocks "hanging" on the hillside, the simile would have been a catachresis, a shift in (or abuse of) categories. Since sheep often cling or seem to cling to hillsides, they can more "literally" be said to "hang" than inanimate trees or rocks can. The Shakespearean lines, which are in fact quoted from Virgil, are exactly parallel: the samphire-gatherer who "hangs" clings to the rocks much as Meliboeus's flock cling to the hillside. But as a figure that assists a patent fiction of hazard in a scene whose relative security constitutes an imagined or mythic interlude before a tragic denouement, the *Lear* simile illustrates the scale of increasing complexity at work in these examples.

Milton's use of "hangs" is the most complex of the three. As an epic simile, it is the one least like the simple, unextended figure of the first example, which exhibits the figurative reticence of Virgilian pastoral.[22] By contrast, Milton's simile begins by signaling the figurative status of the image that is to follow ("As when far off at sea a fleet descried . . ."). As Wordsworth observes, the power of this simile is the effect of the verb *hangs* on the entire figure:

Here is the full strength of the imagination involved in the word *hangs*, and exerted upon the whole image: First, the fleet, an aggregate of many ships, is represented as one mighty person, whose track, we know and feel, is upon the waters; but, taking advantage of its appearance to the senses, the Poet dares to represent it *as hanging in the clouds*, both for the gratification of the mind in contemplating the image itself, and in reference to the motion and appearance of the sublime object to which it is compared. (*Prose*, 3:31)

Satan's "track upon the waters" is nowhere made visible in the text yet "we know and feel" its existence, as we expect to do with sublime figures. The poet who "dares" to compare Satan to an entire fleet recapitulates Satan's daring, colossal, and eccentric path from hell to earth. If a personification of this magnitude and singularity is unquestionably sublime, it is also among the most self-conscious of traditional figures.

Two features of this passage are striking. First, its attitude toward personification is singularly unlike that offered in the *Preface* to *Lyrical Ballads*. To be sure, one reason for the difference is the poetic occasion for the earlier *Preface*, which defends narrative experiments with the limits and language of the traditional ballad. But Wordsworth's later experiments with other, more "elevated" genres like epic and romance demonstrate the reorientation that preceded the 1815 *Preface*, which examines poetic figures Wordsworth would have been silent about or critical of in 1800. Second and more specifically, his interest in this Miltonic simile has an intriguing prehistory. He first mentions it in an 1811 letter to Sir George Beaumont in which he explains that he has seen a ship at sea that reminds him of Milton's text. In describing his visual re-experience of the Miltonic order of things (first the ship, then Satan), Wordsworth presents the image as one of aesthetic cooperation:

The visionary grandeur and beautiful form of this *single* vessel, could words have conveyed to the mind the picture which Nature presented to the eye, would have suited his purpose as well as the largest company of Vessels that ever associated together with the help of a trade wind, in the wide Ocean. Yet not exactly so, and for this reason, that his image is a permanent one, not dependent upon accident.[23]

This rare cooperation between sublimity and beauty echoes the way that poetic figures as forms capture sublime tenors. The most extraordinary sentence in the passage is probably the last, where Wordsworth retracts his preference for the visual image. As a sight made possible by the "atmosphere," the appearance of the ship "hang[ing] in the air" is transient, whereas Milton's image is permanent. This riposte to the pleasures of the visual image carries an unspecified aesthetic freight. For Wordsworth permanence – whether visual or verbal – is always preferable and more often attained by situating meaning in forms, those inhabitations in language and nature that are the sign of the beautiful.

Wordsworth's 1815 analysis of Milton's epic simile and its sublime tenor witnesses a collaboration between poetic devices and sublime ideas that could have been a struggle between opposing rhetorical and aesthetic perspectives. No struggle occurs either here or in Words-

Conclusion: aesthetics and poetic language

worth's discussion of two stanzas from "Resolution and Independence." Some of the logic of his 1807 decision to retitle the poem "Resolution and Independence" instead of "The Leech-Gatherer" (*Poems*, 1807, 123n.) is, I suggest, his recognition of whose sublimity is at issue in the poem. In Milton's simile, the poet dares to imitate Satan's daring by impersonating him as an entire fleet, at once de-personifying him and magnifying his epic, heroic stature. But in "Resolution and Independence" the poet's daring is his own. In both texts similes give figurative shape and definition to unseen and sublime powers – in Milton's case, they belong to Satan and the poet; in Wordsworth's case, to the speaker who uses similes to make a poetic figure of the leech-gatherer.

Using quicker poetic eyes than some have used to read Wordsworth's analysis of the figures he created to represent the leech-gatherer, Lawrence Lipking observes that the "just comparison" between sea-beast, stone, and leech-gatherer that Wordsworth adduces is "a specimen of Lockean wit, 'by affinity to take one thing for another'."[24] "Take" rather than naturally or unobtrusively "acquire" is the appropriate term for the way in which these similes constitute, by an amphibious process of accretion, the figure of the leech-gatherer. As Lipking notes, the resulting image is not "a clear and distinct picture." It is, moreover, ordinary only in the sense that figures of speech are ordinary poetic events. In a more particular and more business-like sense, the work that poetic figures do always requires the wrenching or seizing of meaning that Wordsworth's insistence on the proximity of the images of sea-beast, stone, and leech-gatherer dramatizes. Lipking emphasizes the Romantic blurring of vision which these images illustrate. I am interested in the matter-of-fact tone Wordsworth employs to describe the process by which distinct images become "blurred" as they are made to signify aspects of the leech-gatherer:

In these images, the conferring, the abstracting, and the modifying power of the Imagination, immediately and mediately acting, are all brought into conjunction. The stone is endowed with something of the power of life to approximate it to the sea-beast; and the sea-beast stripped of some of its vital qualities to assimilate it to the stone; which intermediate image is thus treated for the purpose of bringing the original image, that of the stone, to a nearer resemblance to the figure and condition of the aged Man; who is divested of so much of the indications of life and motion as to bring him to the point where the two objects unite and coalesce in just comparison. (*Prose*, 3:33)

Wordsworth might have emphasized the gaps in the leech-gatherer's figurative lineage which the indefinite phrases ("something of," "some

204

of," "a nearer resemblance," "so much of," "unite and coalesce") indicate. Instead he pays more attention to adjunct points of definiteness – the stone being endowed with life, the sea-beast stripped of vital qualities, and so on. Seen against the stream of images and speech which the speaker of the poem initiates or to which he responds, Wordsworth's prose reins in the blurred, visionary energies of the poem. Wordsworth calls his procedure in the poem an instance of "the conferring, the abstracting, and the modifying power of the Imagination, immediately and mediating acting." The same could be said for his analysis.

To illustrate how the imagination shapes and creates as well as modifies and abstracts, Wordsworth returns to the same Miltonic simile. But this time he foregrounds the unlimited sublime perspective which the concluding line of the simile ("so seemed / Far off the flying Fiend") makes available:

"So seemed," and to whom seemed? To the heavenly Muse who dictates the poem, to the eye of the Poet's mind, and to that of the Reader, present at one moment in the wide Ethiopian, and the next in the solitudes, then first broken in upon, of the infernal regions! (*Prose*, 3:34)

As Wordsworth's as well as Milton's sublime object, Satan prompts a telling excursus to another Miltonic figure, the synecdoche used to represent the Messiah "going forth to expel from heaven the rebellious angels, 'Attended by ten thousand thousand Saints / he onward came: far off his coming shone'." Numbered though his retinue be, the figure of the Messiah is for Wordsworth "lost almost and merged in the splendour of that indefinite abstraction 'His coming!'" (*Prose*, 3:34). The 1815 *Preface* illustrates the difference between Wordsworth's admiration for this sublime figure (with its implied affiliation to the sublimity of the figure that precedes it) and his "complex and revolutionary" response to sublime figures in other poems and essays. What matters here is the power and complexity of Milton's "indefinite abstraction." This preoccupation with "the business of poetry," its representational task, is beauty's contribution to Wordsworth's poetics. Elsewhere it suppresses the sublime; here it authorizes the poet's regard for figures that convey sublime ideas.

APPENDIX

Matters of chronology: "The Sublime and the Beautiful"

In their edition of Wordsworth's prose, W. J. B. Owen and Jane W. Smyser conclude that Wordsworth composed "The Sublime and the Beautiful" between September, 1811 and about November, 1812 (*Prose*, 2:128). I suggest instead that although Wordsworth probably did compose its middle section during this time, the opening section may be a palimpsest of materials written between 1806 and 1819 and the last was almost certainly written after his return to the Continent in 1820. As Owen and Smyser observe, the manuscripts which comprise "The Sublime and the Beautiful" are written on the same kind of paper used for "An Unpublished Tour," a manuscript which probably represents Wordsworth's first effort to extend the argument of his anonymous 1810 text for Wilkinson's *Select Views* (*Prose*, 2:139). As such, this manuscript stands between the 1810 text and later editions of the *Guide*, beginning with its 1820 publication in the *River Duddon* volume and its first appearance as a separate work in 1822. As the editors also note, the middle section of Wordsworth's fragmentary essay on aesthetics, which lists the parts of the mind's response to the sublime, reiterates points scattered throughout "An Unpublished Tour." This contextual resemblance strongly suggests that Wordsworth drafted this portion of "The Sublime and the Beautiful" at about the same time that he began to develop early *Guide* materials.

The similarity among the papers used for both manuscript groups suggests one possible objection to my claim that "The Sublime and the Beautiful" is a much later fair copy of several stages of revision. Most of the manuscripts which Owen and Smyser link to early versions of Wordsworth's *Guide*, including the fragment on aesthetics, are written on a paper watermarked 1806 with a design which "looks somewhat like an anchor." (It looks more like a "P" to me.) However, Mark Reed observes some variations in paper color and weight.[1] If the

Appendix

Wordsworths used or repurchased paper with the same watermark at different times for the manuscripts in the group, as I suspect they did, Reed suggests they probably bought a new batch of the 1806 paper after 1811. He adds that something like this must have happened at least once before: "among the W[ordsworth] papers there was heavy use of a paper [watermarked] '1798' in 1806 and again in 1810–11."[2]

One other objection to the chronology I propose is the fact that the opening pages of "The Sublime and the Beautiful" elaborate a discussion of the Pikes of Langdale which appears in "An Unpublished Tour." Owen and Smyser point out that Wordsworth seems to have decided in mid-argument "to write another kind of book" (*Prose*, 2:132). I agree, but I doubt that the new "book" took its present shape or argument in 1811 or 1812. My sense of what may have happened is a more extended version of the layering of manuscript fragments which Owen and Smyser describe for the beginning of "The Sublime and the Beautiful." They note that Ms. 28ª (the first fifty-eight lines in the published transcription) probably replaces a rejected passage about the Pikes which they designate Ms. 28ᵇ (*Prose*, 2:451n.). I surmise that we catch Wordsworth's process of revision and displacement somewhere in the middle, and that it began before 1811 and becomes more persistent after 1811.

My evidence for this hypothesis is contextual and textual in about equal measure. Wordsworth added the passage on sublimity and beauty in nature's successive dealings with the earth's surface to the 1820 text of his *Guide* (*Prose*, 2:181–84, ll. 858–976). Of Ms. Prose 30, an early version of this passage, Owen and Smyser agree that it "must have been written for the 1820 edition" (*Prose*, 2:136). As I argue in Chapter 2, some of the geological observations which Wordsworth borrowed for this passage can be traced to Whitaker's *Antiquities of Craven*, which he read in 1808, but more of them derive from later speculations among friends and acquaintances about the stratigraphy of the Lake District. If Wordsworth wrote the *Guide* passage in question as late as 1819, it either recapitulates the allied argument about the mind's aesthetic progress in the opening lines of his essay on aesthetics, or it foreshadows it. It is impossible to say which came first. Indeed, it is probable that no clear stratigraphy of composition exists for the beginning of "The Sublime and the Beautiful," which may well summarize arguments Wordsworth had been considering for years, some of which he seems to have written down in 1806, when he gave some remarks on the sublime to someone, perhaps Beaumont, to show to Uvedale Price.

The aesthetic stratigraphy of the last section of "The Sublime and the Beautiful," where Wordsworth presents the Rhinefall as an illustration of the role of resistance in sublime experience, is easier to trace. If he had written this section by 1812, he would hardly have discussed the Rhinefall as a sublime scene, as his experience of it in 1790 had been disappointingly un-sublime. This anomaly disappears if we suppose instead that Wordsworth wrote this section after his 1820 tour, when he apparently felt the sublimity of the scene as he had not felt it thirty years earlier (see Chapter 7). The outcome of the long prehistory which I have described for this aesthetic revision is recorded in several of Wordsworth's emendations and insertions in the 1822 and 1823 editions of his *Guide*. Thus the section on Alpine scenery, new in 1822, praises the "great Fall of the Rhine at Schaffhausen" as an exception to the general rule that Alpine waterfalls tend to disappoint travellers (*Prose*, 2:237). A related motif in "The Sublime and the Beautiful" – an adult stranger's likely aesthetic response to a mountainous region (*Prose*, 2:350) – appears just once in "An Unpublished Tour" but repeatedly in the 1822 and 1823 emendations of the *Guide* (*Prose*, 2:230–31, 237). The autobiographical sub-text for Wordsworth's general claim that strangers to a mountainous region gradually learn how to respond to its sublimity after initial disappointments is summarized by the difference between his 1790 and 1820 responses to the Rhinefall. By 1820, Wordsworth was a traveller who had been educated by Coleridge, by Kant, and by recent events in European political history. He had learned, in short, how and why to avoid aesthetic disappointments. Other minor revisions in the 1822 and 1823 editions of the *Guide* discussed in Chapter 2 display an attention to aesthetic details that is infrequent in *Select Views*, more often present in "An Unpublished Tour," and insistent in the 1820 and subsequent editions of the *Guide*.

As a fair copy text that probably collates different stages of composition, "The Sublime and the Beautiful" summarizes the larger aesthetic terrain of Wordsworth's poetry and prose.

Notes

1 Introduction

1 DeQuincey, "William Wordsworth," *Collected Writings*, ed. David Masson, (15 vols. Edinburgh: Adam and Charles Black, 1863), 2:169. See also John Jones, *The Egotistical Sublime: A History of Wordsworth's Imagination* (London: Chatto and Windus, 1970), 156–58 and 165.

2 *The Prelude, 1799, 1805, 1850*, eds. Jonathan Wordsworth, M. H. Abrams, and Stephen Gill (New York: W. W. Norton, 1979), 5:49–165, pp. 154–60. Subsequent references to this edition appear in the text, cited as *Prel.*, followed by book, line(s), and page. Unless otherwise indicated, the 1805 text is cited.

3 Keats to Richard Woodhouse, *Letters, 1814–21*, ed. Hyder E. Rollins (2 vols., Cambridge, Mass.: Harvard University Press, 1958), 1:387; Hazlitt, "Coriolanus," in *Complete Works* (21 vols., London: J. M. Dent, 1930), 4:214. See also Hazlitt's remarks concerning Wordsworth's poetical character in his 1814 review of *The Excursion* (*Complete Writings*, 19:11) and a longer essay "On Mr. Wordsworth's *Excursion*" (4:112–13). For an analysis of Hazlitt's ambivalent critique of Wordsworthian sublimity, see David Bromwich, *Hazlitt: The Mind of a Critic* (New York: Oxford University Press, 1983), 183–87.

4 *The Sublime: A Study of Critical Theories in XVIII-Century England* (1935 repr.; Ann Arbor: University of Michigan Press, 1960), 231–32; Geoffrey H. Hartman, *Wordsworth's Poetry, 1787–1814* (New Haven: Yale University Press, 1964), 242.

5 *Descriptive Sketches*, ed. Eric Birdsall (Ithaca: Cornell University Press, 1984), 792–95, p. 116 (1836 text, p. 117). This passage does not appear in the 1836 version. See also Thomson, "Summer," ll. 423–31 in *The Seasons and the Castle of Indolence*, ed. J. Logie Robertson (Oxford: Clarendon Press, 1891), 77. Paul Sheats notes the role of the revolutionary sublime in Wordsworth's text in *The Making of Wordsworth's Poetry 1785–98* (Cambridge, Mass.: Harvard University Press, 1973), 68–72.

6 Neil Hertz, "The Notion of Blockage in the Literature of the Sublime," in *Psychoanalysis and the Question of the Text*, ed. Geoffrey H. Hartman (Baltimore: The Johns Hopkins University Press, 1978), 62–85.

7 Browning to Ruskin, in *The Works of John Ruskin*, eds. E. T. Cook and Alexander Wedderburn (39 vols., London: Allen, 1909), 36:xxxiv. Cited by

Notes to pages 5–7

Herbert F. Tucker, *Browning's Beginnings* (Minneapolis: University of Minnesota Press, 1980), 11; Wordsworth, *Prose Works*, eds. W. J. B. Owen and Jane W. Smyser (3 vols., Oxford: Clarendon Press, 1974), 3:65. Hereafter cited as *Prose*, volume, page.

8 See especially Virgil Nemoianu, *The Taming of Romanticism: European Literature in the Age of Biedermeier* (Cambridge, Mass.: Harvard University Press, 1984); W. J. T. Mitchell, "Metamorphoses of the Vortex: Hogarth, Turner, and Blake," in *Articulate Images*, ed. Richard Wendorf (Minneapolis: University of Minnesota Press, 1983), 161; Elizabeth R. Napier, "The Problem of Boundaries in *Wuthering Heights*," *Philological Quarterly* 63 (Winter 1984): 95–106; Frances Ferguson, "Shelley's *Mont Blanc*: What the Mountain Said," in *Romanticism and Language*, ed. Arden Reed (Ithaca: Cornell University Press, 1984), 202–14; William Keach, *Shelley's Style* (New York: Methuen, 1984), 194–200; Angela Leighton, *Shelley and the Sublime* (Cambridge University Press, 1984); and Cynthia Chase, " 'Viewless Wings': Keats's 'Ode to a Nightingale'," in *Decomposing Figures* (Baltimore: The Johns Hopkins University Press, 1986), 65–81.

9 Herbert S. Lindenberger, *On Wordsworth's Prelude* (Princeton University Press, 1963).

10 W. J. B. Owen, "The Sublime and the Beautiful in *The Prelude*," *The Wordsworth Circle* 4 (1973): 67–86; Albert Wlecke, *Wordsworth and the Sublime* (Berkeley: University of California Press, 1973); and Thomas Weiskel, *The Romantic Sublime: Studies in the Structure and Psychology of Transcendence* (Baltimore: The Johns Hopkins University Press, 1976).

11 David Pirie, *William Wordsworth: The Poetry of Grandeur and of Tenderness* (London: Methuen, 1982), 1–7 and David Simpson, *Wordsworth and the Figurings of the Real* (Atlantic Highlands, NJ: Humanities Press, 1982), xvi–xxv.

12 Iris Murdoch, "The Sublime and the Beautiful Revisited," *The Yale Review*, NS 49 (1959): 247–71 and Richard Kuhns, "The Beautiful and the Sublime," *New Literary History* 13 (1978): 287–307.

13 In his discussion of why Wordsworth might have been suspicious of Kantian philosophy, James Chandler quotes Jules Michelet's famous anecdote about Kant's reaction to the Fall of the Bastille and George Herbert Mead's claim that Kant was "the philosopher of the French Revolution" (Michelet, *History of the French Revolution*, tr. Charles Cocks, ed. Gordon Wright [University of Chicago Press, 1967], 455; Mead, *Movements of Thought in the Nineteenth Century*, ed. Merritt H. Moore [University of Chicago Press, 1936], 25–30). See Chandler, *Wordsworth's Second Nature* (University of Chicago Press, 1984), 254–56. Even if Kant did alter his daily walk to get news from France after the Bastille fell, as Michelet claims, one wonders how much sympathy the philosopher of practical and pure reason could have had for revolutionary excesses in the name of reason. More specifically, his redefinition of the sublime as the *product* of reason rather than might or magnitude suggests a thoroughly Kantian suspicion of revolutionary power.

14 Jerome Christensen, "The Sublime and the Romance of the Other," *Diacritics* 7 (1978): 10–23.

210

15 McGann contends that Wordsworth is among the chief protagonists of the sublime, transcendent imagination, which is, he argues, the Romantic ideology. See Jerome McGann, *Romantic Ideology* (University of Chicago Press, 1983), 81–92. Gene W. Ruoff argues to the contrary in "Religious Implications of Wordsworth's Imagination," *Studies in Romanticism* 12 (Summer 1973): 670–92. Kenneth R. Johnston implicitly challenges the claim that Wordsworth celebrates the ideology of transcendence when he argues that the task of integrating Imagination, Nature, and poetry in *The Recluse* "implies [Wordsworth's] necessary accommodation of poetic inspiration to ordinary forms of human life." See Johnston, *Wordsworth and The Recluse* (New Haven: Yale University Press, 1984), 150.

16 Hartman argues to the contrary in *Wordsworth's Poetry*, 212.

17 *Guide through the District of the Lakes* and "The Sublime and the Beautiful," *Prose*, 2:181, 349.

18 Michel Foucault, *The Archaeology of Knowledge*, tr. A. M. Sheridan Smith (New York: Harper and Row, 1976). Foucault did not, however, valorize the archeological relation of depths and surfaces. See Hubert L. Dreyfus and Paul Rabinow, *Michel Foucault: Beyond Structuralism and Hermeneutics* (University of Chicago Press, 1982), 104–6.

19 In recent Marxist criticism, the difference between Hegel and Blake on this point tends to be slight. As William C. Dowling observes, for Frederic Jameson genuinely dialectical thinking is Blakean. See Dowling, *Jameson, Althusser, Marx* (Ithaca: Cornell University Press, 1984), 51 and 112.

20 Freud, "Fragments of an Analysis of a Case of Hysteria," vol. 7 in *Complete Psychological Works*, tr. James Strachey (London: Hogarth Press, 1953), 12, cited by Peter Gay, *Freud, Jews, and Other Germans* (New York: Oxford University Press, 1978), 46.

21 See especially Freud, *Interpretation of Dreams*, tr. James Strachey (New York: Avon Books, 1965), 374–85 and Margaret Ferguson, "Border Territories of Defense: Freud and the Defenses of Poetry," in *The Literary Freud: Mechanisms of Defense and the Poetic Will*, ed. Joseph Smith (New Haven: Yale University Press, 1980), 150–56.

22 Weiskel, *Romantic Sublime*, 197.

23 Lawrence Lipking, "Quick Poetic Eyes," in *Articulate Images*, 5. See note 8, above. Gerald L. Bruns opposes Romantic genius to classical rhetorical invention in *Inventions: Writing, Textuality, and Understanding in Literary History* (New Haven: Yale University Press, 1982), 101–2.

2 Archeologies

1 Bacon, *The Advancement of Learning*, ed. William A. Wright (Oxford: Clarendon Press, 1891), Book II, sec. 2:3, 90.

2 For a summary of changing attitudes toward antiquarianism and archeological evidence, see Arnaldo Momigliano, "Ancient History and the Antiquarian," in *Studies in Historiography* (London: Weidenfeld and Nicolson, 1966), 1–39. As Momigliano observes, although the meaning of archeology shifted in the eighteenth and nineteenth centuries, for much of this period it retained its ancient meaning – the study of antiquities and the past – as it

acquired its more specialized modern meaning. Wordsworth's understanding of history as retrieval echoes both definitions.

3 *The Excursion*, III, in *Poetical Works*, eds. Ernest de Selincourt and Helen Darbishire, 2nd edn (5 vols., Oxford: Clarendon Press, 1949), 5:79–80, ll. 125–48, 172–89. Subsequent references to this edition appear parenthetically in the text as *PW*, followed by volume, page, and line. In 1822, John Hodgson offered a similar distinction between "vulgar" (i.e. superficial) and "judicious" antiquarianism. See his "On the Study of Antiquities," *Archaeologia Aeliana* 1:9–19. Cited by Frank Hole and Thomas Heizer, *An Introduction to Prehistoric Archeology*, 3rd edn (New York: Holt, Rinehart and Wilson, 1973), 4. In his 1816 *Letter to a Friend of Robert Burns*, Wordsworth chastizes "remorseless hunters after matter of fact." He also insists he would not have welcomed the discovery of a "Boswellian" account of the life of Horace had one been "unearthed among the ruins of Herculaneaum." See his *Letter*, *Prose*, 3:123. Both points of course serve Wordsworth's immediate purpose: to argue against digging up the more unsavory aspects of Burns's life.

4 Letter to Scott, May 14, 1808 in *The Letters of William and Dorothy Wordsworth: The Middle Years, I, 1806–11*, eds. Ernest de Selincourt and Mary Moorman, 2nd edn rev. (Oxford: Clarendon Press, 1969), 237.

5 *A Guide through the District of the Lakes*, *Prose*, 2:195. Subsequent citations of this work appear parenthetically in the text. The final text of "Long Meg and her Daughters" appears in *PW*, 4:47. See also Wordsworth's letter of January 10, 1821, *Letters: Later Years, I, 1821–28*, 4–5. Owen and Smyser review Wordsworth's fascination with "Druid" structures in their commentary on his *Guide*, *Prose*, 2:403n.

6 William Stukeley, *A Temple Restored to the British Druids* (London: W. Innys, 1740).

7 See Owen and Smyser, eds., *Guide*, *Prose*, 2:132–33, and "The Sublime and the Beautiful," *Prose*, 2:349–60.

8 Wordsworth owned numerous maps and guidebooks. See Chester L. and Alice C. Shaver, *Wordsworth's Library: A Catalogue* (New York: Garland, 1979). See 3, 47, 63, 81–82, 96, 108, 130–31, 169, 191, 249, and 307. Owen and Smyser note Wordsworth's use of earlier guidebooks in their *Guide* commentary, *Prose*, 2:379–429. For recent analyses of maps as models, see Stephen Toulmin, "Theories and Maps," in *The Philosophy of Science: An Introduction* (London: Hutchinson's University Library, 1953), 105–9, and Arthur H. Robinson and Barbara B. Petchenik, "Structure in Maps and Mapping," in *The Nature of Maps* (University of Chicago Press, 1976), 108–23.

9 Owen and Smyser summarize this debate in their *Guide* commentary, *Prose*, 2:388–89. See also DeQuincey, "William Wordsworth," *Collected Writings*, 2:163 and Coleridge, "On the Principles of Genial Criticism," *Biographia Literaria*, ed. John Shawcross (2 vols., 1817; repr. London: Oxford University Press, 1967), 2:233. See a similar account of aesthetic wholes and parts in *The Table Talk and Omnia of Samuel Taylor Coleridge*, ed. T. Ashe (London: George Bell, 1884), 232.

10 Owen and Smyser, eds., *Guide* Introduction, *Prose*, 2:132–33.

11 Thomas Burnet, *The Sacred Theory of the Earth*, ed. J. M. Cohen (2 vols.,

1684; repr. Carbondale, Ill.: Southern Illinois University Press, 1965), 1:67, 77, 140, and Marjorie Nicolson, *Mountain Gloom and Mountain Glory: The Development of the Aesthetics of the Infinite* (1959; repr. New York: W. W. Norton, 1963), 184–224.

12 Burke, *A Philosophical Enquiry into the Origin of Our Ideas of the Sublime and Beautiful*, ed. J. T. Boulton (1858; repr. University of Notre Dame Press, 1968), 58–60.

13 Longinus insisted both that the sublime ratifies the use of exaggerated figures and of those which are inadequate (thus the "silence" of Ajax becomes an emblem of Homer's sublime style), and that broken metrics "debase sublimity" while a dignity of words is requisite to it. See *Dionysius Longinus On the Sublime*, tr. William Smith, 4th edn corrected (London: E. Johnson, 1770), 78, 95–96, 101. English writers tended to identify simplicity as requisite to sublime expression. See Joseph Addison, "The Pleasures of the Imagination," in *The Spectator*, no. 412, ed. Donald F. Bond (5 vols., Oxford: Clarendon Press, 1965), 3:540–44; Hugh Blair, *Lectures on Rhetoric and Belles Lettres* (2 vols., London: W. Strahan, 1783), 1:57; Edward Greene, *Critical Essays* (London: T. Spilsbary, J. Ridley, 1770), 32; Joseph Priestley, *A Course of Lectures on Oratory and Criticism*, eds. Vincent M. Bevilacqua and Richard Murphy (1777; repr. Carbondale, Ill.: Southern Illinois University Press, 1965), 160. William Duff approved exaggeration and other "faults" produced in the expression of sublime ideas or passion in *Critical Observations on the Writings of the Most Celebrated Original Geniuses in Poetry*, ed. William Bruce Johnson (1770; repr. Delmar, New York: Scholar's Facsimiles and Reprints, 1973), 123–24, 165. For a survey of eighteenth-century accounts of the relation between the sublime and poetic figures, see David A. Hansen, "Addison on Ornament and Poetic Style," in *Studies in Criticism and Aesthetics, 1660–1800*, eds. Howard Anderson and John Shea (Minneapolis: University of Minnesota Press, 1967), 94–127.

14 William Gilpin, *Observations relative chiefly to Picturesque Beauty, made in the year 1772, on several parts of England; particularly the Mountains and lakes of Cumberland and Westmoreland* (2 vols., London: R. Blamire, 1786), 1:101–2. Gilpin's phrase is "line of boundary." For an assessment of Gilpin's significance, see Martin Price, "The Picturesque Moment," in *From Sensibility to Romanticism*, eds. Frederick W. Hilles and Harold Bloom (New York: Oxford University Press, 1965), 259–92.

15 Uvedale Price, *Essays on the Picturesque* (2 vols., London: J. Robson, 1796–98), 1:82–123, 188–89; Knight, *An Analytical Inquiry into the Principles of Taste*, 2nd edn (London: L. Hansard, 1805); Repton, *An Enquiry into the Changes of Taste in Landscape Gardening* (London: J. Taylor, 1806). For a discussion of the picturesque debate, see W. J. Hipple, Jr., *The Beautiful, the Sublime, and the Picturesque in Eighteenth-Century Aesthetic Theory* (Carbondale, Ill.: Southern Illinois University Press, 1957); John R. Nabholtz, "Wordsworth's *Guide to the Lakes* and the Picturesque Tradition," *Modern Philology* 61 (1964): 288–97; Russell Noyes, *Wordsworth and the Art of Landscape* (1968; repr. New York: Haskell House, 1973), 45–48; and J. R. Watson, *Picturesque Landscape and English Romantic Poetry* (London: Hutchinson, 1970), especially 93–107. Wordsworth objected to the "delicate

and fastidious" taste of Price's landscaping at Foxley in a letter to Sir George Beaumont, 28 August, 1811, in *MY*, 1, 505–6. Cited by Owen and Smyser, eds., *Guide* commentary, *Prose*, 2:458. See also Coleridge's criticism of tourists who confused distinct aesthetic categories in *Shakespearean Criticism*, ed. Thomas M. Raysor (2 vols., Cambridge, Mass.: Harvard University Press, 1930), 2:62–63. For another contemporary reaction against Gilpin, see William Green, *The Tourist's New Guide* (Kendall: R. Lough, 1819), 1:396.

16 Coleridge, "On the Principles of Genial Criticism," in *Biographia Literaria*, 2:232); Francis Hutcheson, *An Inquiry into the Original of our Ideas of Beauty and Virtue* (London: J. Darby, 1726), 17; Coleridge, *Shakespearean Criticism*, 1:222. Raysor notes this echo of Schlegel (222n.).

17 Thomas Whitaker, *The History and Antiquities of the Deanery of Craven*, 2nd edn (London: T. Nichols, 1812), 1. Cited by Nabholtz, "Wordsworth's Guide," 288–97. Wordsworth received a copy of Whitaker's book in October of 1807. See Mark L. Reed, *Wordsworth: The Chronology of the Middle Years* (Cambridge, Mass.: Harvard University Press, 1975), 700, and Alice P. Comparetti, ed., *The White Doe of Rylstone* (Ithaca, NY: Cornell University Press, 1940), 41–45, 200–46.

18 Addison, *The Spectator*, no. 412, 3:542; for review of geological discoveries during this period, see Charles C. Gillispie, *Genesis and Geology* (New York: Harper and Row, 1951), 96–120.

19 John Housman, *A Topographical Description of Cumberland, Westmoreland, Lancashire, and a part of the West Riding of Yorkshire* (Carlisle: F. Jollie, 1800), 282. To the May 1920 issue of *The Lonsdale Magazine*, Dr. Campbell contributed a brief essay, "Stratification in the County of Lancaster" (1:199–201). In the October issue Jonathan Otley published his first account of Lakes strata, "On the Succession of Rocks, in the District of the Lakes" (1:433–36).

20 Erasmus Darwin, *Botanic Garden* (1791; repr. Menston: Scholar Press, 1973), 192–93.

21 Georges Leclerc (Buffon), *Les Époques de la Nature*, ed. J. Roger (Paris: Éditions du Museum, 1962). Wordsworth owned an abridged English edition titled *The System of Natural History*. See Shaver, *Wordsworth's Library*, 155; James Hutton, *Theory of the Earth* (1788 repr.), vol. 5 in *Contributions to the History of Geology* (New York: Hafner, 1973); John Playfair, *Illustrations of the Huttonian Theory of the Earth*, ed. George W. White (1802; repr. New York: Dover, 1956); Georges Cuvier, *Recherches sur les ossemens fossiles de quadrapèdes* (4 vols., Paris: Deterville, 1814); and Jean Andre De Luc, "Geological Letters addressed to Professor Blumenbach," *British Critic*, October 1793 to March 1795. I am indebted to Alan Bewell for his notice of these early discussions of stratigraphic principles. See also Frere, Letter dated "1797," *Archaeologia* (1800), 204. Cited by Glyn Daniel, *The Origins and Growth of Archeology* (New York: Thomas Y. Crowell, 1967), 30–46. See also Daniel, *A Hundred-Fifty Years of Archeology* (Cambridge, Mass.: Harvard University Press, 1976), 18–30.

22 Sedgwick recalled his promise in the first of three "Letters on the Geology of the Lake District," which were appended to the 1842 edition of Wordsworth's *Guide*. By 1845, Sedgwick had sent a fourth letter. See Owen and Smyser,

Introduction, *Guide, Prose,* 2:134. Although Sedgwick's letters were written long after they could have influenced Wordsworth's *Guide* revisions, they demonstrate the rapid expansion of geological knowledge during the first decades of the nineteenth century. See also: Marilyn Gaull, "From Wordsworth to Darwin: 'On to the Fields of Praise'," *The Wordsworth Circle* 10 (Winter 1979): 36, and Paul H. Barret, "The Sedgwick-Darwin Geologic Tour of North Wales," *Proceedings of the American Philosophical Society* 118 (1974): 146–64. Cited by Gaull, 47n.

23 Dr. Campbell, "Stratification in the County of Lancaster," *The Lonsdale Magazine* 1 (May 1820): 199–201; Jonathan Otley, "The Floating Island On Derwent Water, In Cumberland," 1 (January 1820): 15–16; "Dews and Fogs in the Lake District," 2 (March 1821): 92–94; and "On the Succession of Rocks," 1 (October 1820): 433–36. An anonymous 1842 guidebook included a long and detailed essay on various strata. See *A Guide to the Lakes of Cumberland, Westmoreland, and Lancashire, with a sketch of Carlisle,* 3rd edn (Carlisle: H. Scott, 1842), ii and 138–63. See also W. G. Collingwood, *The Lake Counties* (London: Frederick Warne and Co., 1932), 228–41.

24 Jonathan Otley, "On the Succession of Rocks," 434, and *A Concise Description of the English Lakes* (Keswick: J. Richardson, 1823), 94–105. For a discussion of recent hypotheses concerning "plate techtonics" in the Borrowdale Volcanic Group (which includes Scawfell and Great Gavel), see R. V. Davis, *Geology of Cumbria* (Clapham, North Yorkshire: Dalesman Books, 1977), 7–21.

25 Ramond de Carbonnières, *Lettres de M. William Coxe à M. W. Melmoth sur l'État politique, civil et naturel de la Suisse* (2 vols., Paris: Belin, 1781), 2: 96ff. For an analysis of the significance of geological time in Ramond and the Romantic sense of history, see Charles Rosen, "Now, Voyager," *New York Review of Books,* November 6, 1986, 58–60. See also Paul Sheats's discussion of Ramond, Alpine geology, and deluge in *The Making of Wordsworth's Poetry 1785–98* (Cambridge, Mass.: Harvard University Press, 1973), 64.

26 William Green, *Tourist's Guide,* 2:317–23. Owen and Smyser describe the Green–Wordsworth friendship in their Introduction, *Prose,* 2:124–25.

27 Otley's "Pocket Map," engraved "Kendal, 1818," was reissued with his *A Concise Description of the English Lakes.* Wordsworth acquired the second edition of 1825. See Shaver, *Wordsworth's Library,* 91. Elevations taken from an 1811 trigometrical survey and published in the November 1820 issue of *The Lonsdale Magazine* also identify the Scawfell Pikes as higher than Helvellyn.

28 *Guide, Prose,* 2:175 and Otley, "On the Succession of Rocks," 433–36. Like many contemporaries, Wordsworth avoids taking a position in the debate between the uniformitarian and catastrophic hypotheses of the earth's formation. Except for the affective power of the deluge as the sublime cataclysm of his poetry, he tends to describe geological processes as though they are uniform over time. For a review of this debate, see Gillispie, *Genesis and Geology,* 96–145.

29 Cited by C. W. Ceram, *Gods, Graves, and Scholars,* 2nd edn rev. (New York: Knopf, 1970), 14.

30 Rev. Henry Rowlands, *Mona Antiqua Restaurata; an Archeological Discourse on the Antiquities, Natural and Historical, of the Isle of Anglesey, the Ancient Seat of the British Druids* (Dublin: Robert Owen, 1723), Preface. Cited by Glyn Daniel, *Origin and Growth of Archeology*, 30–31.

31 But see Owen, "The Sublime and the Beautiful," 67–86, "Wordsworth's Aesthetics of Landscape," *The Wordsworth Circle* 4 (1976): 70–82; and Patrick Holland, "Wordsworth and the Sublime," *The Wordsworth Circle* 5 (1974): 17–22.

32 Raimonda Modiano discusses this problem and Wordsworth's echoes of Kant in "The Kantian Seduction: Wordsworth on the Sublime," a paper presented at "Cross-currents and Controversies," a conference on English and German Romanticism, University of Houston, February 25–28, 1981. See also Wordsworth, *Kendal and Windermere Railway* (1845), *Prose*, 3:342.

33 See the narrator's attitude toward Emily's "sensibility" in Radcliffe's *Mysteries of Udolpho* (London: Oxford University Press, 1970).

34 Burke, *Enquiry*, 63–68, 113–117. See Frances Ferguson, "The Sublime of Edmund Burke, or the Bathos of Experience," *Glyph* 8 (1981): 66–75 and "Legislating the Sublime," in *Studies in Eighteenth-Century British Art and Aesthetics*, ed. Ralph Cohen (Berkeley: University of California Press, 1985), 134. Other critics have argued that Wordsworth's aesthetics is primarily modelled on Burkean principles. See Owen, "The Sublime and the Beautiful in *The Prelude*," 67–86 and J. A. W. Heffernan, *Wordsworth's Theory of Poetry* (Ithaca: Cornell University Press, 1969), 158–65.

35 See the discussion of perspective and landscape gardening, s.v. *gardening, Encyclopaedia Britannica*, 1st and 3rd edns. Wordsworth owned the third edition of 1797. See Shaver, *Wordsworth's Library*, 88. Noyes reviews Wordsworth's interest in landscape gardening in *Wordsworth and the Art of Landscape*, 91–113.

36 Weiskel, *Romantic Sublime*, 51–59.

37 Burke, *Enquiry*, 60–64.

38 Burke, *Enquiry*, 57. In "The Sublime and the Beautiful," Owen cites this passage to argue that the Wordsworthian sublime is Burkean in character (70). Yet Wordsworth's principle of individual form contradicts Burke's claim that objects which are perceived as sublime must be obscure. Unlike Wordsworth, Coleridge agreed with Burke on the role of obscurity or indistinct form in sensations of sublimity. See Coleridge's 1799 letter to Josiah Wedgwood, in *Letters of Samuel Taylor Coleridge*, ed. E. H. Coleridge (2 vols., London: W. Heinemann, 1895), 1:117. Quoted by Clarence DeWitt Thorpe, "Coleridge on the Sublime," in *Wordsworth and Coleridge: Studies in Honor of George McLean Harper* (Princeton University Press, 1939), 210.

39 See Stuart Peterfreund, "Wordsworth and the Sublime of Duration," *Publications of the Arkansas Philological Association* 2 (1975): 41–46. For an assessment of an allied principle in Romantic painting, see Karl Kroeber, "Romantic Historicism: The Temporal Sublime," in *Images of Romanticism*, eds. Kroeber and William Walling (New Haven: Yale University Press, 1978), 149–65.

40 Burke, *Enquiry*, 68.

41 Addison, *Spectator*, nos. 412 and 413, 3:540–45. Unlike later theorists, who

often used *great* and *sublime* interchangeably, Addison reserves the term *sublime* for sublimity of thought or expression. See, for example, his *Spectator* discussions of Milton, Longinus, and the sublime: no. 339 (1712), 3:254–55; no. 303 (1712), 3:85–86; no. 279 (1712), 2:587. See also George Miller's late eighteenth-century recapitulation of this and other features of the sublime in "An Essay on the Origin and Nature of our Idea of the Sublime," *Transactions of the Royal Irish Academy* 5 (1794): 17–38.

42 Ephraim Chambers's *Cyclopedia: or, an Universal Dictionary of Arts and Sciences* (1728 and 1751) appears to be the first dictionary to record a specific association of the sublime with the pathetic. However both Nathaniel Bailey's *Dictionarium Britannicum* (1712) and Darnell's *Essays on the Different Stiles of Poetry* (1713) describe the pathetic as that which raises the passions, likewise a theme of the sublime in Longinus's treatise. Noted by Monk, *The Sublime*, 13n.

43 John Baillie, *Essay on the Sublime* (London: Dodsley, 1747), 4, 31–33.

44 Longinus, *On the Sublime*, 30–69.

45 Burke, *Enquiry*, 68.

46 Burke, *Enquiry*, 61–63. See Weiskel, *Romantic Sublime*, 83–107, and Ronald Paulson, *Representations of Revolution* (New Haven: Yale University Press, 1983), 66.

47 See John Dennis, "The Advancement and Reformation of Modern Poetry" (1701) in *The Critical Works of John Dennis*, ed. Edward N. Hooker (2 vols., Baltimore: The Johns Hopkins University Press, 1939), 1:219; and Addison, *Spectator*, nos. 279 and 303. As J. T. Boulton points out in his introduction to Burke's *Enquiry* (lxxxv–lxxxvii), both Hugh Blair and James Beattie echo Burke's use of Milton and Job, while Richard Payne Knight echoes his description of Milton's Satan.

48 Hugh Blair, *Lectures on Rhetoric and Belles Lettres*, 1:55–56; Alexander Gerard, *An Essay on Taste*, 3rd edn (1780; repr. Gainesville, Fla.: Scholars' Facsimiles and Reprints, 1963), 16; Priestley, *A Course of Lectures on Oratory and Criticism*, 158–59; Thomas Reid, *Essays on the Active Powers of the Human Mind* (2 vols., 1788, repr. Cambridge, Mass.: MIT Press, 1962), 2:778; and Archibald Alison, *Essays on the Nature and Principles of Taste* (Dublin: P. Byrne, 1970), 15.

49 Sir William Jones, "On the Arts, commonly called imitative," in *Poems consisting Chiefly of translations from the Asiatic Languages* (Oxford: Clarendon Press, 1772), 217; Uvedale Price, *Essays on the Picturesque*, 1:188–90.

50 Burke, *Enquiry*, 57; Knight, *Analytical Inquiry*, 55–56, 367–70.

51 Kant, *Critique of Judgement*, tr. J. H. Bernard (New York: Hafner, 1951), sec. 25–29, 86–120, especially 88–89. In the German text, *Kritik der Urteilskraft*, in *Sämmtliche Werke* (10 vols., Leipzig: L. Voss, 1867), 5:255–74, especially 257.

52 For discussions of Coleridge's rejection of sublime fear, see Thomas M. Raysor, "Unpublished Fragments in Aesthetics by S. T. Coleridge," *Studies in Philology* 22 (1925): 530–33, and *The Notebooks of Samuel Taylor Coleridge*, ed. Kathleen Coburn (3 vols., Princeton University Press, 1957–1973), Bollingen Series 50, 2 (1794–1804): no. 2093, cited by Raimonda Modiano,

"Coleridge and the Sublime," *The Wordsworth Circle* 9 (1978): 119. See also Coleridge's marginalia in a copy of Herder's *Kalligone*, published in part by John Shawcross, "Coleridge's Marginalia," *Notes and Queries* 4 (1905): 341. Cited by Modiano, "Coleridge and the Sublime," 115. Coleridge's term "endless allness" appears in Thomas Allsop, *Letters, Conversations, and Recollections of S. T. Coleridge* (2 vols., London: Oxford University Press, 1936), 1:97–99. Cited by Clarence DeWitt Thorpe, "Coleridge on the Sublime," 210.

53 Wordsworth and Coleridge probably discussed sublimity and fear when they read Knight's *Analytical Inquiry* together, possibly in 1806, when Wordsworth was apparently trying to compose some portion of his manuscript on aesthetics or, less probably, sometime after 1806 but before their quarrel in 1810. On June 3, 1806 Wordsworth wrote to Lady Beaumont from Coleorton that someone (Mark Reed suggests Sir George Beaumont) had discussed his ideas on the sublime with Uvedale Price. See *MY*, 1, 35 and Reed, *Wordsworth: The Chronology of the Middle Years, 1800–1815* (Cambridge, Mass.: Harvard University Press, 1975), 310. See also Edna A. Shearer, "Wordsworth and Coleridge Marginalia in a Copy of Richard Payne Knight's *Analytical Inquiry into the Principles of Taste*," *Huntington Library Quarterly* 1 (October 1937): 63–99. Reed discusses the probable dates of the marginalia in *Wordsworth: Middle Years*, 344.

54 Kant, *Critique of Judgement*, sec. 25, 88–89; in the German text, 5:257.

55 Kant, *Critique of Judgement*, sec. 28, 101. In the German text, 5:269. Kant argues in his early essay on aesthetics, *Beobachtungen über das Gefühl des Schönen und Erhabenen* (1764), that the sublime is understanding ("Verstand"). But this claim should be understood in context. Here it refers to a polarity between the sublime and the beautiful: "Verstand ist erhaben, witz ist schön" (the sublime is understanding, the beautiful is wit). This implied distinction between sublime depths and beautiful surfaces anticipates the essential polarity of Wordsworth's aesthetics. The text of Kant's 1764 essay appears in his *Sämmtliche Werke*, 2:229–80, especially 233.

56 Kant, *Critique of Judgement*, sec. 27, 97. In the German text, 5:264–65.

57 Jacques Derrida analyzes Kant's uneasiness in "Parergon," in *La Verité en Peinture* (Paris: Flammarion, 1978), 158–68. Frances Ferguson imagines how Kant might have regarded Frankenstein's monster in "Legislating the Sublime," 145–46. Paul de Man observes that, unlike the discussion of the mathematically sublime, Kant's consideration of the dynamically sublime suggests an allegorized combat among the faculties. See de Man, "Phenomenality and Materiality in Kant," in *Hermeneutics: Questions and Prospects*, eds. Gary Shapiro and Alan Sica (Amherst, Mass.: University of Massachusetts Press, 1984), 140–41. Like modern critics, Wordsworth may have been attentive to Kant's description of the dynamically sublime precisely because this section is as much a story as a philosophical disquisition.

58 "Lines composed a few miles above Tintern Abbey," in *PW*, 2:262, ll. 95–97.

59 Kant states (*Critique of Judgement*, sec. 27, 96–97, in the German text, 5:264–65): "Now the idea of the comprehension of every phenomenon that can be given us in the intuition (*Anschauung*) of a whole is an idea prescribed to us by a law of reason, which recognizes no other measure, definite, valid for

everyone, and invariable, than the absolute whole. But our imagination, even
in its greatest efforts, in respect of that comprehension which we expect from it
of a given object in a whole of intuition (and thus with reference to the
presentation of the idea of reason) exhibits its own limits and inadequacy ...
This makes intuitively (*anschaulich*) evident the superiority of the rational
determination of our cognitive faculties to the greatest faculty of our sensibility."

60 Kant, *Critique of Judgement*, sec. 28, 100. In the German text, 5:268–69. An
 intermediate target may be Coleridge, who in 1813 explained why celebrated
 waterfalls often disappoint those who see them for the first time. See
 Coleridge, *Shakespearean Criticism*, 2:273. Cited by Owen and Smyser,
 Commentary, "Sublime and Beautiful," *Prose*, 2:456n. For a discussion of
 how Wordsworth managed his initial 1790 disappointment concerning the
 Rhinefall, see chapter 7.

61 Friedrich von Schiller, "On the Sublime," in *Naive and Sentimental Poetry
 and On the Sublime*, tr. Julius A. Elias (New York: Frederick Ungar, 1966),
 193–210; in the German text, *Schillers Werke* (Weimar: Herman Böhlaus
 Nachfolger, 1962), 20:171–95; Schiller, *On the Aesthetic Education of Man*,
 Letters XVII and XVIII, tr. Elizabeth Wilkinson and L. A. Willoughby
 (Oxford: Clarendon Press, 1967), 117–19 (dual language text); Johann
 Gottfried Herder, *Kalligone* (Weimar: Herman Bölaus Nachfolger, 1955),
 2:191–93 and 202–38; Friedrich Schleiermacher, *Aesthetik* (Berlin and
 Leipzig: Walter de Gruyter and Co., 1931), 102–5, translated by E. F. Carritt
 in *The Theory of Beauty*, 6th edn rev. (London: Methuen and Co., 1962),
 175; Friedrich Wilhelm J. von Schelling, *Philosophie der Kunst*, in *Werke*
 (Munich: C. H. Bech und R. Oldenbourg, 1959), 3:134–337, and *System of
 Transcendental Idealism* (1800), tr. Peter Heath (Charlottesville, Va.: University of Virginia Press, 1978), 225–26, in the German, Vol. III of *Sämtliche
 Werke* (1856–61). For further consideration of parallels between Coleridge's
 aesthetics and the tendency among these German theorists to blend the
 sublime and the beautiful, see Modiano, "Coleridge and the Sublime,"
 114–16, 119–20n. and Elinor Shaffer, "Coleridge's Revolution in the Standard of Taste," *Journal of Aesthetics and Art Criticism* 28 (1969): 213–21.

62 Bruce Clarke, "Wordsworth's Departed Swans: Sublimation and Sublimity in
 Home at Grasmere," *Studies in Romanticism* 19 (1980): 355–74. Peter
 Larkin reiterates this view in "Wordsworth's 'After-Sojourn': Revision and
 Unself-Rivalry in the Later Poetry," *Studies in Romanticism* 20 (Winter
 1981): 409–36.

63 For allied discussions of the relation between Kant's ethics, politics, and
 aesthetics, see David Simpson, ed., *German Aesthetic and Literary Criticism:
 Kant, Fichte, Schelling, Schopenhauer, Hegel* (Cambridge University Press,
 1984), 10 and Frances Ferguson, "Legislating the Sublime," 141.

64 Schiller, *Aesthetic Education*, 118.

65 G. W. F. Hegel, *Aesthetics: Lectures on Fine Art*, tr. T. M. Knox (2 vols.,
 Oxford: Clarendon Press, 1975), 1:362–77.

66 See, for example, Schiller's ideologically charged notice of "the terrifying and
 magnificent spectacle of change which destroys everything and creates it anew,
 and destroys again" (*On the Sublime*, 209–10).

Notes to pages 34–43

67 Letter to Fletcher, April 6, 1825, in *The Letters of William and Dorothy Wordsworth: The Later Years: I, 1821–1828*, eds. Alan G. Hill and Ernest de Selincourt, 2nd edn rev. (Oxford: Clarendon Press, 1978), 335. Dates for other relevant letters to Fletcher in the same volume are: January 17, 1825, 302ff.; February 25, 1825, 321ff.

68 Coleridge makes a similar objection. See *Coleridge's Miscellaneous Criticism*, ed. T. M. Raysor (Cambridge, Mass.: Harvard University Press, 1936), 320. For a discussion of the etymology of Longinus's title and its translations, see Theodore E. B. Wood, *The Word 'Sublime' and Its Context* (The Hague: Mouton, 1972), 34–35.

69 Florio, *Queen Anna's New World of Words, or Dictionarie of the Italian and English Tongues* (London: M. Bradwood for Blount and Barnet, 1611), s.v. *sublime*. Cited by Wood, *The Word 'Sublime'*, 189.

70 OED, s.v. *sublime*.

71 Johnson, *A Dictionary of the English Language* (2 vols., London: J. Knapton, 1756 and [2nd edn] 1760), s.v. *sublime, sublimity*. Also noted by Geoffrey Tillottson, "Imlac and the Business of the Poet," in *Studies in Criticism and Aesthetics, 1660–1800*, eds. Howard Anderson and John Shea (Minneapolis, Minn.: University of Minnesota Press, 1967), 301.

72 "The Definition of Taste," in *Coleridge's Shakespearean Criticism*, 1:182–83.

73 Owen and Smyser, Introduction, *Guide, Prose*, 2:133.

74 *The Notebooks of Samuel Taylor Coleridge*, 1:213–19. Cited by Kathleen Coburn, *In Pursuit of Coleridge* (London: The Bodley Head, 1977), 117.

75 Monk, *The Sublime*, 193–94, and Paulson, *Emblem and Expression: Meaning in English Art of the Eighteenth Century* (Cambridge, Mass.: Harvard University Press, 1975), 23–24.

76 Ernest de Selincourt notes the allusion to *Paradise Lost*, III, ll. 36–42, in *PW*, 2:521n.

77 *Home at Grasmere*, ed. Beth Darlington (Ithaca: Cornell University Press, 1977), Ms. B, 992–96, p. 102.

78 Gilpin, *Observations, in Cumberland and Westmoreland*, 2:54.

79 *The Poetical Works of William Wordsworth* (London: Longman, Hurst, Rees, 1827), Table of Contents.

80 My use of the terms *refuge* and *hazard* is indebted to Jay Appleton, *The Experience of Landscape* (London: John Wiley and Sons, 1975), 74.

81 Thomas McFarland discusses the "disparactive" structure of the ode in *Romanticism and the Forms of Ruin* (Princeton University Press, 1981), 54. Although he does not specify the ode form he has in mind, he describes the Pindaric.

3 The scene of aesthetic instruction

1 Cited by Harold Bloom, *Wallace Stevens: Poems of our Climate* (Ithaca: Cornell University Press, 1977), 375. My analysis of Wordsworthian *topoi* is indebted to Bloom's discussion of *topoi* as poetic crossings in Wallace Stevens's poetry.

2 Quintilian, *Institutio oratoria*, tr. H. E. Butler, (4 vols. London: Heinemann,

1921), 4:211–43, Book XI, ii. Cited by Yates, *The Art of Memory* (University of Chicago Press, 1966), 3, 31.

3 Cicero, *De Oratore*, tr. E. W. Sutton (2 vols., London: Heinemann, 1942), 2:351–54, lxxxvi. Cited by Yates, *Art of Memory*, 1.

4 Jonathan Wordsworth argues that the "Prospectus" was probably composed early in January of 1800 in "On Man, on Nature, and on Human Life," *Review of English Studies* n.s. 31 (1980): 17–29.

5 Included in *Home at Grasmere*, Part First, Book First, of *The Recluse*, ed. Beth Darlington (Ithaca: Cornell University Press, 1977), Ms. B, 984–96, p. 102. Subsequent references to this edition appear parenthetically in the text as *HG*, followed by line and page. In "Wordsworth's Departed Sublimation and Sublimity in *Home at Grasmere*," 355–74, Bruce Clarke rightly observes that Wordsworthian sublimity is frequently displaced or sublimated; however, he neglects the discussion of beauty's tents in the "Prospectus." See chapter 2 for a discussion of Clarke's "counter-sublime" as the beautiful. Karl Kroeber defends Wordsworth's choice of aesthetic enclosure in "*Home at Grasmere*: Ecological Holiness," *PMLA* 89 (1974): 132–41.

6 See, for example, Addison, *The Spectator*, no. 279, 2:587 and no. 303, 3:85–86; Dennis, *Critical Works*, 2:122; Burke, *Enquiry*, 60–62. For a fine analysis of Wordsworth's response to Milton in the 1800 "Prospectus," see James A. Rieger, "Wordsworth Unalarm'd," in *Milton and the Line of Vision*, ed. Joseph A. Wittreich (Madison, Wisc.: University of Wisconsin Press, 1975), 185–208.

7 Hartman discusses the sublime ambitions of the "Prospectus," but neglects its consideration of beauty in "A Touching Compulsion: Wordsworth and the Problem of Literary Representation," *Georgia Review* 31 (Summer 1977): 347, 351.

8 Heffernan uses 1:14 ("And the Word was made flesh, and pitched His tent among us") as an epigraph for his study, *Wordsworth's Theory of Poetry*. See too Donald Wesling, *Wordsworth and the Adequacy of Landscape*, 64.

9 *PW*, 1:3. For probable dates of composition, see Mark L. Reed, *Wordsworth: The Chronology of the Early Years, 1770–1799* (Cambridge, Mass.: Harvard University Press, 1967), 305–6.

10 *PW*, 2:208. See Reed, *Wordsworth: Early Years*, 29, 215. Critical discussions of "A Night-Piece" have until recently emphasized its sublime or visionary qualities. See, for example, David Ferry, *The Limits of Mortality* (Middleton, Conn.: Wesleyan University Press, 1959), 30–31; James Kissane, " 'A Night-Piece': Wordsworth's Emblem of the Mind," *Modern Language Notes* 71 (1956): 183–86; and Neil Hertz, "Wordsworth and the Tears of Adam," *Studies in Romanticism* 7 (1967): 15–33. Owen argues that the poem is descriptive but not imaginative ("The Object, the Eye, and the Imagination," *The Wordsworth Circle* 14 (Winter 1983): 15–21, and, from another perspective, Lawrence Lipking agrees in "Quick Poetic Eyes," in *Articulate Images*, 9.

11 Burke, *Enquiry*, 124; Johnson, *Dictionary*, s.v. (adj.) *sublime*.

12 *PW*, 4:80. See Reed, *Wordsworth: Middle Years*, 40.

13 Burke, *Enquiry*, 36; Kant, *Critique of Judgement*, sec. 28, 101. In the German text, 5:269.

14 *Poems, 1807* (London: Longman, Hurst, Rees, 1815), Table of Contents;

Poems, in Two Volumes, and Other Poems, ed. Jared Curtis ((Ithaca: Cornell University Press, 1983), 72 and 72n. Subsequent citations of this edition appear parenthetically in the text as *Poems, 1807*. In his account of the incident on which "Fidelity" is based, the death of a "Mr. Gough" below Helvellyn, DeQuincey notes that Wordsworth and Sir Walter Scott both chose to emphasize "the sublime and mysterious fidelity of the secondary figure" [the dog] instead of "the naked fact of [Gough's] death amongst the solitudes of the mountains." DeQuincey also observes that neither Scott nor Wordsworth mention the probability that Gough died of starvation. See DeQuincey, "William Wordsworth," in *Collected Writings*, 2:29–30n.

15 *PW*, 3:76. See Reed, *Wordsworth: Middle Years*, 291–92.
16 *PW*, 2:80–94.
17 Simpson, *Wordsworth and the Figurings of the Real*, 147.
18 Levinson, "Spiritual Economics: A Reading of Wordsworth's 'Michael',"
   ELH 52 (Fall 1985): 716–22. For other assessments of Michael's choice, see:
   Peter J. Manning, "Michael, Luke, and Wordsworth," *Criticism* 19 (Summer
   1977): 195–211; Karl Kroeber, "Constable: Millais / Wordsworth: Tennyson," *Articulate Images: The Sister Arts from Hogarth to Tennyson*, ed.
   Richard Wendorf (Minneapolis, Minn.: University of Minnesota Press, 1983),
   230; Paul Magnuson, "The Articulation of 'Michael' or, Could Michael
   Talk?," *The Wordsworth Circle* 13 (Spring 1982): 72–79; and Stephen
   Parrish, " 'Michael' and the Pastoral Ballad," *Bicentenary Wordsworth
   Studies*, eds. Jonathan Wordsworth and Beth Darlington (Ithaca: Cornell
   University Press, 1970), 50–75.
19 Dorothy Wordsworth, *Journals*, 1:66. Cited by de Selincourt, ed., *PW*,
   2:479n. See Paul J. Alpers's analysis of Virgilian pastoral in *The Singer of the
   Eclogues* (Berkeley: university of California Press, 1979), 84–95.
20 Stephen Parrish describes the role of the JJ manuscript in Wordsworth's
   composition of *The Prelude* in his edition, *Prel. 1798*, 3–9. Subsequent
   citations of this edition appear parenthetically in the text as *Prel. 1798*,
   followed by page.
21 For a summary of the differences between the 1799 and 1805 versions of the
   "spots of time," a term Wordsworth used for the Penrith Beacon and Waiting
   for the Horses episodes which appear in Book XI of the 1805 *Prelude*, and a
   discussion of their 1799 placement with episodes that were later assigned to
   Book I of the 1805 *Prelude*, see Parrish's Introduction, *Prel. 1798*, 25;
   Jonathan Wordsworth and Stephen Gill, "The Two-Part *Prelude* of
   1798–99," *Journal of English and Germanic Philology* 77 (1973): 503–25;
   and Jonathan Bishop, "Wordsworth and the 'Spots of Time'," *ELH* 26
   (1959):45–65.
22 See, for example, Sybil A. Eakin, "The Spots of Time in Early Versions of *The
   Prelude*," *Studies in Romanticism* 12 (1973): 389–405.
23 According to the speaker, the actions reported in the Book I "spots of time"
   occurred before he "had seen / Nine summers" (309–10, p. 44). See Piaget and
   Barbel Inhelder, *The Child's Conception of Space*, tr. F. L. Langson and J. L.
   Lunzer (1948; repr. New York: W. W. Norton, 1967), 4–10, 210–25, 153,
   194. Lee M. Johnson suggests that topological distinctions account for a
   continuity among the poet's different selves in *Wordsworth's Metaphysical*

Verse: Geometry, Nature, and Form (University of Toronto Press, 1982), 70.

24 Christopher Ricks, "Wordsworth: 'A Pure Organic Pleasure from the Lines',"
Essays in Criticism 21 (1971): 18; D. G. Gillham, "Wordsworth's Hidden
Figures of Speech," in *Generous Concourse*, ed. Brian Green (Capetown:
Oxford University Press, 1980), 82–83. See also Karl R. Johnson, Jr., *The
Written Spirit: Thematic and Rhetorical Structure in Wordsworth's The
Prelude* (Salzburg: Institut für Englische Sprache und Literatur, 1978), 46–74.

25 Except for minor variants, W. J. B. Owen records the same text in his edition
of the fourteen-book *Prelude*, which was, Owen argues, written between 1832
and 1839. See Owen, ed., *The Fourteen-Book Prelude* (Ithaca: Cornell
University Press, 1985), 11 and 39. Subsequent citations of this edition appear
as *Fourteen-Book Prel.*, followed by page. The Norton edition of the three
Preludes identifies this as the "1850" version. To avoid confusion, I refer to
this version as the 1832–50 *Prelude*.

26 For a late eighteenth-century account of triangulation as a method for
surveying mountainous topography, see *Encyclopaedia Britannica*, 1771, s.v.
geometry. In *The Excursion*, I, the boy Wanderer uses the "altitude" of a crag
to locate himself (ll. 271–75). For another reading of the role of boundary-
lines in the boat-stealing episode, see Jonathan Arac, "Bounding Lines: *The
Prelude* and Critical Revision," *Boundary* 2 7 (Spring 1979): 31–48.

27 Martin Price, "The Sublime Poem: Pictures and Powers," *Yale Review* 58
(1969): 199.

28 Hartman, *Wordsworth's Poetry*, 213.

29 *PW*, 2:262, ll. 115–59. Richard Matlak describes the rhetorical occasion and
structure of the poem in "Classical Argument and Romantic Persuasion in
'Tintern Abbey'," *Studies in Romanticism*, 25 (Spring 1986): 113–28. For
further discussion of how Wordsworth's speaker manages aspiration and
doubt in the poem, see Susan Wolfson, *The Questioning Presence: Wordsworth, Keats, and the Interrogative Mode in Romantic Poetry* (Ithaca: Cornell
University Press, 1986), 60–70. See also Wesling's discussion of the poem as
Wordsworth's "mapping of the self with relation to a significant landscape,"
in *Wordsworth and the Adequacy of Landscape*, 25–26.

30 See Mary Jacobus, " 'Tintern Abbey' and Topographical Prose," *Notes and
Queries*, n.s. 18 (1971): 366–69, and John D. Hunt, *The Figure in the
Landscape: Poetry, Painting, and Gardening during the Eighteenth Century*
(Baltimore: The Johns Hopkins University Press, 1976), 206–16.

31 J. R. Watson, "A Note on the Date in the Title of 'Tintern Abbey'," *The
Wordsworth Circle* 10 (Autumn 1979): 379–80; Little, " 'Tintern Abbey' and
Llyswen Farm," *The Wordsworth Circle* 8 (Spring 1977): 80–82. Recent
critics offer different assessments of the political (sub)terrain of the poem. See
especially Kenneth R. Johnston, "Wordsworth and the Politics of 'Tintern
Abbey'," *The Wordsworth Circle* 14 (Winter 1983): 6–14, and McGann,
Romantic Ideology, 87–88.

32 Reed, *Wordsworth: Early Years*, 243. Cited by Watson, "Title of 'Tintern
Abbey'," 379.

33 Archibald Alison uses the phrase in *Essays on the Nature and Principles of
Taste*, 227; Shelley, "Hymn to Intellectual Beauty" (l. 25) and *Adonais*
(l. 42), *Selected Poetry and Prose*, eds. Donald Reiman and Stephanie Powers

(New York: W. W. Norton, 1977), 94 and 193. Wlecke (*Wordsworth and the Sublime*, 8) uses the sublime of "Tintern Abbey" as the normative definition of the Wordsworthian sublime, as does Carl Woodring in "The New Sublimity in 'Tintern Abbey'," in *The Evidence of the Imagination*, eds. Donald H. Reiman, Michael C. Jaye, Betty T. Bennett (New York University Press, 1978), 86–100.

34 McGann, *The Romantic Ideology*, 85–88. For Paul de Man, this return to surfaces announces the "chiastic exchange" between mind and nature which distinguishes the Wordsworthian sublime from the architectonic features of the Kantian sublime. See de Man, "Phenomenality and Materiality in Kant," in *Hermeneutics*, eds. Shapiro and Sica, 135. Here and elsewhere in Wordsworth's poetry, chiasmus serves at least in part to signal the presence of a competing aesthetic.

35 See especially Frederic Jameson, *The Political Unconscious* (Ithaca: Cornell University Press, 1981) and William C. Dowling's perceptive analysis of Jameson's conception of "a genuinely Marxist style" in *Jameson, Althusser, and Marx*, 11–13.

36 Milton, "Psalm 84," in *Paradise Regained, the Minor Poems, and Samson Agonistes*, ed. Merritt Y. Hughes (New York: Odyssey Press, 1937), 1, p. 37. See *Dictionary of Hymnology*, ed. John Julian (2 vols., 1907; repr. New York: Dover, 1957), 1:737; Sidney, *The Psalms of Sir Philip Sidney and the Countess of Pembroke* (New York University Press, 1963), 1, p. 201. For textual comparisons of the versions of this Psalm in the *King James Bible*, see A. C. Partridge, *English Biblical Translation* (London: André Deutch, 1973) and *New English Bible* (London: Oxford University Press, 1970).

4 Revolution and the egotistical sublime

1 See Stephen Gill's introduction to *The Salisbury Plain Poems of William Wordsworth* (Ithaca: Cornell University Press, 1975), 5–14. Subsequent references to this edition appear in the text.

2 Fenwick note, *PW*, 1:342n. Robert Osborn discusses the setting of the play in his introduction to *The Borderers* (Ithaca: Cornell University Press, 1982), 17–18. Subsequent references to this edition appear in the text. See also Roger Sharrock, "*The Borderers*: Wordsworth on the Moral Frontier," *Durham University Journal* 56 (1964): 174.

3 Schiller, "On the Sublime," in *Naive and Sentimental Poetry and On the Sublime*, 209. Schiller's definition of the historical sublime makes its revolutionary character apparent: "a terrifying and magnificent spectacle of change which destroys everything and creates it anew." Hayden White cites this definition in praise of Schiller's historical sublime as a model for modern politics and criticism in "The Politics of Interpretation: Discipline and De-Sublimation," *Critical Inquiry* 9 (September 1982), 125–26. Wordsworth offers a more skeptical account of sublime radicalism.

4 Reeve Parker discusses the significance of tales in *The Borderers* in "Oh could you hear his voice: Wordsworth, Coleridge, and Ventriloquism," in *Romanticism and Language*, ed. Arden Reed (Ithaca: Cornell University Press 1984), 125–43. Carolyn Warmbold explores narrator–audience relations in the

traditional ballad in an unpublished essay, "Double Visions: The Broadside Ballad and the Supermarket Tabloid."

5 See the parallel texts for "Salisbury Plain" (102, p. 24) and "Guilt and Sorrow" (130, p. 235) in *The Salisbury Plain Poems*.

6 My notice of this phrase is indebted to Ian Reid's fine essay, "'A Naked Guide-post's Double Head': The Wordsworthian Sense of Direction," *ELH* 43 (1976): 538–50.

7 See *entrevoyer*, "to see between" and *flüchtig blicken*, "fugitive" or "evanescent" "glance."

8 *The Italian*, ed. Frederick Garber (London: Oxford University Press, 1968).

9 Ronald Paulson, "Gothic Fiction and the French Revolution," *ELH* 48 (1981): 532–54.

10 Paulson argues to the contrary that gothic thrills like de Sade's do suggest the sublime ("Gothic Fiction," 536).

11 *Prose*, 1:334. See the editors' introduction (1:19–25) for a discussion of the political context of Wordsworth's unpublished *Letter*. Nicholas Roe discusses Wordsworth's political radicalism between 1791 and 1795 in "Citizen Wordsworth," *The Wordsworth Circle* 14 (1983): 21–30.

12 "Lectures on Allegory and Spenser," in *Coleridge's Miscellaneous Criticism*, 28–38.

13 *Encyclopaedia Britannica*, 13th edn, s.v. *hanging*. Michel Foucault discusses the power relations inscribed in public scenes of crime and punishment in *Discipline and Punish*, tr. Alan Sheridan (New York: Pantheon, 1977), 32–59.

14 Martin Heidegger uses the term *clearing* or *Lichtung* in *Being and Time* (tr. John Macquarrie and Edward Robinson [New York: Harper and Row, 1962], 171) to convey his idea of "clarification." In this study I use the term to indicate Wordsworth's tendency to regard rhetorical places in a text as though they were "clearings" in a figurative as well as literal sense.

15 "An Unpublished Tour," *Prose*, 2:128 and 334. See *Encyclopaedia Britannica*, 13th edn, s.v. *hanging*.

16 Gill reviews Wordsworth's use of the Spenserian stanza and its echoes of *The Faerie Queene* in his edition of *The Salisbury Plain Poems* (6n., 23n.).

17 These charges appear in private letters which were written between 1791 and 1796 and are not included among Burke's published correspondence. Cited by Conor Cruise O'Brien in his introduction to Burke's *Reflections on the Revolution in France* (London: Penguin, 1970), 31n. For an analysis of Burke's response to the French Revolution as a sublime terror, see Paulson, "Burke's Sublime and the Representation of Revolution," in *Culture and Politics from Puritanism to the Enlightenment*, ed. Perez Zagolin (Berkeley: University of California Press, 1980), 241–70. See also Paulson's *Representations of Revolution*, 57–87.

18 Letter to Earl Fitzwilliam, 12 November 1789, *The Correspondence of Edmund Burke*, ed. Thomas Cope (10 vols., University of Chicago Press, 1967), vol. 6: July 1789–December 1791, eds. Alfred Cobban and Robert A. Smith, 36. Cited by O'Brien, 16.

19 Paulson, "Gothic Fiction and the French Revolution," 536–38. R. F. Storch discusses oedipal conflicts in *The Borderers* and their revolutionary impli-

cations in "Wordsworth's *The Borderers*: The Poet as Anthropologist," *ELH* 36 (1969): 340–60.

20 Burke, *Reflections*, 164–65. See also Paulson, "Burke's Sublime and the Representation of Revolution," 244–46.

21 Osborn, Introduction, *The Borderers*, 18.

22 Marijane Osborn, "Wordsworth's *Borderers* and the Landscape of Penrith," *Transactions of the Cumberland and Westmoreland Antiquarian and Archeological Society* n.s. 76 (1976): 144–45.

23 James Clarke, *Survey of the Lakes*, 2nd edn (London: Printed for the Author, 1789). Clarke remarks: "If the day be clear, you can see Cumberland spread like an immense map before you" (22). See also Marijane Osborn's discussion of this and other eighteenth-century guidebooks that mention Penrith Beacon ("Wordsworth's *Borderers*," 144–53).

24 Gilpin, *Observations in Cumberland and Westmoreland*, 54.

25 *Ibid.*, 74.

26 Hutchinson, *Excursion to the Lakes in Cumberland and Westmoreland* (London: J. Wilkie, 1776), 11–12.

27 Burke, *Reflections*, 92. Cited by Paulson, "Burke's Sublime," 252. See W. P. Albrecht, *The Sublime Pleasures of Tragedy* (Lawrence, Kansas: University Press of Kansas, 1975), 4–10.

28 Cited by Hannah Arendt, *On Revolution* (New York: Viking Press, 1963), 42; Carlyle, *The French Revolution* (3 vols., London: Chapman and Hall, 1869), see especially 3:134–41.

29 Wordsworth rewrote the Margaret/Robert scenes several times. See manuscripts published in the Cornell edition as part of the *Ur-Borderers*. In the most affirmative of them, "Matilda at the Cottage Door Scene," Robert and Margaret bring the dying Herbert back to his daughter (*The Borderers*, 52–60).

30 David V. Erdman, "Wordsworth as Heartsworth; or, Was Regicide the Prophetic Ground of those 'Moral Questions'?" in *The Evidence of the Imagination*, eds. Donald H. Reiman, Michael C. Jaye, and Betty T. Bennett (New York University Press, 1978), 12–41 and "The Man Who Was Not Napoleon," *The Wordsworth Circle* 12 (1981): 92–96; H. F. Watson, "Historical Detail in *The Borderers*," *Modern Language Notes* 52 (1937): 577–79; Sharrock, "*The Borderers*: Wordsworth on the Moral Frontier," especially 172–74. Robert Osborn summarizes possible antecedents for Rivers in his Introduction, *The Borderers*, 17–18. See also his essay, "Meaningful Obscurity," in *Bicentenary Wordsworth Studies*, ed. Jonathan Wordsworth (Ithaca: Cornell University Press, 1970), 393–424.

31 *Prel.*, 1805, 10:115–27, p. 364. See chapter 5.

32 White articulates this ideological extension of the post-structuralist enthusiasm for the sublime in "The Politics of Interpretation," 113–37. Paul de Man offers a more wary assessment of the ideological uses of sublime negativity in "Hegel on the Sublime," in *Displacement: Derrida and After*, ed. Mark Krupnick (Bloomington, Ind.: Indiana University Press, 1983), 153.

33 W. P. Albrecht, "Tragedy and Wordsworth's Sublime," *The Wordsworth Circle* 8 (1978): 83–94.

34 Addison, *The Spectator*, no. 303 (1712), 3:85–6; Hugh Blair, *Lectures on*

Rhetoric and Belles Lettres, 1:69; Burke, *Enquiry*, 62. However, Burke's point is the sublime obscurity of Milton's description of Satan.

35 See Osborn, Introduction, *The Borderers*, 28–30.

36 For a discussion of Rivers's literary antecedents, see Peter L. Thorslev, Jr., "Wordsworth's *Borderers* and the Romantic Villain-Hero," *Studies in Romanticism* 5 (1966): 84–103. See also O. J. Campbell and P. Mueschke, "'Guilt and Sorrow': A Study in the Genesis of Wordsworth's Aesthetics," and "*The Borderers* as a Document in the History of Wordsworth's Aesthetic Development," *Modern Philology* 23 (1926): 293–306, 465–82. James K. Chandler observes that Wordsworth does not fully reject the Reign of Terror and revolutionary principles until after 1794, but sometime before 1800 and perhaps during the winter in Goslar (1797–98). See Chandler, "Wordsworth and Burke," *ELH* 47 (1980): 41–71.

37 Hartman describes these repetitions as a version of Rivers's desire to have Mortimer reenact his pattern of betrayal and crime in "Wordsworth, *The Borderers*, and Intellectual Murder," *JEGP* 62 (1963): 767.

38 Hume, "Of Eloquence," in *The Philosophical Works*, eds. T. H. Green and T. H. Gross (4 vols., 1882; repr. Aalen: Scientia Verlag, 1964), vol. 3, *Essays Moral and Political*, 167–69.

39 Noted by Osborn, ed., *The Borderers*, 176n.

40 See, for example, the emblem for Justice in Cesare Ripa's *Iconologia*. The last English edition appeared in 1779, edited by George Richardson (2 vols., London: G. Scott). For a discussion of the significance of this work, see D. J. Gordon, "Ripa's Fate," in *The Renaissance Imagination*, ed. Stephen Orgel (Berkeley: University of California Press, 1975), 75ff.

41 For a discussion of the pressure of echoes of *Othello* on this courtship, see Peter Manning, "Reading Wordsworth's Revisions: Othello and the Drowned Man," *Studies in Romanticism* 22 (Spring 1983): 3–28.

42 Freud, "The Uncanny," *The Psychological Works of Sigmund Freud*, tr. James Strachey (24 vols., London: Hogarth Press, 1955), 17:224. Freud quotes Schelling's definition.

43 *Prel.*, 9:482–520, pp. 356, 358. See chapter 5.

44 Mortimer's supposition that if Herbert is innocent someone will save him suggests the naive superstition of medieval ordeals of innocence and a similar naivety in the French revolutionary tribunals which Carlyle describes in *The French Revolution*, 3:38–41.

45 Noted by Osborn, ed., Introduction, *The Borderers*, 28.

5 Revisionary aesthetics

1 Except where otherwise indicated, I cite the 1805 *Prelude* because its aesthetic argument is the most emphatic. Whenever possible I have indicated relevant 1832–50 revisions. W. J. B. Owen's edition of the *Fourteen-Book Prelude* is the 1832–39 text (referred to as 1832) and the Norton edition of the 1799, 1805, and 1850 *Preludes* is the source for the 1805 and 1850 texts (like Owen, the editors of the Norton *Prelude* frequently rely on Ms. D).

2 J. R. MacGillvray first made this argument in an influential essay, "The Three Forms of *The Prelude*," in *Essays in English Literature from the Renaissance*

to the Victorian Age, Presented to A. S. P. Woodhouse, eds. Miller Maclure and F. W. Watt (University of Toronto Press, 1964), 99–115. Jonathan Wordsworth and Stephen Gill reiterate MacGillvray's view in "Two-Part Prelude of 1798–99," JEGP (1973): 503–25.

3 See, for example, Jonathan Bishop's important essay, "Wordsworth and the 'Spots of Time'," ELH 26 (1961):45–65. Bishop makes a superb case for reading Wordsworth's "spots of time" as "key moments in the history of his imagination" (45) and thus as passages that give us "a sense of the poem" (46). My point is not so much to contest these claims, but to identify the revisionary aesthetics that characterize Wordsworth's presentation of these passages.

4 I am indebted to Gene W. Ruoff, who organized an MLA special session on the the Drowned Man, and to fellow panelists Peter Manning, Susan Wolfson, Clifford Siskin, Jonathan Arac, and James Averill for their comments on earlier versions of this chapter. See Manning, "Reading Wordsworth's Revisions," 3–28; Wolfson, "The Illusion of Mastery: Wordsworth's Revisions of the Drowned Man," PMLA 99 (October 1984): 917–35; Siskin, "Revision Romanticized: A Study in Literary Change," Romanticism Past and Present 7 (1983): 1–16.

5 Nathan Drake described the uses of terror and gothic superstition in Literary Hours (Sudbury: J. Burkitt, 1798), 88–94. For a different assessment of sublime fear, see Knight, Analytical Inquiry, 364–67; Wordsworth, "The Sublime and the Beautiful," in Prose, 2:353; and chapter 2 of this study.

6 Cynthia Chase, "The Accidents of Disfiguration: Limits to Literal and Rhetorical Reading in Book V of The Prelude," Studies in Romanticism 18 (Winter 1979): 547–65, reprinted in Chase, Decomposing Figures, 13–31. See too Timothy Bahti, "Figures of Interpretation, The Interpretation of Figures: A Reading of Wordsworth's 'Dream of the Arab'," Studies in Romanticism 18:601–20, and Mary Jacobus, "Wordsworth and the Language of the Dream," ELH 46 (Winter 1979): 618–44.

7 Hertz, "A Reading of Longinus," Critical Inquiry 9 (March 1983): 585.

8 See Douglas H. Thompson, "Wordsworth's Warning Voice: A Miltonic Echo in Book II of The Prelude," The Wordsworth Circle 12 (Spring 1981): 132, citing Paradise Lost, 4:1–8, pp. 108–9.

9 Dorothy Wordsworth, Journals, 1:5. Cited by the editors of the Norton Prelude (144n).

10 See Beth Darlington's analysis and transcriptions, "Two Early Texts: 'A Night-Piece' and 'The Discharged Soldier'," in Bicentenary Wordsworth Studies, 425–48. My discussion of "boundary" figures is indebted to Hartman, Wordsworth's Poetry, 200–2, 224–25.

11 For a debate concerning evidence for this intervening version, see Jonathan Wordsworth, "The Five-Book Prelude of Early Spring 1804," JEGP 76 (January 1977): 1–25 and Reed, Wordsworth: Middle Years, 628–53.

12 Shakespeare's Sonnets, ed. Martin Seymour-Smith (London: Heinemann, 1963), 72. Cited by the editors of the Norton Prelude, 152n. Geoffrey Hartman notes a reversed pair of implicit and explicit allusions to Milton and Shakespeare in Wordsworth's 1816 poem, "A Little Onward" in "Diction and Defense in Wordsworth," in The Literary Freud (see Chapter 1, note 21), 213.

13 Burnet, The Sacred Theory of the Earth, 1:77 and chapter 2 of this study.

14 *Paradise Lost*, 11:754–61, p. 383.
15 *Ibid.*, 12:646, p. 412 and *Prel.*, 1:15, p. 28. Flavius Josephus, *Works*, tr. William Whiston, ed. Samuel Burger, rev. edn (2 vols., Boston: S. Walker, 1821), 1:15–16. Wordsworth owned this edition. See Shaver, *Wordsworth's Library*, 142. For a discussion of the eighteenth-century interest in this Deluge narrative and Wordsworth's revision of this source, see my essay, "Spirit and Geometric Form: The Stone and the Shell in Wordsworth's Arab Dream," *Studies in English Literature* 22 (1982): 563–82.
16 In the 1805 text the dreamer is "a friend" of the speaker (49, p. 154), but in 1832–50 he is the speaker (1832, 56–70, pp. 94–95). In this instance the later text retrieves what the earlier one suppresses.
17 *Paradise Lost*, 10: 282–305, pp. 323–24. Cited by the editors of the Norton *Prelude* (170n.).
18 Burke, *Reflections*, 99–110. See also James K. Chandler, *Wordsworth's Second Nature: A Study of the Poetry and Politics* (University of Chicago Press, 1984), especially 31–61.
19 Addison, *The Spectator*, no. 412, 3:540–44, Wordsworth, *Essays upon Epitaphs*, 1 in *Prose*, 2:51 and chapter 2 of this study. Subsequent citations of these essays appear parenthetically in the text.
20 Ovid, *The Fifteen Books of Publius Ovidius Naso entytuled "Metamorphosis"*, tr. Arthur Golding, ed. John F. Nims (1576; repr. New York: Macmillan, 1965), 1:9. Wordsworth owned the George Sandys and Golding translations. See Shaver, *Wordsworth's Library*, 192.
21 *Paradise Lost*, 2:891–92, 956, 961, 973, pp. 70–73, also noted by Michael Ragussis, "Language and Metamorphosis in Wordsworth's Arab Dream," *Modern Language Quarterly*, 36 (1975), 155–56; Burnet, *Sacred Theory*, 1:67–77.
22 Sheats observes Wordsworth's omission of these disappointments in *Descriptive Sketches* in *The Making of Wordsworth's Poetry*, 69. I am indebted to Jeffrey C. Robinson for his comments on this passage.
23 *Prelude*, ed. de Selincourt, 198–99n.
24 *Descriptive Sketches*, ed. Birdsall, 1793, 42–118. For a review of this period in French/Swiss history, see E. Bonjour, *et al.*, *A Short History of Switzerland* (Oxford: Clarendon Press, 1952), 220–35. Joseph Kishel discusses this inserted text in "Wordsworth and the Grande Chartreuse," *The Wordsworth Circle* 12 (Winter 1981): 82–88.
25 The sublimity of the passage is by now a critical commonplace. See especially Weiskel, *Romantic Sublime*, 200–3; and Monk, *The Sublime*, 231–32. Liu discusses Wordsworth's echoes of Napoleon's speeches to his troops in the Alps in "Wordsworth: The History in 'Imagination'," *ELH* 51 (Fall 1984): 534–36.
26 Ernest Bernhardt-Kabisch reviews the topographical invention of the Crossing of the Alps and Ravine of Arve passages in "Wordsworth and the Simplon Revisited," *The Wordsworth Circle* 10 (Autumn 1979): 381–85; Susan Luther discusses the syntactic and compositional obscurities of Wordsworth's apostrophe in "Wordsworth's *Prelude*, VI. 592–616 (1850)," *The Wordsworth Circle* 12 (1981): 253–61. See also Hartman, *Wordsworth's Poetry*, 238–42.
27 Pirie, *Poetry of Grandeur and of Tenderness*, 22; Ramond de Carbonnières,

Notes to pages 107–14

Lettres de M. William Coxe à M. W. Melmoth, sur l'État politique, civil et naturel de la Suisse, traduites de l'Anglois (2 vols., Paris: Belin, 1781), 2:96ff. Cited by Sheats, *The Making of Wordsworth's Poetry*, 64.

28 Earl R. Wasserman defines *concordia discors* in *The Subtler Language* (Baltimore: The Johns Hopkins University Press, 1959), 104–13. Paul Sheats notes the anomalous relation between this technique and the sublime style in *The Making of Wordsworth's Poetry*, 61.

29 Abrams, *Natural Supernaturalism*, 98 and 106–12.

30 Chapter 3 reviews eighteenth-century debates about figures and the sublime style.

31 Paul de Man defines *prosopopoeia* in "Autobiography as De-facement," *Modern Language Notes* 94 (December 1979): 926.

32 *Paradise Lost*, 2:951, p. 73. Noted by the editors of the Norton *Prelude*, 238n.

33 In Wordsworth's 1817 Poem "To—: On Her First Ascent to the Summit of Helvellyn" (*PW*, 2:287, ll. 29–32), a similar point of view is explicitly satanic. See chapter 2 of this book.

34 W. P. Albrecht, *The Sublime Pleasures of Tragedy*, 4–10ff. and Mary Jacobus, "'That Great Stage Where Senators Perform': *Macbeth* and the Politics of Romantic Theater," *Studies in Romanticism* 22 (Fall 1983), 353.

35 W. J. B. Owen, "'A Second-Sight Procession' in Wordsworth's London," *Notes and Queries* 214 (1969): 49.

36 Jacques Lacan, *Écrits* (Paris: Seuil, 1966), 99–120. See Leo Bersani, *Baudelaire and Freud* (Berkeley: University of California Press, 1977), for an analysis of the role of the superego in the symbolic (116–17).

37 In France, political suppressions of theatrical entertainment at fairs during the last years of the *ancien régime* inadvertently made fairs into protorevolutionary theater. See Marie Helene Huet, *Rehearsing the Revolution*, tr. Robert Hurley (Berkeley: University of California Press, 1982), 17–18.

38 Jon P. Klancher discusses this passage and the emergence of the idea of a mass audience in *The Making of English Reading Audiences, 1790–1832* (Madison: University of Wisconsin Press, 1987), 76–92. For an analysis of the realist "urban vista," see Linda Nochlin, *Realism* (New York: Penguin, 1971), 68–69.

39 In "Wordsworth and the Sublime" Patrick Holland notes that these lines reiterate the parts of the sublime (outline, duration, power) listed in Wordsworth's essay on aesthetics (18). What they omit, however, is fear. See as well Lindenberger, *On Wordsworth's Prelude*, 250–51.

40 Chandler, "Wordsworth and Burke," 754–55. David Simpson argues concerning a similar portrait of Grasmere in *Home at Grasmere* that its details "hold together ... the polymorphous or antithetical predications of passion" (*Figurings of the Real*, 122–23). Yet this adhesion is less a natural by-product of rural, social harmony in Grasmere, as Simpson implies, than a measure of the speaker's *management*, and hence his need to find coherence there.

41 Jonathan Wordsworth, *William Wordsworth: The Borders of Vision* (Oxford: Clarendon Press, 1982), 290–91. The text cited in *Measure for Measure* is 3.1.125–27.

42 Paul Alpers, "What is Pastoral?" *Critical Inquiry* 8 (1982), 444–47 and Lore

Metzger, "Coleridge in Sicily: A Pastoral Interlude in *The Prelude*," *Genre* 11 (1978): 63–81.

43 *Paradise Lost*, 11:203–7, pp. 361–62. Noted by the editors of the Norton *Prelude*, 308n.

44 Coleridge, *Table-Talk*, 171–72.

45 Mary Jacobus explores relations between genre and gender in Vaudracour and Julia in "The Law of/and Gender: Genre Theory and *The Prelude*," *Diacritics* 14 (Winter 1984): 47–57.

46 Burke, *Reflections*, 117–23.

47 The editors of the Norton *Prelude* argue (362n.) that the 1850 revision "spoiled" the apocalyptic lines of the 1805 text. In fact, the revision extends the catastrophic imagery of the earlier text by adding the implied risk of deluge, transmitted by the Biblical resonance of *deep* and the discussion of retreating but returning tides.

48 The 1832–50 texts eliminate the aesthetic marker "place of fear" (1832, 88–92, p. 198). See Ronald Paulson on tigers as figures of revolutionary power in "Blake's Revolutionary Tiger" in *Articulate Images*, 172, and Alan Liu, " 'Shapeless Eagerness': The Genre of Revolution in Books 9–10 of *The Prelude*," *Modern Language Quarterly*, 43 (1982): 11–16.

49 DeQuincey, "William Wordsworth," *Collected Writings*, 2:185n.

50 For recent analyses of Wordsworth's anti-Godwinism, see Alan Grob, "Wordsworth and Godwin: A Reassessment," *Studies in Romanticism* 6 (1967): 98–119 and Robert Osborn's Introduction to *The Borderers*, 30–33, 37.

51 *PW*, 2:213. See Reed, *Wordsworth: Middle Years*, 35.

52 *An Unpublished Tour* in *Prose*, 2:338. See also H. S. Cowper, *Hawkshead* (London: Bemrose and Sons, 1899), 43. Cited by Owen and Smyser in *Prose*, 2:445–46n. See also Moorman, *Wordsworth: A Biography*, 1: 68 and de Selincourt and Darbishire, eds., *Prelude*, 614n.

53 See chapter 3 for further discussion of Wordsworth's use of Clarke's *Survey*.

54 See, for example, Jonathan Wordsworth, "The Growth of a Poet's Mind," *The Cornell Library Bulletin* 11 (Spring 1970), 6.

55 Ian Reid discusses the "images of divestment" in the Penrith Beacon "spot of time" in " 'A Naked Guide-Post's Double Head'," 539. Although I agree with Jim S. Borck's contention that this and similar *Prelude* episodes mark the inadequacy of poetic language, others in the poem insist that the speaker's discourse fully represents his meaning. See Borck, "Wordsworth's *Prelude* and the Failure of Language," *Studies in English Literature* 13 (1973): 605–16.

56 DeQuincey, "William Wordsworth," in *Collected Writings*, 2:135.

57 Cited by Lacan, *Écrits*, 171.

58 Carl H. Ketcham, Introduction, *Letters of John Wordsworth* (Ithaca, New York: Cornell University Press, 1969), 24.

59 Geoffrey Hartman uses the term "avoidance" in *Wordsworth's Poetry* to describe the Ascent of Snowdon in *Prelude*, XIII, especially 226, and "domestication" to discuss Wordsworth's later poetry in "Blessing the Torrent," 198.

60 According to W. J. T. Mitchell, this passage illustrates the visionary, as opposed to sight oriented, nature of Romantic texts because it "defamiliar-

ize[s] ... ordinary sight." Yet the lines that immediately follow familiarize the unordinary, sublime vision the speaker has just offered. See Mitchell, "Metamorphoses of the Vortex: Hogarth, Turner, and Blake," in *Articulate Images*, ed. Wendorf, 133.

61 *PW*, 4:80–83. See chapter 4.

62 *Prometheus Unbound*, 2.4.116, in *Shelley's Poetry and Prose*, 175. Arden Reed describes the mist on Snowdon as a figure for the imagination in *Romantic Weather*, 190. Unlike the "unfathered vapor" of Book VI, however, this mist calls attention to its representational task.

63 *Paradise Lost*, 7:285–87, pp. 229–30. Noted by the editors of the Norton *Prelude*, 460n. Jonathan Wordsworth describes the composition of this text in "The Climbing of Snowdon," in *Bicentenary Wordsworth Studies*, eds. Jonathan Wordsworth and Beth Darlington (Ithaca, New York: Cornell University Press, 1970), 451. As W. J. B. Owen and the Norton editors note, Wordsworth sharply revised the natural supernaturalism of this passage in 1832–50. See as well Richard Schell, "Wordsworth's Revisions of the Ascent of Snowdon," *Philological Quarterly* 54 (1975): 592–603 and *The Wordsworth Circle* 10 (1979): 3–16.

64 Wordsworth wrote to Sir Walter Scott about Park's death on 18 August 1806. See *MY*, 1, 73.

65 *Paradise Lost*, 9:489–93, p. 288. The editors of the Norton *Prelude* note the Miltonic echo (470n.).

66 8 April 1808, *MY*, 1, 207–9. Reed suggests that Wordsworth composed "St. Paul's" approximately when he wrote to Beaumont (*Wordsworth: Middle Years*, 381).

67 F. J. MacCunn, *The Contemporary English View of Napoleon* (London: G. Bell, 1914), 12–19 and *passim*.

68 David Pirie, *Wordsworth: The Poetry of Grandeur and of Tenderness*, 7, 39.

69 William Galperin considers the Wanderer's preference for communicable values in " 'Imperfect While Unshared': The Role of the Reader in Wordsworth's *Excursion*," *Criticism* 22 (1980): 193–210.

6 The aesthetics of containment

1 The phrase "strategies of containment" is Dowling's. See his *Jameson, Althusser, and Marx*, 77. Althusser's definition appears in part seven, "Marxism and Humanism," in *For Marx*, tr. Ben Brewster (London: Allen Lane, 1969), 233.

2 Chandler traces Wordsworth's advocacy of Burkean principles in *Wordsworth's Second Nature*, 31–61. For a different perspective on Wordsworth's conservatism, see Michael H. Friedman, *The Making of a Tory Humanist: William Wordsworth and the Idea of Community* (New York: Columbia University Press, 1979), 1–12.

3 Owen and Smyser describe DeQuincey's supervision in their introduction to Wordsworth's *Concerning the Convention of Cintra*, *Prose*, 1:201–14. Citations of this pamphlet appear parenthetically in the text.

4 Owen and Smyser summarize the sequence of events prior to the Convention of Cintra in their introduction (*Prose*, 1:193–97). For an analysis of this

episode in English political history and the political argument of Words-
worth's pamphlet, see Gordon Kent Thomas, *Wordsworth's Dirge and
Promise: Napoleon, Wellington, and the Convention of Cintra* (Lincoln,
Nebraska: University of Nebraska Press, 1971), especially 59–85.

5 MacCunn, *Contemporary View of Napoleon*, 88.

6 M. J. Sydenham, *The First French Republic, 1792–1804* (Berkeley: University
of California Press, 1973), 281. Friedman suggests that Wordsworth's attacks
on Napoleon signal his repudiation of his own aggressive egotism (*Making of
a Tory Humanist*, 251–55). The diction of the attacks makes it clear that the
sublime is the mode of egotism at issue.

7 See Derrida's analysis of Kant on colossality and the sublime in "Parergon,"
La Vérité en Peinture, 158–64.

8 Wordsworth's argument concerning resistance to Napoleon is partly confirmed by the modern historian Charles Breunig, who argues that the
Peninsular War marked a "turning point in the emperor's military fortunes"
precisely because he "underestimated the degree of resistance" this campaign
would invite. See Breunig, *The Age of Revolution and Reaction, 1789–1850*,
2nd edn (New York: W. W. Norton, 1977), 102.

9 Owen and Smyser, eds., Introduction, *Reply to 'Mathetes'*, *Prose*, 2:3–5.
Citations of this essay appear parenthetically in the text.

10 *Paradise Lost*, 5:756–58, p. 175. Also noted by Owen and Smyser, *Prose*,
2:36n.

11 James Butler, ed. *The Ruined Cottage and the Pedlar* (Ithaca: Cornell
University Press, 1979), xi–xii, 5–20. Citations of this edition appear
parenthetically in the text as *RC*, followed by line and page. For a discussion
and transcription of Ms. D, the manuscript version of *The Pedlar*, see
Jonathan Wordsworth, *The Music of Humanity: A Critical Study of Wordsworth's 'Ruined Cottage'* (New York: Harper and Row, 1969), especially
157–68. See too Manning, "Wordsworth, Margaret, and the Pedlar," *Studies
in Romanticism* 15 (1976): 195–220; and William Galperin, " 'Then the
Cottage Was Silent': The Wanderer vs. *The Ruined Cottage*," *ELH* 51 (1984):
343–63. For a critical assessment of Wordsworth's interpolation of the
Pedlar's story, see Margaret Homans, *Woman Writers and Poetic Identity*
(Princeton University Press, 1980), 24–28. The most extensive analysis of the
role of suffering in Wordsworth's early poetry is James A. Averill's *Wordsworth and the Poetry of Human Suffering* (Ithaca: Cornell University Press,
1980), 116–18, 125–26, and 135–36.

12 *Benjamin the Waggoner*, ed. Paul F. Betz (Ithaca: Cornell University Press,
1981), Introduction, 5–6. Citations of this edition appear parenthetically in
the text by line and page.

13 Letter to Wordsworth, June 7, 1819, *Letters of Charles Lamb to Which Are
Added Those of His Sister Mary Lamb*, ed. E. V. Lucas (3 vols., London: J. M.
Dent, 1935), 2:249 and Crabb Robinson, *Diary*, Betz's transcriptions. Both
cited by Betz, ed., *Benjamin the Waggoner*, 3.

14 Byron, *Don Juan*, eds. T. G. Steffan, E. Steffan, W. W. Pratt (New Haven: Yale
University Press, 1982), 3:98, p. 184.

15 See Hans Robert Jauss, *Toward an Aesthetic of Reception* (Minneapolis,
Minn.: University of Minnesota Press, 1982), 32–41, for a discussion of

reception theory and Don H. Bialostosky's *Making Tales* (University of Chicago Press, 1984) for an analysis of Wordsworth's narrative experiments in *Lyrical Ballads*.

16 David G. Chandler, *The Campaigns of Napoleon* (New York: Macmillan, 1960), 212–60 and MacCunn, *English View of Napoleon*, 12–19.

17 I am indebted to Peter Manning for his notice of the English patriotism implied in Wordsworth's presentation of Benjamin as a comic, yet admirable character.

18 De Selincourt quotes Coleridge's objections in *PW*, 3:545n.

19 January 18, 1816, *The Letters of William and Dorothy Wordsworth: The Middle Years, II, 1812–20*, eds. Ernest de Selincourt, Mary Moorman, 2nd edn rev. Alan G. Hill (Oxford: Clarendon Press, 1970), 276.

20 Manning, "Tales and Politics: *The Corsair*, Lara, and *The White Doe of Rylstone*," *Seventh International Byron Symposium: Byron's Poetry and Politics* (Salzburg: Studien zur Anglistik und Amerikanistik, Band 13, 1981), 222–24.

21 Manning observes: "these prefatory materials [ ] give initial shape to the volume" ("Tales and Politics," 226).

22 Heffernan, *Wordsworth's Theory of Poetry*, 210–25.

23 *Paradise Lost*, 2:636–43, p. 62.

24 Barbara Stafford, "Toward Romantic Landscape Perception: Illustrated Travels and the Rise of Singularity as an Aesthetic Category," *Art Quarterly*, n.s. 1 (1977): 89–124.

25 Letter to Coleridge, May 5, 1809, *MY*, 1, 334–36. De Selincourt uses the classification but queries its logic (*PW*, 1:ix–xi). For representative arguments against the classification, see W. J. B. Owen, *Wordsworth as Critic*, 153–55; Heffernan, "Mutilated Autobiography: Wordsworth's *Poems* of 1815," *The Wordsworth Circle* 10 (1979): 107–12.

26 Donald Ross, "Poems 'Bound Each to Each' in the 1815 Edition of Wordsworth's *Poems*," *The Wordsworth Circle* 12 (1981): 133–40 and Gene W. Ruoff, "Critical Implications of Wordsworth's 1815 Categorization, with Some Animadversions on Binaristic Commentary," *The Wordsworth Circle* 9 (1978): 75–82.

27 Judith B. Herman argues that the classification responds to specific criticisms of the 1807 *Poems* in "Wordsworth's Edition of 1815," *The Wordsworth Circle* 9 (1978): 82–87. Even so, it also creates a text which exerts its own pressures on critics and readers.

28 The "Intimations Ode" is placed at the end of Wordsworth's classifications (but before *The Excursion*) in the 1827, 1832, and 1841–43 editions of his *Poetical Works*.

29 *The Correspondence of Henry Crabb Robinson with the Wordsworth Circle 1808–66*, ed. Edith J. Morley (2 vols., Oxford: Clarendon Press, 1927), 2:838–39. Cited by Manning, "Wordsworth's Intimations Ode and its Epigraphs," *JEGP* 82 (October 1983), 527. Manning astutely summarizes the implications of Wordsworth's abandonment of the Virgilian epigraph. See also Helen Vendler, "Lionel Trilling and the *Immortality Ode*," in *The Liberal Imagination* (Garden City, New York: Doubleday Anchor, 1950), 129–59.

30 Ruoff, "Critical Implications," 81. For a valuable analysis of Wordsworth's ode and the 1815 classification, see Joseph C. Sitterson, Jr., "The Genre and Place of the Intimations Ode," *PMLA* 101 (January 1986): 24–37.

31 Letter to Alexander Dyce, December 23, 1837, *The Letters of William and Dorothy Wordsworth: The Later Years*, III, 1835–39, ed. Alan G. Hill, 2nd edn, rev. (Oxford: Clarendon Press, 1982). p. 502. Cited by de Selincourt (*PW*, 2:526n.), who notes the presence of the Virgilian epigraph in early manuscripts for "On the Power of Sound."

32 Reed, *Wordsworth: Middle Years*, 480.

33 Ketcham, correspondence, October 12, 1983.

34 Ruoff, "Religious Implications," 679.

35 Coleridge, *Biographia Literaria*, 2:109.

36 Ferry, *The Limits of Mortality*, 9; Simpson, "Criticism, Politics, and Style in Wordsworth's Poetry," *Critical Inquiry* 11 (September 1984), 63; Ruoff, "Religious Implications," 680–81.

37 Simpson, "Criticism, Politics, and Style," 56–61.

38 Crabb Robinson, *Diary, Reminiscences, and Correspondence of Henry Crabb Robinson*, ed. Thomas Sadler, 3rd edn (1872; repr. New York: AMS Press, 1967), 1:252; Coleridge, *Biographia Literaria*, 2:152; Hazlitt, "On Manner," in *The Round Table, Complete Works*, 4:45–46n.; and Keats, October 28–30, 1817 letter to Benjamin Bailey, in *Letters*, 1:173–74. Ruoff, who quotes Crabb Robinson's and Coleridge's comments in "Wordsworth's 'Yew-Trees' and Romantic Perception," *Modern Language Quarterly* 34 (1973), 146, offers a phenomenological reading based on Merleau-Ponty's analysis of perception and presence (154). See as well Riffaterre's influential and controversial essay, "Interpretation and Descriptive Poetry: A Reading of Wordsworth's 'Yew-Trees'," *New Literary History* 4 (1973), 230 and Geoffrey Hartman's reply, "The Use and Abuse of Structural Analysis: Riffaterre's Interpretation of Wordsworth's 'Yew-Trees'," *New Literary History* 7 (1975): 165–89. Roger Fowler challenges Riffaterre's emphasis on formal patterning with a semiotic account of "the reader's engagement with the poem as *speech* act." See Fowler, "'The Reader' – a Linguistic View," in *Literature As Social Discourse: The Practice of Linguistic Criticism* (Bloomington: Indiana University Press, 1981), 129–41.

39 Hartman, "Use and Abuse of Structuralist Analysis," 168–69.

40 See the reading texts and facsimile transcriptions in Curtis's edition, *Poems, 1807*, 605–06, 663–71 and Scholes, *Semiotics and Interpretation* (New Haven: Yale University Press, 1982), 13.

41 Manning points out that readings of "Yew-Trees" (including this one) tend to fill in the "hollow" of figurative meaning suggested by the Borrowdale grove. In an attentive discussion of the personifications that inhabit the grove, Steven Knapp reviews their allegorical lineage in Spenser, Milton, and Gray to point out Wordsworth's resistance to that lineage. See Knapp, *Personification and the Sublime: Milton to Coleridge* (Cambridge, Mass.: Harvard University Press, 1985), 125–29.

42 DeQuincey, "William Wordsworth," *Collected Writings*, 2:152.

43 Ruoff, "Wordsworth's 'Yew-Trees'," 150–51.

44 Riffaterre, "Interpretation and Descriptive Poetry," 41–42, citing Cleanth

Brooks and Robert Penn Warren, *Understanding Poetry*, 3rd edn (New York: Holt, Rinehart, Wilson, 1960), 276.

45 Addison, *The Spectator*, no. 501, 4:277. Wordsworth indicates his admiration for Addison's Winter Garden (*The Spectator*, no. 477, 4:191–92), a garden comprised of evergreens, when he describes his plan for a similar garden (including yews) at Coleorton, the Beaumont estate in Leicestershire. Letter to Lady Beaumont, n.d. [probably December 23, 1806], *MY*, 1, 112–20. Horace Walpole notes the earlier use of yews for topiary gardens (as, wonderfully, "mottoes") in his influential *History of the Modern Taste in Gardening*, in *Anecdotes of Painting in England*, 3rd edn (4 vols., London: J. Dodsley, 1786), 4:286.

46 Whateley, *Observations on Modern Gardening* (London: T. Payne, 1771), 46. Whateley's account parallels Wordsworth's description of the Borrowdale four: "the character of a grove is *beauty*; fine trees are lovely objects; a grove is an assemblage of them; in which every individual retains much of its own peculiar elegance; and whatever it loses, is transferred to the superior beauty of the whole."

47 Several readers have analyzed the role of Coleridge's Gloss in the poem's reception. See especially Susan Wolfson, "The Language of Interpretation in Romantic Poetry: A Strong Working of the Mind," in *Romanticism and Language*, ed. Arden Reed, 26–28; Raimonda Modiano, "Words and 'Languageless Meanings': Limits of Expression in *The Rime of the Ancient Mariner*," *Modern Language Quarterly* 38 (1977): 44–61; and Frances Ferguson, "Coleridge and the Deluded Reader," *Georgia Review* 31 (1977): 617–35.

48 Arden Reed discusses mists as signs of semiotic indeterminancy in Romantic texts in *Romantic Weather*, 83–84.

49 Wordsworth's revisions of *Peter Bell* reiterate his aesthetics of containment by re-contextualizing the *Prelude* figure of a drowned man. See John E. Jordan's edition of *Peter Bell* for full transcriptions of all versions (Ithaca: Cornell University Press, 1985).

7 "Family of Floods"

1 Wordsworth tends to use these words interchangeably to refer to waterfalls. See also French equivalents for the English *torrent: torrent, déluge, cours violent*.

2 Longinus, *On the Sublime*, tr. Smith, sec. 32, 73–74. Boileau uses the phrase "*un torrent rapide*" in his influential translation. See *Oeuvres Diverses avec Le Traité du Sublime* (Paris: De La Coste, 1674), sec. 26, 63. In *The Spectator*, no. 412, Addison gives "falls of water" as one example of "greatness" (Addison's term for the natural sublime).

3 Riffaterre, "Interpretation and Descriptive Poetry," 254.

4 For a discussion of "dual signs," see Riffaterre, *The Semiotics of Poetry* (Bloomington: Indiana University Press, 1978), 86ff. Riffaterre claims that such signs reveal a fundamental incompatibility between two tenors which results in semantic and visual blockage. In these cases, he argues, reading "can never yield a stable, secure grasp of the whole meaning, can never, above all, yield visualization" (90). Yet, as a dual sign of a different kind, the Rhinefall does present two contradictory tenors simultaneously.

5 May 23, 1812, *The Love Letters of William and Mary Wordsworth*, ed. Beth Darlington (Ithaca: Cornell University Press, 1981), 174.

6 June 3–4, 1812, *Love Letters*, 227.

7 Fenwick note, *PW*, 3:450n.

8 *Recollections of a Tour Made in Scotland*, in *Journals*, 1:223–24.

9 Coleridge refers to the incident on three different occasions. See *Coleridge's Shakespearean Criticism*, 2:62–63, and other passages which (re)locate the incident at the Lodore waterfall: "On the Principles of Genial Criticism," in *Biographia Literaria*, 2:224, and "On the Definition of Taste," in *Shakespearean Criticism*, 1:182.

10 "Cora Linn, or the Falls of the Clyde," *The Complete Poetical Works of Thomas Campbell*, ed. J. Logie Robertson (1907; repr. New York: Haskell House, 1968), 252–53.

11 Charles Gilliard, *Histoire de la Suisse* (Paris: Presses Universitaires de France, 1949), 82.

12 See Carl R. Woodring, *Politics in English Romantic Poetry* (Cambridge, Mass.: Harvard University Press, 1970), 14, 222–24.

13 September 6 and 16, 1790. *The Letters of William and Dorothy Wordsworth: Early Years, 1787–1805*, ed. Chester L. Shaver, 2nd edn (Oxford: Clarendon Press, 1967), 35.

14 *Lettres de William Coxe à M. W. Melmoth sur l'État Politique, Civil et Naturel, de la Suisse*, 1:10–19. See Reed, *Wordsworth: Early Years*, 97, and Charles N. Coe, *Wordsworth and the Literature of Travel* (1935; repr. New York: Octagon Books, 1979), 46–48. Subsequent English translations of the same work are titled *Travels in Switzerland*. Unless another edition is specified in the text, I cite the third English edition (London: J. Edwards, 1796). For this note, the citation is 1:9. In the fourth edition (London: A. Strahan, 1801) Coxe reissued the earlier text to which he added extensive notes and a preface describing the changes that had occurred as a result of the French invasion of Switzerland in 1799.

15 For a fuller discussion of traditional definitions of the sublime and Wordsworth's essay on aesthetics, see Chapter 2.

16 *Prose*, 2:237.

17 John Murray, *Handbook for Travellers in Switzerland* (1838; repr. New York: Humanities Press, 1970), 19.

18 Coxe, *Travels in Switzerland*, 1:10.

19 September 6 and 16, *EY*, 35.

20 Dorothy Wordsworth, *Journals*, 2:88–90.

21 See Plate 1 in the 1801 edition of Coxe's *Travels* (Plate 2 in this study).

22 Two of Mechel's engravings of the scene are reproduced and a third is discussed in Lukas Heinrich Wüthrich, *Das Oeuvre des Kupferstechers Christian von Mechel* (Basel, 1959), nos. 211, 212, 213. The Loutherbourg drawing is reproduced in *Philippe-Jacques de Loutherbourg, R.A.* (London: Greater London Council, 1972), no. 39.

23 Dorothy Wordsworth, *Journals*, 2:89.

24 *Prose*, 2:352–56. My understanding of the consequences of a viewer's absorption in a painting is indebted to Michael Fried, *Absorption and*

Theatricality in the Age of Diderot (Berkeley: University of California Press, 1980).

25 Turner's 1806 *Falls of the Rhine* is in the Museum of Fine Arts, Boston. See Martin Butlin and Evelyn Joll, *The Paintings of J. M. W. Turner*, 2 vols. (New Haven: Yale University Press, 1977), Text, 40–41. See also Joseph Farington, *Diaries*, 8 vols. (London: Hutchinson and Co., 1924): May 1, 1806, 3:210; May 6, 1806, 3:216–17.

26 Wordsworth to Beaumont, April 8, 1808, in *MY*, 1, 209. Martha Shackleford reviews Wordsworth's comments on Turner in *Wordsworth's Interest in Painters and Pictures* (Wellesley, Mass.: The Wellesley Press, 1945), 48, 60. See also Wordsworth's *Guide, Prose*, 2:234 and 421–22n.

27 One Swiss sketch is reproduced in *Sir Beaumont and his Circle*, Leicester Art Gallery, June 1952, no. 20. For a discussion of Turner's Swiss sketches during these years, see A. J. Finberg, *The Life of J. M. W. Turner, R.A.*, 2nd edn rev., Hilda F. Finberg (Oxford: Clarendon Press, 1961), 479. I am indebted to Kathleen Nicholson for discussion of Turner's attention to topographical features in his art and in that of his predecessors. For an analysis of Turner's response to Loutherbourg, see John Gage, *Colour in Turner* (New York: Praeger, 1969), 29–31 and 229n.

28 Finberg, *Turner*, 138, 369.

29 Loutherbourg's 1788 painting is reproduced and discussed in J. H. Kunin, "Date of Loutherbourg's Falls of the Rhine near Schaffhausen," *Burlington Magazine* 114 (1972): 554–55.

30 Dorothy Wordsworth, *Journals*, 2:90.

31 Described by Hugh Honour, *Romanticism* (New York: Harper and Row, 1979), 33.

32 See chapter 2.

33 Gilliard, *Histoire de la Suisse*, 66–70 and Bonjour *et al.*, *Short History of Switzerland*, 220–21. Mary Moorman also notes the curious timing of the sonnet on the subjugation of Switzerland (*William Wordsworth: A Biography*, 2 vols. [Oxford University Press, 1965] 1:68).

34 Wordsworth's political interests and activities during this period are well documented in poems, pamphlets, and essays. One instance of the specificity of his reactions to the Napoleonic Wars is his 1806 sonnet "November, 1806" (*PW*, 3: 122), which deplores Napoleon's defeat of Prussia at Jena. See Reed, *Wordsworth: Middle Years*, 339.

35 *PW*, 3:115. For another analysis of this sonnet, see J. C. Maxwell, "Wordsworth and the Subjugation of Switzerland," *Modern Language Review* 65 (1970), 16–17.

36 See chapter 5.

37 Burke, *Reflections*, 149.

38 Cited by Liu, "Wordsworth: The History in 'Imagination'," 536.

39 Cited by Hannah Arendt, *On Revolution* (New York: Viking Press, 1963), 41. See too "Desmoulins," *Chambers' Biographical Dictionary* (New York: St. Martin's Press, 1969), 376.

40 "The Sublime and the Beautiful," *Prose*, 2:353–54 and Dorothy Wordsworth, *Journals*, 2:128, 90–91.

41 *Memorials of a Tour of the Continent, 1820 (PW, 3:164–201)*. See especially: "After visiting the Field of Waterloo," "On approaching the Staub-Bach, Lauterbrunnen," "The Fall of the Aar – Handec," "Memorial near the Outlet of the Lake of Thun," and "The Column intended by Buonaparte for a Triumphal Edifice in Milan, now lying by the Way-side in the Simplon Pass" (the full title).

42 *PW*, 3:588n.; in Ramond de Carbonnière's French translation, *Lettres de William Coxe* (1781), 1:62.

43 *Descriptive Sketches*, 72n.

44 Dorothy Wordsworth, *Journals*, 2:90.

45 See chapter 6 for a discussion of Wordsworth's pamphlet *Concerning the Convention of Cintra*.

46 Gilliard, *Histoire de la Suisse*, 82.

47 Dorothy Wordsworth, *Journals*, 2:33, 42, 56, 172, 230, 236–38, 241, 256–58, 332–33.

48 Ramsay W. Phipps, *The Armies of the First French Republic: The Rise of the Marshalls* (6 vols., Oxford: Clarendon Press, 1939), 5:94–97.

49 Coxe, *Travels in Switzerland* (1801), 1:10; Dorothy Wordsworth, *Journals*, 2:88.

50 Coxe, *Travels in Switzerland*, 1; map: William R. Shepherd, *Historical Atlas*, 9th edn, (New York: Barnes and Noble, 1964), 151–52, 154.

51 William Martin with Pierre Beguin, *Switzerland from Roman Times to the Present*, tr. Jocasta Innes (New York: Praeger, 1971), 48, and Bonjour, *et al.*, *Short History of Switzerland*, 222–25.

52 Coxe, *Travels in Switzerland* (1796), 1:13.

53 See Wordsworth's remarks in his 1820 *Guide* concerning how erosion modifies the boundaries of lakes, in *Prose*, 2:181–82.

54 *Henry Crabb Robinson on Books and their Writers*, ed. Edith J. Morley, (3 vols., London: J. M. Dent, 1938), 1:253.

55 "Two Addresses to the Freeholders of Westmorland" (1), *Prose*, 3:158.

56 September 24 [1824], *LY* 1, 275–79.

57 Hartman, "Blessing the Torrent," 197.

58 Hartman, "Blessing the Torrent," 202–3n.

59 See de Selincourt's gloss on these lines, *PW*, 3:432.

60 Hartman, "Blessing the Torrent," 203n., and Bloom, *Wallace Stevens*, 396–97.

61 Wordsworth reiterates the power of torrents as force and flood in an 1842 Fenwick note to "The Forsaken," an early "overflow," as he says, of "Margaret's story." In the note he explains that the "natural imagery" of the poem came from "frequent, I might say intense, observation of Rydal torrent," which he compares with other Alpine rivers (*PW*, 2:473n.). I am indebted to Jeffrey C. Robinson for his notice of this passage.

62 Coxe, *Travels in Switzerland* (1801), 1:334n.

63 6 and 16 September 1790, *EY*, 34; Dorothy Wordsworth, *Journals*, 2:188–89. In the 1793 *Descriptive Sketches* (ed. Zall, ll. 243–50), the speaker describes a roofed wooden bridge on the Simplon route, then recalls his descent of the St. Gotthard, but makes no mention of the Devil's Bridge, unusual in the Alps because it was made of stone not wood.

64 Andrew Wilton, *Turner and the Sublime* (University of Chicago Press, 1980), 122; Dorothy Wordsworth, *Journals*, 2:186.

65 John Hollander, "Wordsworth and the Music of Sound," in *New Perspectives on Coleridge and Wordsworth* (New York: Columbia University Press, 1972), 50–75.

66 Jonathan Culler summarizes semiotic queries concerning signs and things in *The Pursuit of Signs* (Ithaca: Cornell University Press, 1981), 48–50.

67 *The Role of the Reader* (Bloomington: Indiana University Press, 1979), 22–23.

8 Conclusion: aesthetics and poetic language

1 *Preface* to *Lyrical Ballads*, *Prose*, 1:122–23, 139, 148–51. Further citations are included parenthetically in the text.

2 *Essay, Supplementary to the Preface*, *Prose*, 3:80. Further citations are included parenthetically in the text.

3 Hegel's dialectical aesthetic temper is complicated by questions about his view of the sublime. For an analysis of the mature Hegel's aesthetics, see Geoffrey Hartman, "From the Sublime to the Hermeneutic," in *The Fate of Reading* (University of Chicago Press, 1975), 114–23.

4 In the *Essay, Supplementary to the Preface*, Wordsworth argues that the "business of poetry" is "to treat of things not as they *are*, but as they *appear*" to the "senses" and the "passions."

5 In his edition of the two-part *Prelude*, Parrish explains that this manuscript is one of several Wordsworth finally excluded from the second part (*Prel. 1798*, 33–35).

6 *Essays upon Epitaphs*, III, in *Prose*, 2:85. Further citations appear parenthetically in the text. See also Frances Ferguson, *Wordsworth: Language as Counter-Spirit* (New Haven: Yale University Press, 1977). Although I agree with Ferguson that language is frequently a "counter-spirit" in Wordsworth's poetry, I situate this claim within a more overtly dialectical understanding of the competition between sublime and beautiful figures and their allied poetic powers.

7 Wordsworth first mentions the figure of incarnation in the third *Essay upon Epitaphs*, *Prose*, 2:84). Owen and Smyser review neoclassical use of the clothes-as-language metaphor in their commentary on this essay (*Prose*, 2:114).

8 Owen and Smyser note Wordsworth's indebtedness to Dennis in their commentary on the *Essay, Supplementary to the Preface* (*Prose*, 3:104–5).

9 Schiller, "On the Sublime," in *Naive and Sentimental Poetry and On the Sublime*, 209. White defends Schiller's admiration in "The Politics of Interpretation," 209. Although I agree with Schiller and White about the dangers of the beautiful, neither recognizes contrary (in the Blakean and Wordsworthian sense) dangers in the sublime.

10 *Appendix* to *Lyrical Ballads*, *Prose*, 1:160–61. Further citations appear parenthetically in the text. See too Blake, *The Marriage of Heaven and Hell*, in *The Complete Poetry and Prose of William Blake*, ed. David V. Erdman, rev. edn (Berkeley: University of California Press, 1982), 38; Shelley, *A Defence of*

Poetry, in *Shelley's Poetry and Prose*, eds. Donald H. Reiman and Sharon B. Powers (New York: W. W. Norton, 1977), 481–82. Rousseau argues instead that the origin of language was not poetry but the "cry of nature" (pain or fear). And what followed was still not poetry but assertions of power over others. See his *Discourse on the Origin of Inequality* (1761; repr. New York: Burt Franklin, 1971), 54–55.

11 See chapter 2 of this study. Owen observes that Wordsworth's objections to personification may echo contemporary distinctions between poetry and prose (*Wordsworth as Critic*), 15–18).

12 For an astute discussion of the consequences of this identification for Coleridge and other Romantic writers, see Steven Knapp, *Personification and the Sublime*, 7–50, 66–97. Representative eighteenth-century commentaries include Johnson's *Dictionary*, Chambers's *Cyclopaedia*, and the 1771 and 1797 editions of *Encyclopaedia Britannica*, s.v. *personification*. Blair objected to Kames's conservative analysis of the strengths and weaknesses of personification. See Blair, *Lectures on Rhetoric and Belles Lettres*, 1:324–25 and Kames, *Elements of Criticism*, 2:228–54. Owen notes that in successive revisions of the poem "Repentance" (probably composed in 1802), the diction becomes more elaborately "poetic" (*Wordsworth as Critic*, 80–82).

13 Ferguson argues that for Wordsworth durability refers to "the fact that they [figures] are seen as figures only through the temporary changes which repeated experience reveals in them" (*Wordsworth: Language as Counter-Spirit*, 20). This, I suggest, is the argument of the "turnings intricate" in *The Prelude*, v. But in the 1800 and 1802 *Preface*, rustic language is "durable" (*Prose*, 1:124) precisely because it resists the fluctuations of traditional poetic figures.

14 Coleridge, *Biographia Literaria*, chapters 17–18, 2:28–68. For a recent critique of Coleridge's evaluation of Wordsworth's faults, see Simpson, "Criticism, Politics, and Style," 54.

15 Longinus, *On the Sublime*, 3, 16, 92–93.

16 *Ibid.*, 124.

17 *Ibid.*, 91.

18 René Wellek, *A History of Modern Criticism: 1750–1950. The Romantic Age* (New Haven: Yale University Press, 1955), 146. Ruoff considers Wordsworth's phrase together with Wellek's objection in "Religious Implications," 677. Owen, "The Object, the Eye, and the Imagination," 15–18.

19 Ruoff, "Religious Implications," 682.

20 Chase, "Accidents of Disfiguration," in *Decomposing Figures*, 17–18.

21 Virgil, *Eclogues*, 1, 76–77, tr. Paul Alpers, *The Singer of the Eclogues*, 15; Shakespeare, *King Lear*, 4.6.15–16. Owen and Smyser note in their commentary that Wordsworth echoes Oliver Goldsmith's discussion of this verb (*Prose*, 3:42n.). Wordsworth uses the same literary examples for Virgil and Shakespeare, but chooses a different one for Milton.

22 See Alpers's analysis of Virgilian reference (*Singer of the Eclogues*, 97–98).

23 August 28, 1811, *Letters: Middle Years, 1806–11*, 508. Cited by Owen and Smyser in their commentary, *Prose*, 3:43n.

24 Lipking, "Quick Poetic Eyes," in *Articulate Images*, ed. Wendorf, 19.

Appendix

1 Reed, *Wordsworth: Middle Years*, 670.
2 Reed, correspondence, October 24, 1981.

Index

Abrams, M. H., 107
Addison, Joseph, 18, 27–28, 102, 166–67, 216–17 n. 41, 221 n. 6, 226 n. 34, 236 n. 2
aesthetics, models for: in nature, 8–9, 14–18, 34; in mind, 9–10, 24–27, 32–33, 49–57, 109, 120; sublimity and beauty, coexistence of: 38–39, 103; conflict between: 7, 30–32, 40–41, 45, 74, 85, 92–93, 139; *see also* sublime, beautiful, picturesque, rhetoric
Albrecht, W. P., 226 nn. 27 and 33, 230 n. 34
Alison, Archibald, 217 n. 48, 223 n. 33
Alpers, Paul, 230–31 n. 42
Althusser, Louis, 137
antiquarianism, 13–14, 142
Appleton, Jay, 220 n. 80
Arac, Jonathan, 223 n. 26
archaeology, as a figure for aesthetic retrieval, 9–10, 13, 14, 22–23, 142
Augustine, 91–92
Averill, James A., 233 n.12

Bacon, Francis, 13
Bahti, Timothy, 228 n. 6
Baillie, John, 27–28
ballads, 64–65
Barret, Paul, 215 n. 22
Beaumont, Sir George, 133, 179, 187, 203, 207
beautiful: defined, 3–4, 7, 24, 40, 47–48, 66; and domestication, 41, 61, 85, 126, 132, 149, 190–91; in landscape, 38, 40; representability and, 3, 66, 106; in society, 88–89; and reason, 7, 32; as shelter or refuge, 45, 60–61, 76, 79; in narrative, 64–65, 72, 75; and time, 156, 160

Bernhardt-Kabisch, Ernest, 229 n. 25
Bersani, Leo, 230 n. 36
Bialostosky, Don H., 234 n. 15
Biedermeier, 5
Bishop, Jonathan, 222 n. 21, 228 n. 3
Blair, Hugh, 213 n. 13, 217 n. 38, 226–27 n. 34, 241 n. 12
Blake, William, 5, 88, 106, 193–94
Bloom, Harold, 220 n. 1
Bonjour, E., 229 n. 24
Borck, Jim S., 231 n. 55
Breunig, Charles, 233 n. 8
Bromwich, David, 209 n. 3
Brontë, Emily, *Wuthering Heights*, 5
Browning, Robert, 5
Bruns, Gerald, 211 n. 23
Buffon, Georges Le Clerc, 20
Burke, Edmund: aesthetic model, 2–3, 24–26, 51, 53; on beauty: custom and, 138; property and, 33, 149, 199; in women, 119; on sublimity: fear, 27–29, on Milton, 221 n. 6 and 227 n. 34; obscurity or indistinctness, 18, 25–26, 77; and French Revolution, 32, 64, 72
Burnet, Thomas, 17, 37, 40, 100, 102
Byron, George Gordon, 89, 126, 150–51

Campbell, Dr., 214 n. 19
Campbell, O. J., 227 n. 36
Campbell, Thomas, 173
Carlyle, Thomas, 75, 227 n. 44
cartography, as practice and aesthetic figure, 11, 15–16, 200, 212 n. 8
Chambers, Ephraim, 217 n. 42
Chander, David G., 234 n. 16
Chandler, James, 210 n. 13, 227 n. 36, 229 n. 18, 232 n. 2
Chase, Cynthia, 95, 201, 210 n. 8
Christensen, Jerome, 7

Index

Cicero, 43
Clarke, Bruce, 219 n. 62, 221 n. 5
Clarke, James, 73, 120–22, 226 n. 23
Coe, Charles N., 237 n. 14
Coleridge, Samuel Taylor: ascent of
    Scawfell, 36; on beauty, 18–19; at
    Cora Linn, 172–73; coach wheel
    image, 16; on picturesque, 214 n. 15;
    Rime of the Ancient Mariner, 168; on
    sublimity, 18–19, 29–30, 216 n. 38;
    on sublimity and fear, 18–19, 29–30,
    217–18 nn. 52 and 53; waterfalls and
    disappointment, 219 n. 60; and
    Wordsworth's poetry: *Prelude*, 119,
    123, 131; *White Doe*, 150;
    "Yew-Trees," 163; *Lyrical Ballads*,
    197; "Gipsies," 160
Cowper, H. S., 231 n. 50
Coxe, William, 20, 174, 176, 179, 181,
    183–85, 189–90, 237 n. 14
Crabb Robinson, Henry, 146, 157, 163,
    186
Culler, Jonathan, 240 n. 66
Cuvier, Georges, 20

Dalrymple, Sir Hew, 139–40
Dampier, William, 130
Darwin, Erasmus, 19–20
De Luc, Jean Andre, 214 n. 21
Deluge: and Alpine geology, 21, 106; in
    Arab Dream, 100–2; and Genesis, 38,
    109; and French Revolution, 118–19,
    170–71, 182–83, 186–87; and Nile
    flood, 11, 105–6; and recovery of
    past, 13; compared to figure of
    torrents, 170–71, 182–3, 186–87
De Man, Paul, 218 n. 57, 224 n. 34, 230
    n. 31
Dennis, John, 28, 221 n. 6
DeQuincey, Thomas, 1, 16, 118, 123, 138,
    164, 222 n. 14
Derrida, Jacques, 218 n. 57, 233 n. 7
De Selincourt, Ernest, 159, 234 n. 25, 235
    n. 31
Desmoulins, Camille, 75, 182
Dowling, William C., 211 n. 19,
    224 n. 35
Drake, Nathan, 228 n. 5
Dreyfus, Hubert L., 211 n. 18
Duff, William, 213 n. 13

Eakin, Sybil, 222 n. 22
Eco, Umberto, 191
eidofusikon, 181
emblem, 81, 153, 156
Erdman, David V., 226 n. 30

Farrington, Joseph, 179
Ferguson, Frances, 30, 210 n. 8, 216 n. 34,
    219 n. 63, 240 n. 6
Ferguson, Margaret, 211 n. 21
Ferry, David, 161, 221 n. 10
Fletcher, Jacob, 34–35
Florio, John, 35
Foucault, Michael, 9, 225 n. 13
Fowler, Roger, 235 n. 38
France: revolutionary period: Burke on,
    74–75; freedom and 3–4, 7, 59, 63,
    83, 116–19; men of "enterprize," 76;
    Penrith Beacon as displaced site for,
    74; in *Prelude*, 96, 101–3, 116–19,
    126–27; in *Excursion*, 133–34;
    Directory: 103, 109, 140, 147,
    184–85; Napoleonic period: 103,
    133, 185 see also Napoleon
Frere, John, 20, 23
Freud, 10, 82, 124
Fried, Michael, 237–38 n. 24
Friedman, Michael, 232 n. 2, 233 n. 6
Friend, The, 142, 160

Gage, John, 238 n. 27
Galperin, William, 232 n. 69
Gaull, Marilyn, 215 n. 22
Genesis, 37–38, 44, 109, 118–19
geology, 8–9, 20–23, 106, 185–86,
    215 n. 28
Gerard, Alexander, 217 n. 48
gibbet, 70–71, 82, 102, 120, 122–23
Gill, Stephen, 225 n. 16, 228 n. 2
Gilliard, Charles, 237 n. 11
Gillham, D. G., 52
Gillispie, Charles C., 214 n. 18, 215 n. 28
Gilpin, William, 18, 38–39, 74
Godwin, William, *Caleb Williams*, 79
Gospel of John, 45
gothic, 52, 56–57, 67, 72–73, 228 n. 5
Green, William, 21, 36, 214 n. 15
Greene, Edward, 213 n.13
Grob, Alan, 231 n. 50

Hansen, David A., 213 n. 13
Hartman, Geoffrey, 2, 5, 45, 163, 187–89,
    210 n. 16, 227 n. 37, 228 nn. 10 and
    12, 229 n. 26, 231 n. 59, 240 n. 3
Hazlitt, William, 1–2, 4, 126, 160
Heffernan, James A. W., 216 n. 34,
    221 n. 8, 234 n. 25
Hegel, G. A. W., 5–6, 9, 33–34, 64, 77,
    104–5
Heidegger, Martin, 225 n. 14
Herder, Johann Gottfried, 32
Herman, Judith B., 234 n. 27

244

Index

Hertz, Neil, 4, 95, 221 n. 10
Hipple, W. J., 213 n. 15
Holland, Patrick, 216 n. 31, 230 n. 39
Hollander, John, 240 n. 65
Homans, Margaret, 223, n. 11
Honour, Hugh, 238 n. 31
Housman, John, 214 n. 19
Huet, Marie Helene, 230 n. 37
Hume, David, 80
Hunt, John D., 223 n. 30
Hutcheson, Francis, 18
Hutchinson, William, 74
Hutton, James, 20

ideology, 60–16, 135, 137–38

Jacobus, Mary, 223 n. 30, 228 n. 6, 230 n. 34, 231 n. 45
Jameson, Frederic, 61, 137
Jauss, Hans Robert, 233–34 n. 15
Johnson, Lee M., 222–23 n. 23
Johnson, Samuel, 35, 46, 47, 60, 131
Johnston, Kenneth R., 211 n. 15, 223 n. 31
Jones, John, 209 n. 1
Jones, Robert, 173–74, 187
Jones, Sir William, 217 n. 49
Josephus, Flavius, 101

Kant, Immanuel: aesthetic model, 3–4, 6–7, 24, 31, 104, 184; on colossal forms in nature, 140, 142; "dynamically sublime," 31, 104; on fear, 29–31; on freedom, 33; on self-preservation; 24; on reason, 7, 24, 218–19 n. 59; 1764 essay on aesthetics, 218–19 n. 55
Keach, William, 210 n. 8
Keats, John, 1–2, 5, 160
Ketcham, Carl H., 159
Kishel, Joseph F., 229 n. 24
Kissane, James, 221 n. 10
Klancher, Jon P., 230 n. 38
Knapp, Steven, 235 n. 41, 240 n. 12
Knight, Richard Payne, 29
Kroeber, Karl, 216 n. 39, 221 n. 5, 222 n. 18
Kuhns, Richard, 210 n. 12
Kunin, J. H., 238 n. 29

Lacan, Jacques, 111
Lamb, Charles, 146
Larkin, Peter, 219 n. 62
Leighton, Angela, 210 n. 8
Levinson, Marjorie, 48
Lindenberger, Herbert, 5, 230 n. 39

Lipking, Lawrence, 204, 211 n. 23, 221 n. 10
Little, Geoffrey, 59
Liu, Alan, 105–6, 231 n. 48
Longinus: *hypsos*, 34–35, 220 n. 68; pathos and fear, 3–4, 6, 27–28; sublime figures, 170, 188, 196, 198–200, 213 n. 13; sublimity in nature, 95
Lonsdale Magazine, 20, 215 n. 27
Loutherbourg, Philippe-Jacques de, 176, 181
Luther, Susan, 229 n. 26

MacCunn, F. J., 232 n. 67
McFarland, Thomas, 220 n. 81
McGann, Jerome, 7, 60, 211 n. 15
MacGillvray, J. R., 227–28 n. 2
McKeon, Richard, 43
Magnuson, Paul, 222 n. 18
Manning, Peter J., 150, 157, 227 n. 41, 233 n. 11, 234 nn. 17, 20, 21, 29, 235 n. 41
Marat, Jean Paul, death of, 59
Martin, William, 239 n. 51
Marxian analysis, 16, 48, 137
Matlak, Richard, 223 n. 29
Maxwell, J. C., 238 n. 35
Mechel, Christian von, 176
memory, in classical rhetoric, 43; *see also topoi*
Metsger, Lore, 230–31 n. 42
Michelet, Jules, 210 n. 13
Miller, George, 217 n. 41
Milton, John: *Lycidas*, 119, 145; *Paradise Lost*: Adam, 107; chaos and creation, 38, 44, 102, 109, 116, 129; sublime style, 1, 28, 78–79, Satan as sublime figure and speaker, 1, 28, 37–38, 73, 78–79, 86–87, 96, 131, 142, 153, 202–5; 84th Psalm, 61
Mitchell, W. J. T., 210 n. 8, 231–32 n. 60
Modiano, Raimonda, 216 n. 32, 219 n. 62
Momigliano, Arnaldo, 211 n. 2
Monk, Samuel, 1
Moorman, Mary, 238 n. 33
Mueschke, P., 227 n. 36
Murdoch, Iris, 210 n. 12
Murray, John, 237 n. 17

Nabholtz, John R., 19, 213 n. 15
Napier, Elizabeth, 210 n. 8
Napoleon, 7, 103, 105–6, 138, 139, 140, 147, 150–51
Nemoianu, Virgil, 210 n. 8
Nicolson, Marjorie, H., 17

245

Index

Index

Index

Index